THE INTERNET REVOLUTION IN THE SCIENCES AND HUMANITIES

The Internet Revolution in the Sciences and Humanities

Alan G. Gross and Joseph E. Harmon

OXFORD
UNIVERSITY PRESS

OXFORD
UNIVERSITY PRESS

Oxford University Press is a department of the University of Oxford. It furthers
the University's objective of excellence in research, scholarship, and education
by publishing worldwide. Oxford is a registered trade mark of Oxford University
Press in the UK and certain other countries.

Published in the United States of America by Oxford University Press
198 Madison Avenue, New York, NY 10016, United States of America.

© Oxford University Press 2016

Library of Congress Cataloging-in-Publication Data
Names: Gross, Alan G., author. | Harmon, Joseph E., author.
Title: The Internet revolution in the sciences and humanities /
Alan G. Gross and Joseph E. Harmon.
Description: Oxford; New York: Oxford University Press, [2016] |
Includes bibliographical references and index.
Identifiers: LCCN 2015039127| ISBN 978-0-19-046593-3 (pbk.: alk. paper) |
ISBN 978-0-19-046592-6 (hardcover: alk. paper) | ISBN 978-0-19-046594-0 (ebook)
Subjects: LCSH: Internet publishing. | Scholarly electronic publishing. | Science publishing—
Technological innovations. | Humanities literature—Publishing—Technological innovation. |
Science and the humanities. | Communication in science. | Communication in the humanities. |
Internet in higher education. | Communication in learning and scholarship—
Technological innovations.
Classification: LCC Z286.I57 G76 2016 | DDC 070.5/7973—dc23 LC record
available at http://lccn.loc.gov/2015039127

9 8 7 6 5 4 3 2 1
Printed by Sheridan, USA

Contents

List of Illustrations ix
List of Videos on Companion Website xiii
About the Companion Website and Endnotes xvii
Acknowledgments xix

1. *The Internet and the Two Cultures* 1
    Ideal Types 2
    The Scientific Culture and Scientist as Ideal Type 5
    The Humanistic Culture and Humanist as Ideal Type 7
    The Sciences and Humanities Transformed 10
    The Book Itself 12
    The Audience 16

2. *The Internet Scientific Article: Reshaping Verbal and Visual Communication* 17
    Revolution or Evolution? 17
    A Survey of the Web Article 23
      Increasing Accessibility 24
      The Changing Nature of Authorship 26
      Coping with Complexity 27
      Increasing Inter- and Intra-textuality 28
      Including Reader Comments and Reader Statistics 33
      Enhancing Visualization 34
    Internet Visualization and the Science of Shape 38
      Birth of a Science of Shape 39
      The Mathematical Visualization of Shape 42

Science of Shape and the Internet 46
Conclusion 50

3. Internet Humanities Essays and Books: Seeing and Hearing Anew 52
Internet Innovation and the Humanities Essay 52
Historians See Anew 55
    Photographs as Historical Evidence 55
    Art as Historical Evidence 60
    Reinterpreting the Civil War: The Role of Visualization 64
    Meeting the Challenge of Urban History: A Multimedia Los Angeles 69
    Reimagining the Roman Forum: Vision as Hypothesis 75
Musicians See and Hear Anew 77
Film Scholars See Anew 79
Conclusion 86

4. Archival Websites in the Humanities and Sciences 88
Websites that Provide Resources for Scholarship 91
Websites that Store Data for Scientific Research 104
Websites that Store Scientific or Scholarly Papers 107
Websites that Create Knowledge Through Volunteer Participation 110
Websites that Codify Existing Knowledge 115
Conclusion 120

5. Evaluation Before Publication: Opening up Peer Review 122
The Case for and Against Peer Review 123
Argument Theory and Peer Review 126
Theory Application 129
Open Internet Peer Review in the Sciences 135
Open Internet Peer Review in the Humanities 144
Peer Sourcing: The Wave of the Future? 151
Conclusion 153

6. Evaluation After Publication: Setting the Record Straight 155
Watchdog Blogs in the Sciences 155
What Watchdog Blogs Reveal 158
How Watchdog Blogs Work 165
Humanities Post-Peer Review 169
Postpublication Peer Review: The Article 172

Postpublication Peer Review: The Book 178
Conclusion 186

7. *Overcoming the Obstacles to Internet Exploitation* 188
   The Opportunities 188
   Gated Access: The First Obstacle 189
   Current Tenure Rules: The Second Obstacle 193
   Digital Preservation: The Third Obstacle 195
   Patents and Copyright: The Fourth Obstacle 197
   Freedom of Information: The Fifth Obstacle 203
   A Path Forward 206

NOTES 209
INDEX 239

Illustrations

Figures

2.1   Screenshot of three-pane format in *Cell* 22

2.2   Screenshot of 2010 digital article from 2010 *PLOS Biology* 25

2.3   Reproduction of first printed page in 1962 article in *Proceedings of National Academy of Sciences (PNAS)* 26

2.4   Example *Journal of Biological Chemistry* article incorporating abstract of abstract followed by traditional heading abstract 29

2.5   Example abstract of the abstract from *Applied Physics Letters* contents page 30

2.6   Sample issue homepage from *Journal of the American Chemical Society* 32

2.7   Graph integrated into text in Goodman and Rich (1962) article 35

2.8   Example of multicomponent figure with caption 37

2.9   A Cartesian grid applied successively between *Diodon* and *Orthagoriscus mola* 39

2.10 Relative growth of the chela (claw) in the prawn *Palaemon malcomsoni* [now *Macrobrachium malcomsonii* or Monsoon River prawn]. Logarithmic plotting 41

2.11 (a) Profile of embalmed Wilkinson Head. (b) Full face of the British Museum wax death mask fitted with the facial outlines of the Wilkinson Head 44

2.12 Profile of Wilkinson Head showing trace of embalmed head (solid line), skull bone (short dashed line), and ordinary flesh allowance (long dashed line) 45

2.13 Three views of a human hemi-mandible, aged one year 47

2.14 Screenshot from video of the development of the human mandible, front and side view 49

2.15 On the left, the Neanderthal skull; on the right, the human skull. In the online version, red indicates shrinkage, green, expansion 50

3.1   Table of competing narratives 58

3.2 Poster from visual archive: "To hell with Afrikaans" 59

3.3 Photo from visual archive: Uncle Tom's Hall truck burned out and flipped 61

3.4 Drawing posted for collaborative analysis in *Imaging the French Revolution*. "Bertier de Sauvignon, Intendant of Paris, is led to his punishment" 62

3.5 Five points of analysis on the 1860 presidential campaign in *The Differences Slavery Made* 66

3.6 Supporting evidence in *The Differences Slavery Made*: cash value of farms per capita 68

3.7 Supporting evidence in *The Differences Slavery Made*: farm size, 1860 69

3.8 Supporting evidence in *The Differences Slavery Made*: agricultural production by precinct in Augusta County, 1860 70

3.9 Interactive map showing complex political boundaries of Los Angeles. Online viewers can choose to see a specific layer by clicking on "layers" on left 71

3.10 Los Angeles from Robbert Flick's artistic display "Along Central," May 16, 2000. Part of 50-photo photomontage 72

3.11 Maps of Hispanic population in Los Angeles for 1970 (a) and 1990 (b) 73

3.12 Building on 2150 South Central Avenue, altered by Photoshop to display ads from 1940 and 1999 74

3.13 Panoramas of Seventh and Broadway: 1905 (top) and 2000 (bottom) 74

3.14 Interactive model of ancient Roman Forum in "Death in Motion" 76

3.15 Interactive visual for *Who Shot Liberty Valence?* Rance (Stewart), on the left, easily sees Donaphon (Wayne) on the right 81

3.16 Mamber's comment on Davis, emphasizing the importance of Ford's choice of black-and-white 82

3.17 Chart mapping the structure of narrative in Kubrick's *The Killing* 83

3.18 Nikki waits to shoot Red Lightning: 3D representation of *The Killing* 84

3.19 Movie posters for three versions of Dashiell Hammett's *Maltese Falcon* 84

3.20 Film clip with superimposed text from *The Maltese Falcon*. The film's dialogue is right from the book 85

3.21 Still frame showing Sydney Greenstreet, shot from a low angle 85

4.1 Proof copy from Walt Whitman's "Song of Myself" 93

4.2 Coded revisions to poem by Walt Whitman in digital repository 95

4.3 Whitman's handwritten manuscript for poem shown in Figure 4.2 96

4.4 Final image in Blake's *Songs of Experience* followed by Giovanni Battista Tiepolo's *Immaculate Conception* (1767–1769) 100

4.5 Final page of Blake's *Europe* followed by bas relief by Artus Quellinus the Elder depicting Aeneas's escape from Troy 102

4.6 Segment of RCSB PDB page for structure of deoxyhemoglobin S 106

4.7   ArXiv monthly submission rates 108

4.8   Screen for user input to Galaxy Zoo Project. Viewer matches shape in astronomical image on left with drawn shapes on right, bottom 111

4.9   Galaxy Zoo image with "blue stuff" below spiral galaxy IC 2497 at center 113

4.10   Radio photometry image of previous Galaxy Zoo image 114

4.11   Snapshot of EOL contents page for *Pomadasys incisus*. Different layers of information accessible through tabs at top 117

4.12   Drilling down in OneZoom fractal tree of life (moving left to right): from animals to vertebrates to mammals to primates to hominoidea to *Homo sapiens* 119

5.1   Interactive discussion page for *Climate of the Past* 139

5.2   Screenshot of open commentary page for *Shakespeare Quarterly* 145

6.1   Mashup illustrating image manipulation in a 1999 retracted article by S. Bulfone-Paus et al. 162

Table

2.1   Example comparison of the Wilkinson Head with masks and busts 46

Videos on Companion Website

1.1   Visual summary of book
[L. Aron et al., *PLOS Biology* 8, no. 4 (2010): e1000349; B. Naranjo, *Nature* 434 (2005): 1115–1117, http://www.nature.com/nature/journal/v434/n7037/ extref/nature03575-s2.mpg; P. Ethington, *American Historical Review* 112 (December 2007), http://www.usc.edu/dept/LAS/history/historylab/ LAPUHK/Locations/Broadway/Bwy+7th/BWY+7th.htm; W. Whitman, "And Yet Not You Alone," Walt Whitman Archive, 1885, http://www. whitmanarchive.org/manuscripts/transcriptions/yal.00050.html; T. Karlberg et al., *PLOS One* 4, no. 10 (2009): e6975; M. Tudeau-Clayton, "Shakespeare and 'the King's English,'" in "Shakespeare and Language," *Shakespeare Quarterly Open Review*, http://shakespearequarterly.folger.edu/openreview/ ?page_id=406; "Endurance," Australia's Audiovisual History Online, 1916, http://aso.gov.au/titles/documentaries/endurance/clip3]

2.1   Tour through main components in online article [L. Aron et al., *PLOS Biology* 8, no. 4 (2010): e1000349]

2.2   Video demonstration of development of the human mandible [M. Coquerelle et al., *Journal of Anatomy* 217 (2010): 507–520]

2.3   Transformations from drawing of chameleon in 17th century to 3D manipulatable simulation in 21st [C. Perrault, "Description anatomique d'un cameleon" (Paris: Frederic Leonard, 1669); S. Suter et al., *IEEE Transactions on Visualization and Computer Graphics* 17 (2011): 2135–2143; B. Wilhelm et al., *Science* 344 (2014): 1023–1028]

2.4   Interactive manipulation of molecular representation and demonstrations of its integration with text [T. Karlberg et al., *PLOS One* 4, no. 10 (2009): e6975]

3.1   Nonlinear hypertext humanities essay from *Vectors* [A. Friedberg, "Virtual Window Interactive," *Vectors: Journal of Culture and Technology in a*

Dynamic Vernacular, 3, no. 1 (2007), http://vectors.usc.edu/projects/index. php?project=79]

3.2 Animated map showing Hispanic population in Los Angeles from 1940 to 1990 [P. Ethington, *American Historical Review* 112 (December 2007), http://www. usc.edu/dept/LAS/history/historylab/LAPUHK]

3.3 Panoramas of Seventh and Broadway: 1905 and 2000 [P. Ethington, *American Historical Review* 112 (December 2007), http://www.usc.edu/dept/LAS/history/ historylab/LAPUHK/Locations/Broadway/Bwy+7th/BWY+7th.htm]

3.4 Interactive model of ancient Roman Forum in "Death in Motion" [D. Favro and C. Johanson, "Google Earth Model: An Image of the Roman Forum and Environs via Google Earth," 2010, http://www.jstor.org/action/showPopup?citi d=citart1&id=figure0&doi=10.1525%2Fjsah.2010.69.1.12]

3.5 Music samples of Bach D minor Partita for violin [D. Fabian and E. Schubert, *Music Performance Research* 3 (2009): 36–55]

3.6 Maltese Falcon posters [C. Galiher, *Mediascape: UCLA's Journal of Cinema and Media Studies*, January 27, 2013, http://www.tft.ucla.edu/mediascape/ Winter2013_ThreeFates.html]

3.7 Maltese Falcon dialogue [C. Galiher, *Mediascape: UCLA's Journal of Cinema and Media Studies*, January 27, 2013, http://www.tft.ucla.edu/mediascape/ Winter2013_ThreeFates.html]

4.1 Perseus Digital Library [Homer, *Odyssey*, Perseus Digital Library, http://www. perseus.tufts.edu/hopper/text?doc=Perseus:text:1999.01.0135]

4.2 Walt Whitman Archive [W. Whitman, "And Yet Not You Alone," Walt Whitman Archive, 1885, http://www.whitmanarchive.org/manuscripts/tran- scriptions/yal.00050.html; Beinecke Rare Book and Manuscript Library, Yale University]

4.3 William Blake Archive [W. Blake, "The Cloud and the Pebble," *Songs of Innocence and Experience*, 1789, http://www.blakearchive.org/exist/blake/ archive/object.xq?objectid=songsie.c.illbk.53&java=no; Lessing J. Rosenwald Collection, Library of Congress. Copyright © 2015 William Blake Archive]

4.4 Protein Data Bank ["The High Resolution Crystal Structure of Deoxyhemoglobin S," RCSB Protein Data Bank, accessed May 2015, http:// www.rcsb.org/pdb/explore/explore.do?structureId=2hbs]

4.5 Encyclopedia of Life ["Pomadasys incisus: Bastard Grunt," EOL, accessed May 2015, http://eol.org/pages/204098/overview]

5.1 Shakespeare Quarterly Open Review [M. Tudeau-Clayton, "Shakespeare and 'the King's English,'" in "Shakespeare and Language," *Shakespeare Quarterly Open Review*, http://shakespearequarterly.folger.edu/openreview/?page_

id=406; to be published in Katie Halsey and Angus Vine, eds., *Shakespeare and Authority* (Basingstoke: Palgrave Macmillan, 2007)]

7.1   ChemSpider ["Tylenol," accessed July 2012, http://www.chemspider.com/Chemical-Structure.1906.html?rid=0a028c92-e470-4049-b89e-9b49bc9f1287]

7.2   Rome Reborn Project [Frischer Consulting, Rome Reborn 2.2, 2008, http://romereborn.frischerconsulting.com/gallery-current.php]

About the Companion Website and Endnotes

WHY IS THIS book not published as a native e-book with figures in color, embedded videos, interactive graphics, and hyperlinks? Are we not in the "post-Gutenberg" era? Faced with difficult decisions concerning the very nature of publishing, academic presses are in a time of transition. In moving in digital directions, they must exercise caution; they must track the habits of their consumers, most of whom still read books the old-fashioned way. Sales figures are as yet unable to justify enhanced e-books.

This time of transition accounts for the occasional poor quality of the black-and-white images in this book. In almost every case, their source is the Internet. On the Internet, these images are generally in color and always look fine; unfortunately, these characteristics do not always transfer to the medium of print.

That Oxford University Press offers a companion website for this book is a step forward. On this site, you will find 20 videos, all except the first running from 30 seconds to a little over two minutes. The first is a five-minute preview of the book's contents. The remaining videos are related to some discussion within the chapters themselves, signaled by a special web icon ⏵. These videos are evidence for our claims and for scholarly and scientific claims in areas as diverse as film criticism and geometric morphometrics.

Given the extraordinary diversity of computers, all with different software, memory, processing speed, virus protection, and mode of Internet connection, we cannot expect all of our videos to work smoothly on all computers. We have run all the videos successfully on a PC desktop, a Mac at home, a PC laptop, and an iPad (they look great on iPad). That suggests to us that our videos will work on most computers.

There are no discursive endnotes in the book. Endnotes can be consulted for bibliographic purposes; they serve no other purpose.

Acknowledgments

IN WRITING THIS book, we corresponded with many of the ingenious creators of the articles, books, and websites we discuss. We interviewed two, Adam Marcus and Ivan Oransky. We corresponded fruitfully with Ed Ayers, Lutz Bornmann, William Caplan, Morris Eaves, Robert Essick, Philip Ethington, Hughes Goosse, James Hepokoski, Lynn Hunt, Christopher Johanson, Robert Kolker, Michèle Lamont, George Landow, Stephen Mamber, Hugo Mercier, Kenneth Price, Ulrich Pöschl, Janet Smalfeldt, William G. Thompson III, and Joseph Viscomi. We apologize if we omitted some of our correspondents; they might have been victims of a computer storm.

We would like to thank Paige Sandvik for making our images presentable and Anne Brataas for referring her to us. We would like to thank our longtime former editor, Christie Henry; her able assistant, Amy Krynak; and their team for support and encouragement and for efforts that led always to a book that met the highest aesthetic and scholarly standards. We would like to thank our former editor at Oxford University Press, Peter Ohlin, for referring us to our current and consistently supportive editor, Hallie Stebbins. Finally, we also thank the whole Oxford team involved in the production of a book with unusual challenges, both those in New York and those in far-away Chennai.

Joseph Harmon performed the research and writing for this book independent of his current employer, Argonne National Laboratory. Obviously, the views expressed are those of the authors and in no way reflect those of Argonne, the Department of Energy, or Oxford University Press.

Alan Gross would like to dedicate this book to the memory of his grandfather, Jacob Jamron, and his father, Jacob Gross. Joseph Harmon dedicates it to his mother, Anne V. Harmon, who at 90 years of age enjoys surfing the Internet on her iPad and keeping up with her 17 grandchildren on Facebook.

THE INTERNET REVOLUTION IN THE SCIENCES AND HUMANITIES

1

THE INTERNET AND THE TWO CULTURES

Video 1.1 ⊙

IN A 1959 lecture delivered at Cambridge University, C. P. Snow famously argues
that Western intellectual life is divided into two polar-opposite cultures—the sciences and the arts. In his view, most scientists are ignorant of the arts, "with the exception, an important exception, of music," and as a whole non-scientist intellectuals—a
group we will be calling "humanists"—have no conception of the "scientific edifice
of the physical world . . . the most beautiful and wonderful collective work of the
mind of man."[1] Moreover, Snow asserts that, besides this mutual ignorance, both
sides underestimate, and even sometimes denigrate, the value of the other. He makes
a telling point about the missed opportunities for intellectual advance entailed by
the lack of lively commerce between the two groups:

> There seems then to be no place where the cultures meet. I am not going to
> waste time saying that this is a pity. It is much worse than that. Soon I shall
> come to some practical consequences. But at the heart of thought and creation
> we are letting some of our best chances go by default. The clashing point of two
> subjects, two disciplines, two cultures—of two galaxies, so far as that goes—
> ought to produce creative chances. In the history of mental activity that has
> been where some of the break-throughs came. The chances are there now. But
> they are there, as it were, in a vacuum, because those in the two cultures can't
> talk to each other.[2]

Nowhere does Snow mention that, despite many cultural differences, the sciences
and the humanities do have three central tasks in common: They generate knowledge, they communicate it, and they evaluate its quality. The thesis of our book is

that, in both camps, the Internet has transformed and is still transforming these tasks in important and even similar ways. Nevertheless, for a variety of reasons, all based on differences between the two cultures, on their very different sets of social habits and attitudes, in the sciences the Internet revolution appears to be further along than in the humanities. It is because of this situation that the humanities can learn from the sciences how better to exploit the Internet in the interest of advancing their own kind of knowledge. In advocating learning from the sciences, we must stress, we are not suggesting the humanities are somehow inferior to the sciences. Ours cannot be an attitude hostile to the humanities, whose practices are at the very center of our intellectual lives and, not incidentally, of this book. Moreover, it is also true that, because the pace of successful innovation is uneven in both the sciences and the humanities, the sciences can learn from the humanities, the humanities from the humanities, and the sciences from the sciences. By aligning the future with the best practices of the present, this book will also point to ways with which the two cultures can institutionalize or even improve upon the positive changes that are now in various stages of implementation or experimentation.

IDEAL TYPES

As the home of a leading idea that spread with great rapidity, *Two Cultures* continues its influence on intellectual life. It was rightly selected by the *Times Literary Supplement* as one of the 100 most influential books of the last half of the 20th century.[3] This persistence, however, does not depend entirely on the cogency of Snow's analysis. Along with a few penetrating insights, he gives us many biased generalizations. Scientific culture is intellectually superior, he says, because it "contains a great deal of argument usually much more rigorous, and almost always at a higher conceptual level, than literary persons' arguments." Scientists are also morally superior, presumably as a result of their training, as they do not read literary books.[4] In contrast, Snow avers, humanists are self-deceived; they pretend that theirs is the whole of culture and remain stubbornly ignorant of scientific achievements.[5] Trained as a scientist, Snow makes clear the culture he admires more. His prejudices have their source, in part, in the image scientists have of themselves. For example, according to anthropologist Sharon Traweek, particle physicists view the world from atop a hierarchy of disciplines. Below them in order are chemistry, engineering, biology, and the social sciences. The humanities are so far below as to be barely visible. Understandably, particle physicists "would agree also that the scale of intelligence and reasoning capacity needed to practice these various specialties corresponds to this sequence."[6]

Clearly, if we are to make sense of the two cultures as twin enterprises that generate, communicate, and evaluate knowledge—a characterization central to our enterprise—we need to leave such biased views far behind. For Snow's offhand remarks and the biases of particle physicists, we substitute Max Weber's method of ideal types, sociological models of typical human behavior designed as means of exploring actual instances of such behavior. In other words, we employ ideal types to make "clearly explicit not the class or average character, but rather the unique individual character of cultural phenomena."[7] Our target is the effect of contrasting sets of social habits and attitudes on the pursuit of knowledge in two very different media—print and the Internet. We will present these contrasting sets as ideal types in this introductory chapter; the rest of our book will grapple with the historical—and of course the current—reality of their effect on the pursuit of knowledge. We use these ideal types to explain the differences in pace in which the two cultures take advantage of the Internet's possibilities.

An example of ideal types might help. In *The Protestant Ethic and the Spirit of Capitalism*, Weber employs these types to contrast the ways in which various emerging Protestant sects transformed traditional Christian asceticism into a secular force, one that "slammed the gates of the cloister, entered into the hustle and bustle of life, and undertook a new task: to saturate mundane *everyday* life with its methodicalness. In the process, it sought to reorganize practical life into a rational life in the world rather than, as earlier, in the monastery."[8] Weber's example is the shift from cottage-industry head to entrepreneur, from one ideal type to another. A cottage-industry head purchased the output of peasants and employed a chain of middlemen to market it. His business was rationally constructed; double-entry bookkeeping kept track of his profits and losses. Nevertheless, his was a traditional business. The head carried out his activities in a leisurely spirit; he was satisfied with a modest return on his investment. In contrast, the entrepreneur who succeeded him created a capitalistic enterprise with workers, who were paid as little as the labor market permitted and housed in a central location. His customers' needs came first, always and invariably. Because they expected low prices, an entrepreneur's profits depended on a high volume of sales, on rapidly developing markets. The extent to which these particular ideal types are true to reality can be determined only by a resort to the evidence in particular cases. The claim is not that they are historically accurate but that they capture something essential about two types of business enterprise and about the change that occurred as a consequence of the infusion of the Protestant ethic into secular enterprises.

Our analysis imitates Weber's; our parallel claim is that the spirit of the Internet, having entered the academy, is changing the nature of academic work at varying paces, a rate of change largely dependent on cultural differences in the sciences and humanities. We do not assume that any actual humanist or scientist or the corresponding cultures have the exact character of our ideal types. We assume only that we are capturing something essential to scholarly and to scientific cultures, something each of these generally exhibits as a pattern of social habits and attitudes.

There are two problems in applying our ideal types to reality. The first stems from the structure of academic bureaucracy. It is a mistake to confuse the bureaucratic place of disciplines within university structures with their place on the cultural map. The colleges of liberal arts that house most humanists are administrative units; typically, they contain departments as diverse as English, history, foreign languages, mathematics, sociology, psychology, and economics. Colleges of science are also administrative units; typically, they contain departments as diverse as botany, biology, chemistry, computer science, and physics. While the sciences as a group have much more in common than those disciplines typically housed in colleges of liberal arts, it would still be a mistake to conflate the social habits and attitudes of descriptive botanists and particle physicists, two very different subcultures. In our analysis, we must look to where they are not on the bureaucratic, but on the cultural map.

There is a second problem, the awkward fact that there are, arguably, *three* academic cultures: the natural sciences, the social sciences, and the humanities. We would not disagree that in many respects the social sciences have a distinct academic identity.[9] Still, we would argue that in their work social scientists will align themselves with one or another of our ideal types. There are anthropologist-scientists like Raymond Dart and Donald Johanson and anthropologist-humanists like Victor Turner and Clifford Geertz. Because of this difference in allegiances, it will certainly be true that some who inhabit colleges of liberal arts, some psychologists and economists for example, will legitimately feel themselves closer to the ideal type of the scientist than that of the humanist. We would also concede that scientists and humanists might, as it were, switch sides. Paul Schilpp's *Albert Einstein, Philosopher-Scientist*[10] testifies to this possibility, as does Descartes's *Meteorology* when coupled with his *Discourse on Method*.[11] It is even possible for humanists to combine the qualitative and quantitative in a single project. This is what Edward Ayers does in *In the Presence of Mine Enemies*[12] and what William Thomas does in *The Iron Way*.[13] And, incidentally, it is what we did ourselves in *Communicating Science*.[14] But, we maintain, any particular research project will fit more comfortably within one ideal type than another, will lead in the one case to an article, deliberately constrained in form and style, in the other case to an essay, deliberately free in form and style. We reiterate that our ideal types are ideal types; they are not historical realities, but means of exploring these realities.

THE SCIENTIFIC CULTURE AND SCIENTIST AS IDEAL TYPE

At the very beginning of modern science, letters were the preferred medium of intellectual exchange, supplemented by informal meetings for those in or near such large cities as Paris or London. At the beginning, in other words, the velocity with which knowledge circulated was held hostage to the postal system and to occasional face-to-face interaction. With the simultaneous mid-17th-century publication of the first two scientific periodicals—the *Philosophical Transactions* in London and the *Journal des Sçavans* (*Journal of the Learned*) in Paris—the velocity with which knowledge circulated markedly advanced. For the first time, thanks to print technology, what had been private became public: In effect, the whole world became, potentially, the audience for scientific advance. In the 17th and 18th centuries, velocity was also increased because modern science organized socially in major cities: The Lincean Academy in Rome, the Royal Society of London, the Royal Academy of Sciences in Paris, the Academy of Experiment in Florence, the Royal Society of Sciences in Berlin, the American Philosophical Society in Philadelphia, and the Imperial Academy of Sciences in St. Petersburg were founded for regular and frequent scientific exchange.[15]

The social interactions these organizations fostered, along with the publications they sponsored, led eventually to the formation of research fronts, the central feature of intellectual advance in modern science. Scientists who may have been separated geographically were united intellectually, focusing on the same families of problems and competing for their solution.[16] As a consequence of this coordinated effort at the research front, duplication of discoveries was less the exception than the rule. (Indeed, such duplication is an infallible sign that a research front exists.) Such duplication need not be wasteful: It increases the chances that a discovery will be noticed and helps to confirm its truth.[17] Nevertheless, for individual scientists, the possibility of preemption menaces careers, a danger best avoided by rapid publication. The desired rapidity was somewhat impeded by the relatively slow transfer from manuscript to print, a barrier that did not decrease markedly with time; in the following centuries, the process was further retarded by peer review, a delay of months in the interest of maintaining knowledge quality and relevance. These delays led to the practice of noting the date of receipt upon publication. But while reputations might thus be preserved, the pace of dissemination was unaltered. Print and peer review continued to slow the circulation of knowledge. The presence of a research front had another effect: A contribution was valuable only insofar as it was incorporated into a front. Once this incorporation occurred (normally within 5 to 10 years), the original document had little citation value, except to historians of science, no matter how renowned the author, no matter how important the contribution. Of course, there are exceptions.

There is a way in which the velocity of knowledge might have been accelerated, even in the age of print. Scientists could have collaborated, pooling their intellectual and technical resources. But until the 20th century, collaboration was by far the exception, becoming more common only in the first half of the last century, and rising exponentially only in the second half.[18-20] This considerable increase was generated more by external than by internal factors. World War II and the Cold War provided the motivation; the Manhattan Project, the space program, and many other research projects were the result. From these large-scale successful enterprises, scientists learned what industrialists had discovered long before: the benefits of the division of labor. This division was of two sorts: the apportioning of labor among those equally skilled, as with carpenters building a barn, and the apportionment among those differentially skilled, as with an operating room team. There is considerable evidence that collaborations not only increased but also led to greater research impact in the later part of the 20th century,[21-23] coincident with the start of the Internet revolution.

Even in the age of print, the speed with which knowledge circulated could have been increased by designing journal articles so as to facilitate their efficient perusal. But science was slow to institute such changes. Article design became more efficient only gradually over the centuries. The current scientific article with its abstracts, its clearly demarcated sections, its keywords, its sophisticated system of citations, and its full array of graphic and photographic aids is a product of the latter half of the 20th century. Only by that century's end could it be said the printed page had been fully exploited so as to maximize its utility and to minimize the investment of readers with varying interests in the article's content. Until the advent of the Internet, another way of increasing the velocity with which knowledge circulated, easy availability to any interested reader, was not technically feasible.

In the sciences, we see that social patterns already in existence paved the way for the ready exploitation of the Internet as a medium in which to generate, communicate, and evaluate knowledge more efficiently. Collaboration was already flourishing; the Internet greatly facilitated it, among not only networked scientists from around the globe but also armies of citizen-scientists participating through websites like Galaxy Zoo. The scientific article already embodied a master finding system well suited to the use of hyperlinked text; the Internet only opened the door to seeing articles more clearly as nodes in networks of knowledge. Scientists already believed that knowledge should be universally shared; the Internet simply made open access a realistic possibility. Scientists were always interested in the quality and quantity of the evidence they could share with peers; now they could share virtually all of the relevant evidence their work generated: photographs, videos, 3D simulations, whole datasets. Scientists already put a high value on new technology, so giving up paper in favor of Internet celerity and flexibility could not generally be perceived as a loss. Scientists also place a high value on the practice of peer review before publication; online, it did not need to be substantively changed but it could be made more efficient and more participatory. Finally, scientists place a high value on the rapid dissemination of new knowledge. The Internet has made it possible, in the interest of increased velocity, to circulate candidate scientific knowledge to the discourse community within a matter of days after manuscript completion. Paul Ginsparg founded the arXiv website in 1991 for that very purpose. This site posts physics articles without peer or editorial review, after which authors typically submit their articles to journals for that review and, if all goes well, official publication.

THE HUMANISTIC CULTURE AND HUMANIST AS IDEAL TYPE

By and large, scientists live in the present; they are fully immersed in what happens today in the laboratory or the field. In contrast, humanists are rooted in the past, in living traditions that nourish their scholarly lives and form the object of their daily reflection. As a consequence of this habitual cast of mind, in which writing and thinking are one and the same, humanists resist the organizational rigidity of the scientific article, the neatly packaged unit of intellectual advance that can be readily abstracted and segmented into discrete chunks in hypertext fashion. Instead, they feel more at home within the relatively unconstrained compass of the essay, the tentative foray into new intellectual territory. Theirs is not primarily a search for new facts, although they often come upon such facts in the course of their work and frequently use them to support their claims. Theirs is primarily an effort at understanding, concerned with the interpretation of the products of culture, the expression of human desires and human ingenuity embodied in texts and artifacts. For the humanist, turning facts into theories, the goal of science, is far from sufficient; at its best, the humanistic essay also explores the foundations of knowledge, those presuppositions that make knowledge possible. In so doing, these forays become models for scholarly activity. Fully to engage with them is to generate additional scholarly activity, some of it equally exemplary, equally generative. What is generated by humanists, however, is not a "research front," the coordinated advance of a whole field of endeavor aimed at a specific target such as the structure of the human genome. Successful humanists instead attempt to establish beachheads whose perimeters others expand and deepen. As a consequence of this interaction over time, there forms an unbroken intellectual chain stretching from Aristotle to Martin Heidegger, from Max Weber to Clifford Geertz, from Karl Marx to Jürgen Habermas. This is, typically, a chain of *individual* achievements. Even in the 21st century, collaboration in the humanities, though more common than previously, is not common at all. When it does occur, only two scholars are usually involved. There is a sense that these achievements *ought* to be individual.

While the best scientists are endowed with an aesthetic sensibility—they speak of a beautiful experiment, an elegant theorem—such sensibility is closer by far to the humanist center. Humanists do not merely strive to interpret the aura that radiates from cultural objects as diverse as the art song and situation comedy; they savor it. Moreover, aesthetic concerns shape their own work, their choice of expository forms, their attitude toward the language they employ. While scientists speak of writing up their results, of communicating clearly, humanists think of writing as the twin of thinking, the means of generating ideas from their existential encounters with the blank page or empty screen. For humanists, unlike scientists, the generation of ideas is never entirely separate from their expression, the search for the most satisfying form of their essay and for *le mot juste*. For humanists also, the book, that privileged vehicle of scholarship, is or should be a work of art. The best of contemporary scholarly books may not rival the masterpieces of the Aldine or Kelmscott presses, but there is no denying the pleasure humanists experience when they hold in their hands someone else's book and, more especially, their own, savoring the cover art, the page design, and the judicious choice of typefaces, all chosen on the basis of criteria that are largely aesthetic.

No better example of humanist preferences exists than Clifford Geertz, an anthropologist of the humanist ideal type. In a series of essays, collected in *The Interpretation of Cultures*, he defines the form and content of his approach:

> rather than following a rising curve of cumulative findings, cultural analysis breaks up into a disconnected yet coherent sequence of bolder and bolder sorties. Studies do build on other studies, not in the sense that they take up where others leave off, but in the sense that better informed and better conceptualized, they plunge more deeply into the same things. [As a consequence of this approach] the essay, whether of thirty pages or three hundred, has seemed the natural genre to present cultural interpretations and the theories sustaining them, and why, if one looks for systematic treatises in the field, one is soon disappointed, the more so if one finds any.[24]

Geertz's description applies to a wide swath of generative scholarly work in the humanities. In Geertz's sense, Aristotle's *Nicomachean Ethics*,[25] John Austin's *How to Do Things with Words*,[26] Northrup Frye's *Anatomy of Criticism*,[27] and Thomas Kuhn's *The Structure of Scientific Revolutions*[28] are essays. These may be as short as Walter Benjamin's "The Work of Art in the Age of Mechanical Reproduction"[29] or Paul Grice's "Logic and Conversation"[30]; they may be as long as John Locke's *Essay Concerning Human Understanding*[31] or Martin Heidegger's *Being and Time*[32]; they may be as idiosyncratic as Plato's *Lysis*[33] or Ludwig Wittgenstein's *Philosophical Investigations*[34]; they may even be in the form of lecture notes, as is the case with Friedrich Schleiermacher[35] and Ferdinand de Saussure.[36] Such work continues to be fresh and to refresh. Unlike the masterpieces of science, the best humanist essays can be read and reread with profit and pleasure long after their publication. This generative longevity does not depend on their being free from controversy. Neither Kuhn's *Structure* nor Heidegger's *Being and Time* is free from contention over its importance. Nor does this perennial quality depend on being right, strictly speaking. While John McTaggert's 1908 argument against the reality of time is almost certainly flawed,[37] it seems not to be so fatally, as it continues to provoke refutations, even a century after its publication.[38]

These works are not the products of isolated sightings deep into the structure of the object of study: the sudden insight, quickly communicated, of Newton on optics[39] or Röntgen on x-rays.[40] Rather, these forays are typically the products of slow growth, long-term cogitation, cumulative thought. As with the sciences, these discoveries are new to the field; as with the sciences, they constitute the fuel of others' intellectual fires. Unlike the sciences, however, these new possibilities are embodied, not only in any conclusions reached, but also in the fine structure of arguments made, the model of a new intellectual style. Such arguments resist abstraction and paraphrase, bearing as they do the stamp of a powerful personality not readily translated into prose. To study these works is to engage in an existential encounter, a meeting of mind with virtual mind. A few works of science, of course, have had similar generative power to the great works in the humanities. Ptolemy's *Almagest*[41] was generative in this sense for many centuries; indeed, it inspired Ibn al-Haytham's *On the Configuration of the World* in the 11th century[42] and Copernicus's *On the Revolutions of the Heavenly Bodies* in the 16th century.[43] We can say the same about the generative power of more recent scientific books, Darwin's *Origin of Species*[44] and E. O. Wilson's *Sociobiology*.[45]

In presenting the humanist ideal type, we are not making the broad claim that every scholarly product is an essay that generates other essays and, as a result, creates over the long term a cottage industry of learning. We are not contending that every scholarly article and book is a masterly artistic performance, shaped as carefully as a novel or a play by a literary master. We are not contending that the aesthetic value of the printed book militates firmly against a scholarly move onto the Internet. Rather, we are contending that the humanities ideal type can be viewed as an encompassing network of longstanding social habits and attitudes, a network also embodied in the tenure and promotion codes of every American research university. It is this network that guides scholars in their investments of professional time. In the case of the sciences, a system of values is in place that encourages the move to the Internet; in the case of the humanities, an analogous system of values discourages this move. This system says that time spent at such tasks will not necessarily pay in terms that count: reputation, the admiration of colleagues, and career success.

THE SCIENCES AND HUMANITIES TRANSFORMED

Our subject is the "Internet revolution" in the sciences and humanities—not the broader "digital revolution" spawned by the invention of the computer. No one has written more eloquently and thoughtfully than Yochai Benkler about the transformative changes that the Internet has wrought in information, knowledge, and culture:

> It seems passé today to speak of "the Internet revolution." In some academic circles, it is positively naïve. But it should not be. The change brought about by the networked information environment is deep. It is structural. . . . One needs only to run a Google search on any subject of interest to see how the "information good" that is the response to one's query is produced by the coordinate effects of the uncoordinated actions of a wide and diverse range of individuals and organizations acting on a wide range of motivations—both market and nonmarket, state-based and nonstate.[46]

Within the vast network of networks that is the Internet our primary concern is the World Wide Web—a virtual library of linked websites consisting of texts, images, and audio instantly accessible to anyone with a networked personal computer and instantly searchable by means of a browser. And on the World Wide Web our interest is limited to those texts, images, and audio contributed by the sciences and humanities and accessed by those communities in the process of generating new knowledge. And within the sciences and humanities, our object of study is primarily the communicative *products* of knowledge generation on the World Wide Web, not the *processes* by which these products are generated by various forms of specialized software or computer technology.

We believe that in identifying the Internet as the cause of a major innovation in scientific and humanistic communication we are simply following in the footsteps of Elizabeth Eisenstein in her classic *The Printing Press as an Agent of Change: Communications and Cultural Transformations in Early Modern Europe*,[47] which traces the cultural changes wrought by Gutenberg's invention in the 15th century. Robert Kahn and Vinton Cerf, the inventors of the Internet, are our Gutenbergs. The contents of our book and companion website constitute the proof of our contention of its transformative effects on the communicative products within the two cultures.

As we shall see in the chapters that follow, in the wake of this Internet revolution, the sciences are already reasonably well along in the process of reinventing the ways in which knowledge is generated, communicated, and evaluated. It is because of this that we think that the humanities—not only writer-scholars but those responsible for publishing journals and books—can learn from the current Internet practices in the sciences how better to harness them in the interest of the advance of knowledge. They will be able to do so, we feel, without altering the distinct character of research in the humanities, its canonization of the tentative, its reflective and reflexive stance, its underpinning in human understanding. In saying that the sciences are ahead in these matters, however, we are not saying that there has been no Internet progress in the humanities; indeed, a transformation is already under way without the assistance of the sciences. Truly impressive efforts that are entirely self-generated exist, though at present they flourish largely at the margins of disciplines. The key difference is this: In the sciences, Internet projects are extensions of the mainstream, while in the humanities such projects exist in a parallel universe that seldom affects the mainstream. While the challenge for the sciences is to move more rapidly in paths that are already marked out, the challenge for the humanities is to transform marginal into central tendencies, with help from forward-looking colleagues and perhaps inspiration from the sciences, to turn pockets of innovation into characteristics of the scholarly mainstream.

Although we are recommending that the sciences and the humanities complete the Internet revolution each has begun, our goal remains conservative. Once the revolution is over—once the Internet has transformed the generation, communication, and evaluation of knowledge in the sciences and humanities—we predict that the orientation toward knowledge of the two cultures will remain as far apart as ever. The products of the humanities will still be essays, the heirs of Plato's dialectic; the products of the sciences will remain quantitatively based articles, the heirs of the earliest learned letters published in their first periodicals.

In reflecting on the Internet revolution, now entering its fifth decade (third decade for the World Wide Web), there is no need to build castles in Spain, to speculate wildly about the Internet future of research and its communication. While we cannot foretell the results of future ingenuity in generating, communicating, and evaluating knowledge on the Internet, we can responsibly predict the future in the near term because, as a result of the uneven adoption of current innovations, what will be the future in some areas already constitutes the present in others. Moreover, while we cannot predict the source of future innovations, we can say that in both the sciences and the humanities change will come at the margins, working its way toward the center, fairly quickly in the sciences, more slowly in the humanities. Given their very different social habits and attitudes, this is hardly surprising.

THE BOOK ITSELF

The next three chapters address knowledge generation and communication in scientific articles, humanities essays in the form of articles and books, and virtual archives or electronic databases in the sciences and humanities.

In Chapter 2, we argue that now is a time of extraordinary fecundity in scientific communication. Scientists were always in the business of ruthlessly exploiting the communicative possibilities of the printed page, and their attitude toward the Internet is no different. In the history of scientific communication, the short article or learned letter soon displaced the lengthy monograph, recognition that as a rule the advance of knowledge comes in small increments, intellectual packages assembled and disseminated, used or discarded, in weeks or months rather than in years.

In the course of the 20th century, the scientific article further accelerated intellectual advance by becoming collaborative, recognition of the power of the division of intellectual labor and teamwork among scientists. Then the Internet intervened. The e-pages of the best journals are now the product of a collaboration among software engineers, journal editors, scientist-authors, and web designers. Journal browsers now find multimedia centers, complete archives of back issues, social media, links to most-cited and most-viewed articles, image albums, abstracts of abstracts, article summaries aimed at general audiences, supplemental information omitted from print articles, reader statistics, reader commentary, and more. This illustrates the scope of change. To illustrate its depth, its reach into the heart of science, we present a case study of the historical evolution of visualization in geometric morphometrics, a relatively recent scientific discipline whose task is to model mathematically and visually the shape of living things as they develop and evolve. Over the course of the 20th century, this task has led to a coincidence between a mathematically based biological science of shape and the intelligent and creative exploitation of the possibilities of its representation on the page and, to much greater effect, on the web. This chapter may seem primarily of interest to those in the sciences, but we believe humanists can learn from our discussion of the elite journals in the sciences, as well as from our case study tracing the evolution of innovative visuals, clearly demonstrating the benefits of the Internet over the printed page.

In Chapter 3, a general survey of a wide selection of prominent humanities journals leads to the conclusion that, in contrast to the sciences, Internet innovation in these disciplines occurs largely at the margins. Nonetheless, searching the humanities online literature assiduously, we find plentiful examples of scholars who meet the challenge of the Internet squarely. In history, we find an innovative collection of e-books, a collection of interactive articles on images of the French Revolution, and an online quantitatively oriented study of the antebellum economies of two Shenandoah Valley communities, one slave and one free. We also find a study of the recent history of Los Angeles heavily reliant on the visual in forms best suited to web display, as well as a study of the architectural history of ancient Rome that includes interactive 3D reconstructions of buildings in the Roman Forum. In music, we find a study of Beethoven's *Tempest* sonata that relies on evidence you can hear online, and a study of historical styles of performance equally indebted to the audible. In film criticism, we find several examples of the use of film clips and 3D reconstructions that serve as evidence for claims these scholars of the movies make. All these examples illustrate humanities scholars exploiting the Internet to create an alternative path through argument, link main text to supporting information, collaborate online to create new knowledge, and incorporate a greater variety of visual and audio representation than is possible or at least practical with print alone.

In Chapter 4, we contend that the rise of web-based digital archives fitted with powerful search algorithms will likely become as important to science and scholarship as were the first learned journals and academic presses. In this chapter, we set out to accomplish two goals: by means of a general survey of the different types of digital archive, to give readers a sense of their variety and protean character, and by means of an analysis of some exemplary cases, to give readers a sense of what it is like to employ such sites in the generation and communication of new knowledge. In the humanities, our exemplary cases are the online Walt Whitman and William Blake archives, which house different editions and handwritten copies of the authors' works along with a host of supporting documents and images not available in any single brick-and-mortar archive. We demonstrate how scholars can use the source materials on these sites for conducting comparative textual analysis in a way not possible before the Internet. Our comparative textual analysis also shows in what ways these sites are superior to printed scholarly editions of Whitman and Blake.

The exemplary websites in the sciences we examine in detail—the Encyclopedia of Life, Tree of Life, Galaxy Zoo, and Protein Data Bank—are also superior to their print-era alternatives. The Encyclopedia of Life and Tree of Life share the goal of documenting the acquired knowledge on all the known species on Earth. They also share the goal of creating a single visual that links all these species according to evolutionary origin, a visual not possible in print. Galaxy Zoo is an

archive of predominantly visual material—hundreds of thousands of astronomical images taken by the Sloan Digital Sky Survey and Hubble Space Telescope. It
and similar citizen science sites seek volunteers to analyze archived visual material and thereby help solve problems virtually insoluble without their participation. Probably the most successful archival site to date in science is the Protein
Data Bank and associated websites, which maintain an archive of structural data,
visualizations of the data, and 3D rotatable images for about 100,000 macromolecules, a population constantly growing. We also show how such web-based databases have become an important adjunct to journal publication, especially in the
biochemical sciences.

It is unfortunately true that the Internet makes it possible to flood virtual space
with material of dubious quality. This situation makes it essential that the current
knowledge evaluation system be retained and enforced. Our next two chapters show
how, through the Internet, the system can be reinvented in the interest of greater
academic rigor.

Chapter 5 deals with a single question: In the age of the Internet, what form will
peer review take? In our opinion, traditional peer review does reasonably well the
task for which it was designed: It provides a preliminary judgment of the value of
articles, a first step in the advance of knowledge. How sound are the researchers'
methods? How cogent are their arguments? How well supported are their interpretations? How original and significant are their conclusions? The answers to
these questions emerge as a consequence of adherence to a practical modification of
the communicative principles inherent in rational debate. In such debate, authors,
reviewers, and editors create an arena as free as possible from the distortions incident on strong emotional investment and the inequities of power. This situation will
be more closely approached, we contend, the more the humanities and science journals adopt the open Internet peer review currently practiced regularly by *Climate of
the Past* and, on special occasion, by *Shakespeare Quarterly*.

In Chapter 6, we show how the Internet offers a new means of achieving the postpublication goal all desire: constant scrutiny that keeps the scholarly and scientific
record straight, a procedure that shares with all interested parties an accurate picture
of the current state of knowledge. In the case of the sciences, in which the chief
vehicle of intellectual advance is the article, the problem is not only unintentional
error but also fraud and plagiarism, the unintended consequences of the fierce competition for scarce twin resources, reputation and research funding. In this case, the
solution has come from an unexpected source outside of science: journalistic blogs
such as "Retraction Watch" and "Abnormal Science," which have reinvented investigative journalism in the interest of keeping science on course. We also show that
serious postpublication conceptual clarification is possible by means of blogs and

discussion forums. In this connection, we analyze a deliberately controversial article by Hugo Mercier and Dan Sperber, "Why Do Humans Reason? Arguments for an Argumentative Theory."[48] It appeared in *Behavioral and Brain Sciences* accompanied by 24 commentaries by other scholars and the authors' response. In the year after this publication, robust debate took place in the public arenas of blogs and discussion groups, as well as online newspapers and magazines. This debate serves as a sterling example of postpublication evaluation by the community at large.

Setting the record straight is also vital for scholarly monographs, the chief vehicle of intellectual advance in the humanities. In the main, this has been the job of book reviews; in the best case, these reveal the significance of monographs and detect any errors of fact and judgment these monographs might contain. At present, however, book reviews are an inefficient vehicle for accomplishing these tasks, scattered as they are behind gates that only high fees will unlock. We suggest that the humanities reinvent the book review in the form of an open-access, web-based aggregate review site that would provide an extended summary of the monograph in question; would compile existing reviews, reader comments, and author responses; and would rate the book on a dual scale of competence and significance.

Although the optimism this book has so far embodied has been true to the Internet's potential, we have deliberately slighted the obstacles that could interfere with and even undermine that potential. In our concluding chapter we address these. Only by overcoming them can both cultures truly harness the Internet in the interest of maximizing the generation, communication, and evaluation of knowledge. The first three obstacles we discuss affect both the sciences and the humanities: the difficulties publishers have in finding a middle path between access to the scholarly and scientific literature and reasonable profitability, the employment of tenure and promotion codes better suited to an era of print, and the difficulties in preserving and updating Internet archives. A fourth obstacle also affects the sciences and humanities, but differently: It concerns limits on the use of existing information. On the one hand, the sciences are being impeded by lack of community access to the massive datasets that are routinely generated but could be easily shared through the Internet coincident with article publication, or even earlier. On the other hand, humanities scholarship is being limited by procrustean copyright legislation that greatly discourages reproduction of 20th- and 21st-century cultural artifacts in essays, thereby limiting comment and critique at the time when the incorporation of those reproductions is technically much easier and less costly than in the pre-Internet era. A final obstacle faces only scholars whose research involves government documents. Historians and political scientists have been impeded in their archival work by unreasonable prohibitions on release of and overclassification of documents at a time when the quantity of material and the demand for its use are increasing exponentially due to the Internet. In the final paragraphs, we suggest various ways of overcoming these obstacles within current legal and institutional systems.

THE AUDIENCE

Our expectation is that scientists, scholars, university administrators, science publishers, and scholarly journal or book editors reading our book—whether the print or electronic versions—will have cause for both self-congratulation and self-criticism. They will see demonstrated their many successful efforts to harness the Internet in the interest of improving the generation, communication, and evaluation of knowledge. They will read about a complex task that reaches beyond the merely cognitive, involving as it does a sophisticated appreciation of computer technology, a high degree of administrative competence, an acute business sense, and deep insight into the possibilities and constraints afforded by legislation and institutional arrangements. While they will be impressed by what they have achieved, they will be humbled, we hope, by the size and complexity of the task ahead: the full exploitation of the possibilities of the Internet in the interest of science and scholarship across the globe.

In our view, the motto of the University of Minnesota—"Driven to Discover"—encapsulates the imperative scientists and scholars share in generating, communicating, and evaluating knowledge. Our book should thus have some professional interest for them. It may come as a surprise, however, that anyone else—any instructor at a college, community college, or high school, or any member of the general public—might find this book worth reading, or its advice worth heeding. But it is a surprise that is embodied in our central message: The knowledge that the Internet makes freely available and the collaborative opportunities it affords—opportunities such as the Perseus Digital Library and Galaxy Zoo—expand the scope and definition of legitimate research and at the same time widen the pool of those who can be involved.

2

THE INTERNET SCIENTIFIC ARTICLE

Reshaping Verbal and Visual Communication

REVOLUTION OR EVOLUTION?

Do the changes in the scientific article incident on Internet publication constitute a revolution in representation and communication? John Stewart MacKenzie Owen insists that they do not. In *The Scientific Article in the Age of Digitization*, he argues that contrary to claims about the impact of digitization on scientific communication, "the journal article as a communicative form for reporting on research and disseminating scientific knowledge does not seem to have been transformed by . . . [the Internet]: it remains a digital copy of the printed form."[1] Owen views the current situation as preserving and extending "existing functions and values rather than as an innovation that radically transforms a communicative practice that has evolved over the centuries."[2]

The conclusion Owen draws cannot be faulted. We do not doubt that the articles and journals in his sample are, on average, to quote Stevan Harnad, "mere clones of paper journals, ghosts in another medium."[3] We do, however, question Owen's sample of online scientific journals. While he includes such journals as the *Brazilian Electronic Journal of Economics*, *Internet Journal of Chemistry*, and *Journal of Cotton Science* (all three now defunct), he excludes the most highly cited scientific journals producing printed and electronic issues, like *Nature, Physical Review, Journal of the American Chemical Society*, or such highly successful open-access journals as those of the Public Library of Science. It is the latter set that contains the journals we need to scrutinize if we are to discover what innovations, if any, have surfaced and are likely to be widely adopted in the future. These journals have the robust readership, the prestige, the financial resources, and the technical capacity necessary to introduce web-based innovations on a large scale. It is in these that the Internet revolution is now most visible.

Still, among all scientific journals today, whether print or electronic, there remains a conservative core at this revolution's center, a still point in the turning world of knowledge generation and communication. As we ourselves noted elsewhere,

> it is the interaction of visual and verbal texts, an interaction enabled and facilitated by devices of style and presentation, that constitutes the heart of scientific argumentative practices at the end of the 20th century. While the "computer revolution" will undoubtedly continue to facilitate this interaction, we do not think this heart will look, or beat, very differently at the end of the 21st century.[4]

Scientific argument is and will remain scientific argument. True, readers can browse through a digital or print scientific article following a nonlinear path: Depending on their interests, they can jump from abstract to methods, or from title to figures, or from abstract to conclusion and back to methods. Nevertheless, they do this fully confident that the text has as its primary axis of organization an argument of Aristotelian rigor. Indeed, it is this axis that makes opportunistic reading possible. In the scientific article, regardless of medium, a research problem will be introduced and contextualized, a method for its solution will be described, the results from having applied the method will be presented and discussed, and conclusions will be drawn. Indeed, whether in print or on the web, the boundaries of these argumentative components will routinely be signaled by section headings. In a 20th-century print article by Goodman and Rich,[5] these are Introduction, Methods and Materials, Results, Discussion, and Summary; in a 21st-century Internet article by Aron et al.[6] these are Abstract, Acknowledgments, Author Summary, Introduction, Results, Discussion, and Supporting Information. If anything, the primary axis of organization of the digital scientific article is even more regimented than ever before: Data-driven articles almost always conform to this argumentative plan, or to a slight variation.

This is not to say that no substantive variation is possible in the basic argumentative structure. In an earlier book we identified a major variation, appearing in the *Journal of the Chemical Society* and *Journal of the American Chemical Society* of the early 20th century.[7] These articles were typically divided in two. Their first part distilled the essence of the discovery; it was aimed at an audience of chemists in general. The second part provided experimental method and results in enough detail to satisfy experts in a particular research area. During the 20th century, this sensible two-part structure did not take hold, but a similar variation is now routine in journals like *Nature, Science*, and *Applied Physics Letters*. In these journals, the article itself is only a few thousand words long. Available in the printed issue or as a PDF from the web, it conforms to the typical argumentative structure but does so with minimal experimental detail and a severely limited number of visuals. It is aimed at scientist-readers from diverse disciplines with little time to spend. But there is also a link to Supplemental Information, available only through the web, conveying that experimental detail to experts with a strong interest in the subject matter.

This Supplemental Information section is a web innovation that deserves further comment. It now routinely appears appended to articles not only in journals that severely limit article length like the three just mentioned, but in many of the online elite journals we have examined. Such sections provide authors with the capacity to include technical details that would be omitted in the print era for lack of space. These supplements also routinely contain videos or audiovisual files that no print edition could possibly accommodate. These sections vary in size from a few pages to more than a hundred. Supplemental Information permits these journals to give us science in depth without alienating readers who lack an intense interest in a particular investigation. It has been reported that scientists have complained about "constraining word limits to achieve 'the smallest publishable unit' ... which often eliminates detailed discussions of methods and room for deeper arguments."[8] These scientists must have been thinking back to the print-only era; today, the Supplemental Information link routinely provides those detailed discussions.

Another variation focuses on a particular difficulty, the translation of the typical methods section into actual practice. In 2006 Moshe Pritsker founded the *Journal of Visualized Experiments* to resolve this key problem in the life sciences by taking "advantage of video technology to transmit the multiple facets and intricacies of life science research." Each article begins with a professionally produced video demonstrating some experimental procedure in the life sciences, such as a method for obtaining RNA samples from human postmortem brain tissue.[9] Accompanying that video are the typical components of a scientific article: a detailed abstract describing the method and its application; a step-by-step protocol, often including additional visuals; and representative results combined with a discussion of their significance. In the past, scientists wanting to replicate a difficult experiment often had to spend weeks or months learning and perfecting a new technique or visiting the authors' laboratory for a demonstration. The goal of this unique journal is no less than greatly reducing this major inefficiency in scientific practice by creating a vast virtual repository of "visualized experiments" that feature video streams of scientists at work in the lab, intermixed with processes captured by video microscopy and microscopic structures rendered by 2D and 3D animation. One can easily project the day when videos of experimental methods are routinely a part of scientific articles in areas where replication based on print alone is not easily managed.

In his blog, Michael Nielsen tackles the question "Is scientific publishing about to be disrupted?" His answer is that there is already "a striking difference between today's scientific publishing landscape, and the landscape of ten years ago. What's new today is the flourishing of an ecosystem of startups that are experimenting with new ways of communicating research, some radically different to conventional journals."[10] By "radically different" he means use of blogs for reporting preliminary research findings, open sharing of data and other information during the research process, and links to a personalized list of recommended reading. Our analysis presented in the next section shows that it is not only "the ecosystem of startups" that reveals experimentation with variations on the traditional form and content of the article in print; it is rather a mixture of the *ancien régime* of elite scientific journals and radical new journals founded to fully exploit the Internet. These deviations from the past include multimedia centers, social media, links to most-cited and most-viewed articles, links to related articles, links to databases, image albums, abstracts of abstracts, summaries aimed at a general audience, supplemental information omitted from print articles, reader statistics, reader commentary, educational videos, exhibitions of visually striking images, interactive visuals, experimental results in video form, audio and video abstracts, and rotatable 2D and 3D animations of microscopic structures. The agents behind these innovations are software engineers, web designers, and the editorial staff of journals, as well as article authors—it is a team effort.

Recently, the largest publisher of scientific literature, Elsevier Publishing, unveiled "The Article of the Future." Because it is really an amalgamation of many of the features already present in elite scientific journals, it might be more accurately called "The State-of-the-Art Digital Article," an attempt to discern and exemplify central tendencies amid proliferating innovation. Elsevier has posted a dozen "prototype" articles for different scientific disciplines on a website. In all these prototypes, the viewer sees three panes of different widths. The left one is for navigation. In this the narrowest pane, the viewer sees the table of contents and thumbnails to all figures and tables. A click on a link in the left pane sends viewers to the corresponding location in the middle and widest pane, which displays the main feature—the article itself, heavily hyperlinked. Within this middle pane, viewers can read or scan the article and save or print a PDF version; they can also watch any videos, and automatically convert tables of data into graphs. For figures composed of multiple discrete images, they can position the cursor over any and read the associated caption. The right pane displays information supplemental to the middle pane. Clicking on links in the middle pane activates elements in the right pane. For instance, if viewers click on an author's name in the middle pane, they will see in the right pane a biography and photograph. If viewers click on a link within the abstract, a video may be activated in the right pane in which an author describes the article's contents. Click on a reference number in the article's text, and in the right pane bibliographic information and the corresponding abstract appear along with a link to the complete referenced article. Click on an image in the text, and the image with caption appears in the right pane. If the image is in an interactive form, the viewer manipulates it in that right pane. Interactive images include rotatable 3D structures, graphs, or tree diagrams. For graphs, the viewer may position the cursor over a data point and its numerical (x,y) values will appear on the screen; click on another link with the graph, and all the data appear in tabular form. Some images are also tied into databases like the Protein Data Base, Google Maps, and ChemSpider. Click on a link, and the viewer sees the information in the database on the right or middle pane. The Elsevier journal *Cell* has already partially implemented some of these features (Fig. 2.1).[11]

Some bloggers were far from impressed with Elsevier's article of the future. Kent Anderson found the prototypes "elaborate, unstable, and disappointing overall," no more than "an article from the past, with some embedded hyperlinks, some AJAX tabs [that permit a switch from one document to another], two basic social media elements, and not much else."[12] The Online Journalism Blog reported that "the prototypes resemble an enthusiastic bash at a multimedia-infused online encyclopaedia circa 1997, when multimedia was still a buzzword, or such as you might have found on a CD-ROM magazine cover mounted giveaway around the same time."[13]

In our view, these prototypes must be seen for what they are: representations of the state of the art in digital scientific communication. More to the point, they are as different from the print version as black-and-white silent movies shot with a stationary camera are different from talking color movies shot with a handheld digital camera. As a result, the experience of "reading" the scientific literature has been transformed in important ways. Readers do not only read text; they also point and click to access a host of related materials (databases, other articles, author biographies, and pictures), rotate 3D structures, interact with graphs and tables, zoom in and out of maps, watch videos of computer simulations and events as they occurred in the laboratory or field, listen to authors talk about their research, share articles they like with friends, and comment upon claims they question. Because the number of viewers, citation counts, blog posts, and social bookmarking are immediately accessible, readers can experience simultaneously the content of an article and the current community judgment of its value.

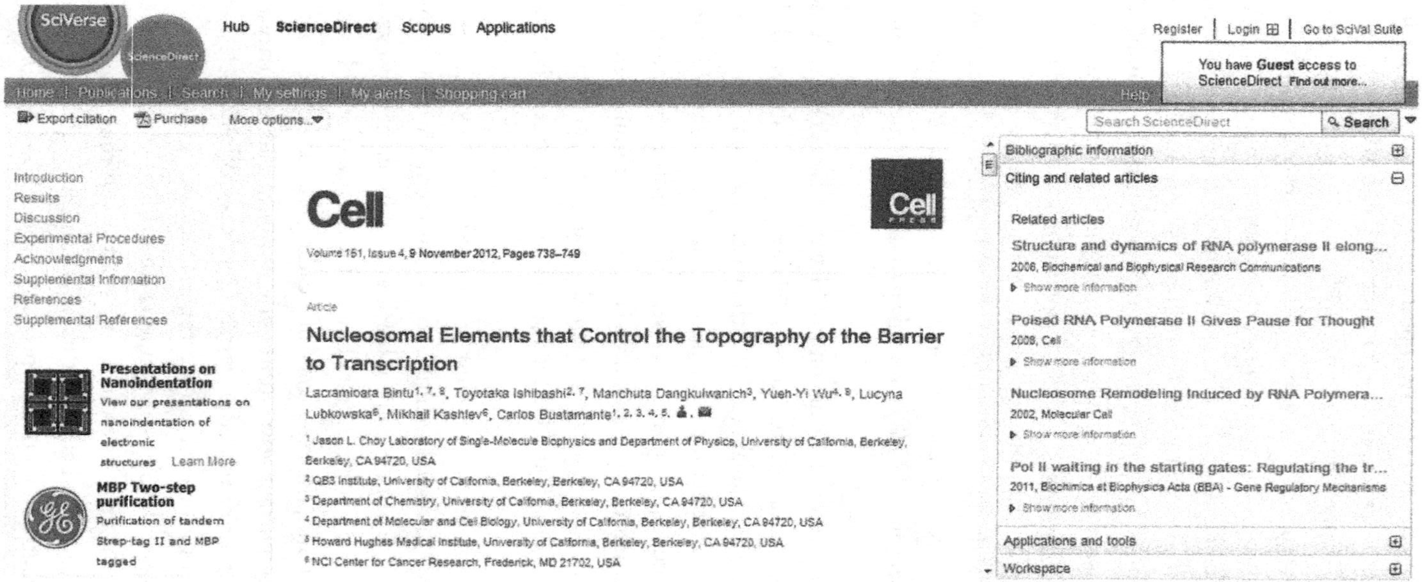

FIGURE 2.1 Screenshot of three-pane format in *Cell* [L. Bintu et al., *Cell* 151 (2012): 738–749].

We need to understand the scope and depth of these rapidly proliferating innovations in the creation and communication of Internet science. To make sense of its scope, we will survey the landscape of 21st-century scientific communication by means of a quantitative analysis of change in a large selection of online scientific articles. To make sense of the depth of change, we focus on a particular case, that of geometric morphometrics, the science of shape, a specialty in which the limitations of the printed page constitute a representational and epistemic imprisonment from which the web offers hope of escape. By means of this combined quantitative analysis and case study, we trace the outlines of the tidal shift from paper to the computer screen.

A SURVEY OF THE WEB ARTICLE

Our first task is to analyze a random selection of scientific research articles published in 2010 and 2011, chosen from the 10 most highly cited science journals for the period 1999 to 2009:[14] *New England Journal of Medicine, Astrophysical Journal, Nature, Journal of the American Chemical Society, Science, Journal of Biological Chemistry, Proceedings of the National Academy of Sciences (PNAS), Physical Review Letters, Applied Physics Letters,* and *Physical Review B.* These are elite journals with a long publication history. The oldest, *New England Journal of Medicine,* has been in existence for over 200 years; the youngest, *Physical Review B,* while itself only 40, is an offshoot of *Physical Review,* founded in 1893. All offer HTML and PDF versions of individual articles, except *Physical Review B* and *Physical Review Letters,* which are PDF only. And while all 10 journals offer free access to some articles, most articles are accessible only to subscribers (individual or institutional) or those willing to purchase or rent selected ones.

Also added to our selection were three journals from the premier publisher of open-access journals—*PLOS (Public Library of Science) Biology, PLOS Medicine,* and *PLOS One.* We had originally included two other open-access journals in our selection, *Journal of Modern Physics* and *International Journal of Geosciences,* which are financed by author charges—$500 per article. We later learned that both these journals are published by Scientific Research Publishing, which Jeffrey Beall has listed on his watchdog website Scholarly Open Access as one of the "potential, possible, or probable predatory scholarly open-access publishers."[15] Sadly, the ease of starting a new online research journal and charging authors to publish in it has given rise to journals that have engaged in dubious practices, like listing bogus advisory committees, misrepresenting the publisher location, and failing to subject submitted manuscripts to legitimate peer review or any other serious means of internal quality control.[16],[17] On his watchdog website Not Even Wrong, for example, Peter Woit reports that two papers in the *American Journal of Modern Physics* (also published by the Scientific Publishing Group) plagiarized material extensively.[18] The potential financial gains here are not trivial: If you become an Internet science publisher and start up 100 journals that each publish 100 articles per year, at author charges of $500 per article, that generates a tidy gross income of $5 million. In any case, having learned that *Journal of Modern Physics* and *International Journal of Geosciences* are included on Beall's list as emanating from a suspect publisher, we decided to drop them from our analysis. (We have more to say about watchdog websites in Chapter 6.)

In total, we analyzed 10 randomly selected articles from each of the 13 journals in our selection. We also gathered information about the homepage and first page for a 2011 issue of each journal. As a means of gauging change, we will be comparing our results for the 21st century with those obtained in our previous study of earlier centuries.[19] We will also be illustrating these changes by examples chosen from the 21st-century scientific article in Figure 2.2[20] and the 20th-century article in Figure 2.3.[21] We look at the ways the Internet has increased accessibility, facilitated changes in the nature of authorship, coped with the increasing complexity of scientific knowledge, increased intra- and inter-textuality, incorporated reader comments and reader statistics, and enhanced visualization. Since we cannot claim our selection of only 130 articles is representative of the "typical" article from the same time period or our analysis results are statistically significant, we mainly stick to qualitative generalizations and, to the extent possible, support the data we do include with citations from previous studies that reached similar conclusions.

Increasing Accessibility

It's 1962. How would you get a copy of the article in Figure 2.3? You would either have to have had a subscription to *PNAS*, known someone with a subscription, written to the author for a preprint, or undertaken a trip to a well-stocked science library. In contrast, anyone with an Internet connection could have read the article in Figure 2.2 immediately upon its publication in the open-access journal *PLOS Biology*. This migration from print to digital was already well under way by the end of the 20th century: Over half of our earlier sample of 35 journals from the 20th century offered web-based versions of their articles.[22] Today, essentially all scientific articles published in the 21st century and a major proportion of those published in the 20th are available through the web. A PDF of the Goodman and Rich article in Figure 2.3 is now freely downloadable to all through the *PNAS* online archives.

Much has been written about the urgent need for a "truly network-enabled research communication system" without access restrictions.[23] But the top 10 journals in our

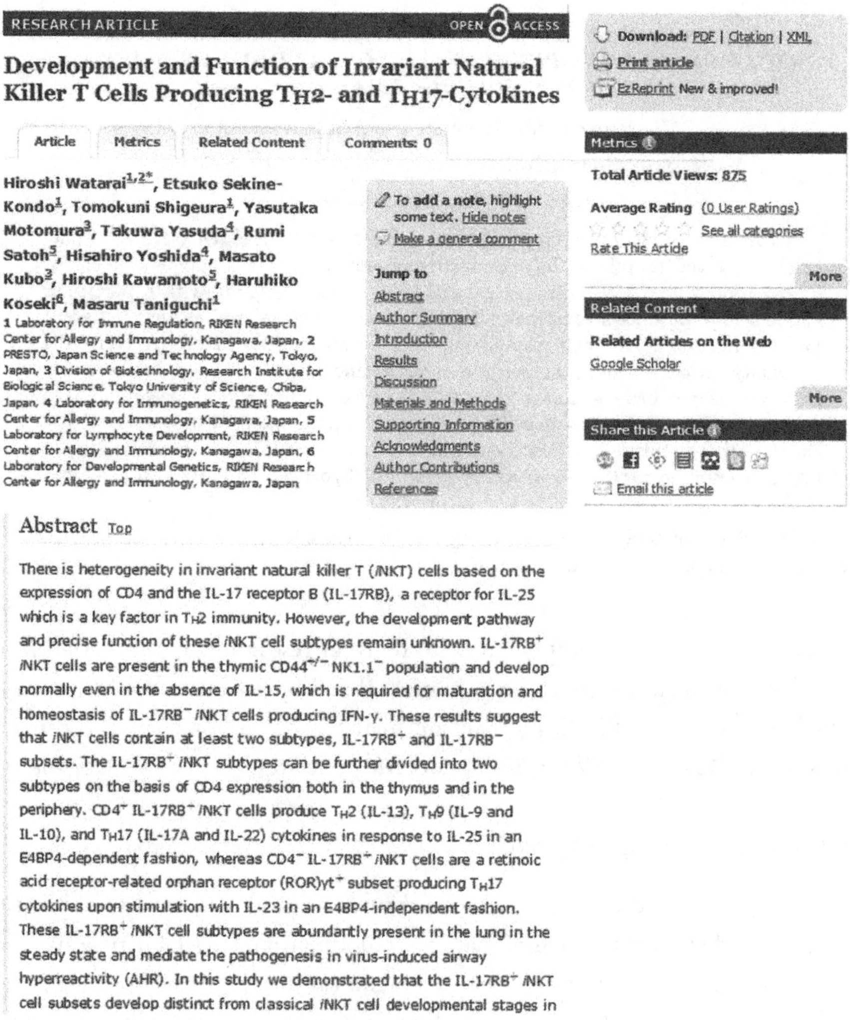

RESEARCH ARTICLE OPEN ACCESS

Development and Function of Invariant Natural Killer T Cells Producing TH2- and TH17-Cytokines

Article | Metrics | Related Content | Comments: 0

Hiroshi Watarai[1,2*], Etsuko Sekine-Kondo[1], Tomokuni Shigeura[1], Yasutaka Motomura[3], Takuwa Yasuda[4], Rumi Satoh[5], Hisahiro Yoshida[4], Masato Kubo[3], Hiroshi Kawamoto[5], Haruhiko Koseki[6], Masaru Taniguchi[1]

1 Laboratory for Immune Regulation, RIKEN Research Center for Allergy and Immunology, Kanagawa, Japan, 2 PRESTO, Japan Science and Technology Agency, Tokyo, Japan, 3 Division of Biotechnology, Research Institute for Biological Science, Tokyo University of Science, Chiba, Japan, 4 Laboratory for Immunogenetics, RIKEN Research Center for Allergy and Immunology, Kanagawa, Japan, 5 Laboratory for Lymphocyte Development, RIKEN Research Center for Allergy and Immunology, Kanagawa, Japan, 6 Laboratory for Developmental Genetics, RIKEN Research Center for Allergy and Immunology, Kanagawa, Japan

To add a note, highlight some text. Hide notes
Make a general comment

Jump to
Abstract
Author Summary
Introduction
Results
Discussion
Materials and Methods
Supporting Information
Acknowledgments
Author Contributions
References

Download: PDF | Citation | XML
Print article
EzReprint New & improved!

Metrics
Total Article Views: 875
Average Rating (0 User Ratings)
See all categories
Rate This Article
More

Related Content
Related Articles on the Web
Google Scholar
More

Share this Article
Email this article

Abstract Top

There is heterogeneity in invariant natural killer T (iNKT) cells based on the expression of CD4 and the IL-17 receptor B (IL-17RB), a receptor for IL-25 which is a key factor in TH2 immunity. However, the development pathway and precise function of these iNKT cell subtypes remain unknown. IL-17RB+ iNKT cells are present in the thymic CD44+/− NK1.1− population and develop normally even in the absence of IL-15, which is required for maturation and homeostasis of IL-17RB− iNKT cells producing IFN-γ. These results suggest that iNKT cells contain at least two subtypes, IL-17RB+ and IL-17RB− subsets. The IL-17RB+ iNKT subtypes can be further divided into two subtypes on the basis of CD4 expression both in the thymus and in the periphery. CD4+ IL-17RB+ iNKT cells produce TH2 (IL-13), TH9 (IL-9 and IL-10), and TH17 (IL-17A and IL-22) cytokines in response to IL-25 in an E4BP4-dependent fashion, whereas CD4− IL-17RB+ iNKT cells are a retinoic acid receptor-related orphan receptor (ROR)γt+ subset producing TH17 cytokines upon stimulation with IL-23 in an E4BP4-independent fashion. These IL-17RB+ iNKT cell subtypes are abundantly present in the lung in the steady state and mediate the pathogenesis in virus-induced airway hyperreactivity (AHR). In this study we demonstrated that the IL-17RB+ iNKT cell subsets develop distinct from classical iNKT cell developmental stages in

FIGURE 2.2 Screenshot of 2010 digital article from 2010 *PLOS Biology* [L. Aron et al., *PLOS Biology* 8 (2010): e1000349]. Video 2.1 [▶]

selection do not permit free public access: They depend heavily upon revenue streams from institutional and individual subscriptions, page charges, and online payment for access to single articles. Yet this business model does not leave open access entirely out of bounds. Six journals grant immediate access upon publication to individual articles if the author has paid a publication fee in the range of $1,500 to $2,700 per article, in most cases an expense covered by a grant. And all 10 journals open at least a small portion of their archive to free viewing without author charges.

Also included in our selection are three PLOS journals, which are open access. The stated mission of PLOS is to "make the world's scientific and medical literature

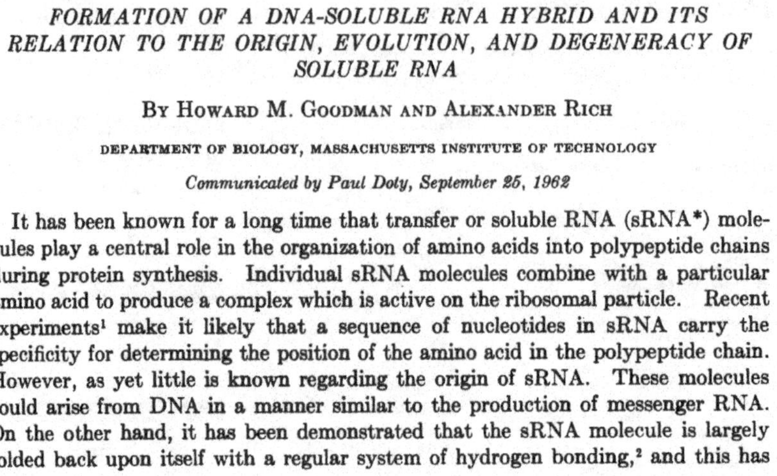

FORMATION OF A DNA-SOLUBLE RNA HYBRID AND ITS RELATION TO THE ORIGIN, EVOLUTION, AND DEGENERACY OF SOLUBLE RNA

BY HOWARD M. GOODMAN AND ALEXANDER RICH

DEPARTMENT OF BIOLOGY, MASSACHUSETTS INSTITUTE OF TECHNOLOGY

Communicated by Paul Doty, September 25, 1962

It has been known for a long time that transfer or soluble RNA (sRNA*) molecules play a central role in the organization of amino acids into polypeptide chains during protein synthesis. Individual sRNA molecules combine with a particular amino acid to produce a complex which is active on the ribosomal particle. Recent experiments[1] make it likely that a sequence of nucleotides in sRNA carry the specificity for determining the position of the amino acid in the polypeptide chain. However, as yet little is known regarding the origin of sRNA. These molecules could arise from DNA in a manner similar to the production of messenger RNA. On the other hand, it has been demonstrated that the sRNA molecule is largely folded back upon itself with a regular system of hydrogen bonding,[2] and this has

FIGURE 2.3 Reproduction of first printed page in 1962 article in *Proceedings of National Academy of Sciences (PNAS)* [H. Goodman and A. Rich, *PNAS* 48 (1962): 2101–2109].

a freely available public resource" and "to reinvent research communication from top to bottom to fully exploit the potential offered by digital media."[24] But there is no free lunch: The PLOS journals are financed by author charges for article publication—$2,900 for *PLOS Biology* and *Medicine* and $1,350 for *PLOS One*.

The Changing Nature of Authorship

One of the marked differences between Figures 2.2 and 2.3 concerns the list of authors and their institutional affiliations. Goodman and Rich's article has two authors, both from the same U.S. research organization; the Aron et al. article has six, from three different German research organizations. This contrast reflects 21st-century practice: The article's composition is a more highly social activity than its 20th-century predecessor, often involving participants from different countries and organizations, exchanging e-mails, texts, data, and images via the Internet. We earlier found that on average 20th-century articles have a little over two authors per article, with a maximum of five. On the basis of these data, we concluded that the practice of 20th-century science was "largely the product of an individual or very small group trying to solve a limited problem within a larger research field."[25] This statement does not apply to the new century. Recent quantitative studies have reported that single authors generated "the papers of singular distinction in science and engineering and social science in the 1950s, but the mantle of extraordinarily cited work has passed to teams by 2000."[26] After 1975, these collaborations increasingly involved multiple universities and research institutes.[27]

Bylines in our 21st-century selection of articles support these conclusions. The average number of authors is 12, with a median of six—much higher than that for our 20th-century sample. There were only two single-author articles, while two had author lists running into the hundreds. The average number of institutions listed in the bylines was also impressively high, just under six, with a median of three; moreover, almost half of the articles involved an international collaboration. Not surprisingly, the most represented countries were the same as those who have been major players in scientific research over the past several centuries: the United States, Russia, Germany, the United Kingdom, and France. One journal, *Applied Physics Letters*, has an interesting variation on the byline that dramatizes the shift to global-ization: world maps with the geographic locations of the authors' home institutions.

One might legitimately ask what it means to be an "author" when a six-page arti-cle can have as many as 242 of them with 131 different institutional affiliations,[28] or even just six authors from one institution.[29] From such bylines, the reader usually has no way of telling who wrote what, or performed what tasks. In fact, some listed authors do not write anything but only review what someone else has written. For that reason, some journals routinely append paragraphs spelling out the authors' roles, as in Aron et al.:

> The author(s) have made the following declarations about their contribu-tions: Conceived and designed the experiments: LA PK RK. Performed the experiments: LA PK. Analyzed the data: LA PK WW RK. Contributed reagents/materials/analysis tools: TTP ERK WW. Wrote the paper: LA RK.[30]

For the entire 21st-century selection, the bylines reflect the fact that scientific prac-tice today is more and more a collaborative effort involving multiple authors from different research institutions, often in different countries, performing tasks that, while they contribute to the whole, are frequently highly specialized. Obviously, these commodious bylines are not directly a product of digital publication, but it is hard to imagine the existence of such collaborative teams without the ease of com-municating messages, images, articles, and data through the Internet, facilitating what would otherwise be a task of daunting proportions.

Coping with Complexity

Clearly, web publication has caused the journals in our selection to think seriously about how to better communicate complex information to a more diverse audience. Observe that the Goodman and Rich article has no abstract, while the Aron et al. article has not only a heading abstract but also an "author summary" of about the same length. Its purpose is "to make findings accessible to an audience of both scientists and non-scientists . . . Ideally aimed to a level of understanding of an undergraduate student," as the PLOS website asserts. All research articles in the three PLOS journals include such author summaries, as do *PNAS* and *Journal of Biological Chemistry* (Fig. 2.4).[31] Moreover, in a given issue nearly all the journals offer links to a synopsis or to news stories for at least some articles. While such author and editor summaries could also be added to print articles, the lack of space restrictions on the web facilitates their widespread adoption. And we must not omit the innovative spirit the web instills.

Other journals have adopted different approaches to combat article complexity. The contents page of *Applied Physics Letters* shows the usual lists of titles and authors, but also a one- or two-sentence abstract of the abstract and the key image. In the example of Figure 2.5,[32] there is a clear division of purpose. The title announces the major claim in a noun phrase; the abstract of the abstract elaborates on that claim in two complete sentences; the graph depicts the claim. Following the link in the lower right corner sends interested readers to the actual heading abstract and byline. The *New England Journal of Medicine* takes yet another tack. Its articles have abstracts divided into four components: a paragraph on the background, another on the methods, another for results, and yet another for conclusions. All are linked to corresponding sections in the main text. In all these journals, there appears to be a genuine effort to ensure that readers, whatever their expertise, can follow the main points with the least effort.

Increasing Inter- and Intra-textuality

Scientific research articles are not only textual but intertextual; all emerge from the existing literature, a context that through citation serves to establish the importance and originality of any new effort: "We create our texts out of the sea of former texts that surround us, the sea of language we live in. And we understand the texts of others within that same sea."[33] Printed scientific articles keep the sea of former texts "spatially distant from the references to them," while hyperlinked text "makes individual references easy to follow and the entire field of interconnections obvious and easy to navigate."[34]

Citation number, format, and placement have evolved over time. In the 17th century, only about a third of articles had any citations. Those few were incorporated into or adjacent to running text. There was minimal bibliographic information and no format consistency.[35] In the 18th and 19th centuries, more than half the articles had citations. These were incorporated into the text or placed at the bottom of the page as footnotes. Citational format still varied widely from journal to journal, even

Journal of Biological Chemistry
www.jbc.org

First Published on October 7, 2011, doi: 10.1074/jbc.M111.290973
December 2, 2011 The Journal of Biological Chemistry, 286, 41312–41322.

F1000 "Recommended" – FREE!

ATP Synthase Complex of *Plasmodium falciparum*
DIMERIC ASSEMBLY IN MITOCHONDRIAL MEMBRANES AND RESISTANCE TO GENETIC DISRUPTION*

Praveen Balabaskaran Nina, Joanne M. Morrisey, Suresh M. Ganesan,

Hangjun Ke, April M. Pershing, Michael W. Mather and Akhil B. Vaidya[1]

⌐+⌐ Author Affiliations

⌐[1] To whom correspondence should be addressed: Drexel University College of Medicine, 2900 Queen Ln., Philadelphia, PA 19129. Tel.: 215-991-8557; Fax: 215-848-2271; E-mail: avaidya@drexelmed.edu.

Capsule

Background: The role of ATP synthase in blood stages of malaria parasites has been unclear.

Results: Canonical subunits were targeted to the mitochondrion, could not be deleted by gene disruption, and were present in large complexes.

Conclusion: *Plasmodium* ATP synthase is likely essential and forms a dimeric complex.

Significance Composition, properties, structure, and drugability of the complex should be fully investigated.

Abstract

The rotary nanomotor ATP synthase is a central player in the bioenergetics of most organisms. Yet the role of ATP synthase in malaria parasites has remained unclear, as blood stages of *Plasmodium falciparum* appear to derive ATP largely through glycolysis. Also, genes for essential subunits of the F_O sector of the complex could not be detected in the parasite genomes. Here, we have used molecular genetic and immunological tools to investigate the localization, complex formation, and functional significance of predicted ATP synthase subunits in *P. falciparum*. We generated transgenic *P. falciparum* lines expressing seven epitope-tagged canonical ATP synthase subunits, revealing localization of all but one of the

FIGURE 2.4 Example *Journal of Biological Chemistry* article incorporating abstract of abstract followed by traditional heading abstract [P. Nina et al., *Journal of Biological Chemistry* 286 (2011): 41312–41322].

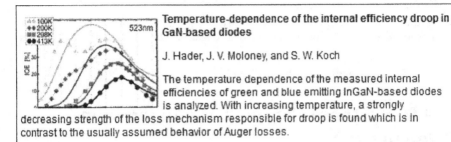

Temperature-dependence of the internal efficiency droop in GaN-based diodes

J. Hader, J. V. Moloney, and S. W. Koch

The temperature dependence of the measured internal efficiencies of green and blue emitting InGaN-based diodes is analyzed. With increasing temperature, a strongly decreasing strength of the loss mechanism responsible for droop is found which is in contrast to the usually assumed behavior of Auger losses.

Appl. Phys. Lett. 99, 181127 (2011)

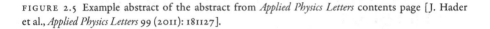

FIGURE 2.5 Example abstract of the abstract from *Applied Physics Letters* contents page [J. Hader et al., *Applied Physics Letters* 99 (2011): 181127].

from article to article in a given journal. During this period, the average number of citations within a section grew and the citational elements grew more uniform. In the 20th century, citational density increased fourfold, citational format became standardized, and the placement of the citations shifted from the bottom of the page to the article's end.[36]

The Goodman and Rich article is typical of the 20th century. Its 25 citations are gathered in full at the end, numbered, and uniformly presented. In each case, Goodman and Rich provide author names, journal name, volume, first page, and year of publication. The key components for finding the article—journal name, volume, and first page—are differentiated by typeface: italics for journal name, bold for volume, plain font for page number. These citations are linked to super-scripted numbers dispersed throughout the text. They are not confined to the beginning or end, turning the entire article into a network of intertextuality. This network serves two purposes: It rewards scientists for having provided the article's authors with productive information, and it provides readers with additional reading concerning the research problem, methods details, and supporting information.[37]

The intertextuality of the scientific article continues to evolve in the 21st century, spurred by the Internet. In Aron et al. reference numbers in the text and in the reference list remain as they were in Goodman and Rich. But in all the digital articles in our selection, reference numbers are linked to actual citations, and actual citations to the corresponding article or at least to its abstract. Readers can thus follow their own hyperlink paths, employing the original article in ways wholly unimagined by the author.

The intertextuality of the digital article has spread beyond the web of citations within it. Articles often include sidebars with links to one or more of the following: published works in the same journal by the authors, articles on the same topic by authors not cited in the reference list, and articles related to key words chosen by the authors. Also linked is information about manufacturers of equipment and materials used in experiments or about databases to relevant subject matter such as the Protein Data Bank. Finally, we have access to articles that cite the subject article after publication, written comments by readers and the authors' responses, even blogs. This dense intertextuality is the one feature of the digital scientific article that profoundly distinguishes it from its brethren in print.

The intratextuality of the scientific article is also important. One of the more remarkable characteristics of the 20th-century scientific article is its elaborate finding system of section headings, graphic legends, numbered citations, and numbered equations, a system that evolved gradually over time.[38] This master finding system also allows readers to navigate more easily among the article's diverse components. Grazing from one section to another, from one graph to another, readers can extract desired bits of theory, methods, results, and conclusions. The finding system acts like a map, allowing readers easily to direct their attention to select components within an argument. In the digital scientific article, this finding system has been augmented by a linked contents component. There are links from a section heading to the actual section, links from a figure or table callout in running text to the actual figure or table, and links from a citation number in text to the bibliographic information in the reference list to the actual reference. The element of greatest interest to any given reader within an article is a click away, whether in the article itself or in the Supplemental Information.

Another component to the finding system for the scientific article is the journal contents page—a listing of authors, article titles, and corresponding page numbers for a single journal issue. This useful index has been around since the 17th century. The most-cited online journals in our selection have two contents pages: one for the journal as a whole, another for each issue. Anyone examining these pages on the web (e.g., Fig. 2.6) will come away with little doubt that a major transformation in journal contents has occurred: These pages are now portals to new knowledge, edification, and even entertainment and social engagement.

Perhaps the most dramatic difference between the contents of the print and digital scientific journals is that the latter also function as virtual libraries. The contents pages for all 13 journals offer portals to browsable electronic archives that cover all previously published articles back to the first issue. Moreover, visitors to a journal's home page can not only view research articles before the print issue is published but can also find which articles are the most viewed, most cited, most downloaded, and most e-mailed, and can go to recently published articles judged by the editors to deserve special attention, both articles on narrow topics and those covered by the news media.

For Selected: View Abstracts   Add to ACS ChemWorx   Download Citations

COMMUNICATIONS

Development of a Highly Selective Fluorescence Probe for Hydrogen Sulfide

Kiyoshi Sasakura, Kenjiro Hanaoka, Norihiro Shibuya, Yoshinori Mikami, Yuka Kimura, Toru Komatsu, Tasuku Ueno, Takuya Terai, Hideo Kimura, and Tetsuo Nagano

pp 18003-18005

Publication Date (Web): October 14, 2011 (Communication)

DOI: 10.1021/ja207851s

Section: Biochemical Methods

Abstract | Supporting Info

ACS ActiveView PDF

Hi-Res Print, Annotate, Reference QuickView

PDF [1321K]

PDF w/ Links [717K]

Full Text HTML

Add to ACS ChemWorx

Subscriber Access

Check for Full Text

In another strategy designed to capture reader attention, four of the most-cited journals offer "multimedia centers" composed of scientific images displayed for the reader's aesthetic pleasure or edification or both, podcasts highlighting the contents of individual issues or other newsworthy matters, instructional webinars and visuals, slideshows on a variety of scientific topics, and short videos produced by the journal or authors of articles. For the most part, the purpose of these multimedia centers is not to convey arguments for new knowledge—the primary function of the research article itself—but to present stories about science meant to reach those without specialized knowledge, to present science and scientists to a wider readership in a more personal light. The *Journal of the American Chemical Society*, for example, has a link called "Video Abstracts," which leads to an archive of short videos produced by the authors of published articles; *Science, Nature, New England Journal of Medicine*, and *Journal of Biological Chemistry* have podcasts summarizing issue contents; *PNAS* has podcasts on various topics as well as interviews with scientists about their research; and for teaching purposes, *New England Journal of Medicine* posts videos of microscopic physical abnormalities in patients.

Including Reader Comments and Reader Statistics

In the print era, scientists who wished to comment on published research articles or sociopolitical issues that concern the journal's readership wrote letters, normally published some weeks or months after submittal. They seldom drew a published response. At best a few such comments would appear in a single journal issue. The Internet may be transforming this once fairly sedate section of the scientific journal. Now, a little more than half the journals in our selection allow online readers to comment on articles after their publication. Links to those comments along with any author responses are then incorporated into the digital article.

In the Goodman and Rich article, obviously, readers cannot append a comment, while Aron et al.'s article has a comments tab at the top. No comments are evident. That is typical: Even though widely available, online commentary remains generally anemic. The problem may be the time, effort, and expertise required to formulate a substantive comment. If readers find something that might possibly be problematic in an article, they normally ignore it in favor of directing their attention to their own research problems. As Michael Nielsen explains:

> The problem all these sites have is that while thoughtful commentary on scientific papers is certainly useful for other scientists, there are few incentives for people to write such comments. Why write a comment when you could be doing something more "useful", like writing a paper or a grant? Furthermore,

if you publicly criticize someone's paper, there's a chance that that person may be an anonymous referee in a position to scuttle your next paper or grant application.[39]

To these strictures, however, controversial articles are an exception, as our chapter on peer review demonstrates (Chapter 6).

But article commentary is not the whole story. With the introduction of social media, journals are entering the freewheeling public sphere of gossiping, complaining, exchanging information on professional experiences, debating, deliberating, even ranting. Readers for about half the journals in our selection can immediately post a tweet, blog, or Facebook comment about some issue and, if it is controversial, spark a lively or even contentious debate. Like article commentary, this feature is still very much in its infancy.

The three PLOS journals also provide reader statistics. The results are surprisingly robust. PLOS journals report the number of views for each article, the average being a striking 4,418 in our selection. In a sense, readers implicitly vote on an article's potential interest simply by viewing or downloading it. In PLOS journals, readers can actually rate articles on a scale of 1 to 5, but they very seldom do so. Taken together, such statistics give scientist-authors a sense of the reception of their writing and scientist-readers a sense of what articles have received major attention. When a healthy number of views or downloads is displayed with the article itself, it adds authority to the contents being reported, a weight that reaches beyond the reputation of the authors or their institutional affiliations, or even the citation impact factor of the journal itself.

Enhancing Visualization

The motto adopted in 1660 at the founding of the first important scientific society in England, the Royal Society of London, was "Nullius in verba." That sentence loosely translates as "Trust no one's word." An amplification in keeping with the intent would be "See for yourself." That phrase aptly describes the ethos of modern science, then and now. And since the early days of the scientific article, that ethos has been manifested to some extent by the routine inclusion of visuals—pictures of plants, animals, rocks, stars, the moon, landscape—that authors saw with their unaided eyes, or by means of instruments such as microscopes, telescopes, and X-ray machines. With these pictures, readers see for themselves what the author saw in the first place. The Internet scientific article is giving a new dimension to "Seeing for yourself."

The visuals in Goodman and Rich are typical of 20th-century practice. The article has one table of data and eight graphs of data trends displayed in five figures. All have numbers and captions and are integrated into the text close to first mention. Figure 2.7 reproduces one of the graphs.[40]

Our present study suggests that—in large part due to the abundance of computer-based instruments for converting data into graphs and the relative ease of incorporating such images into a digital article—the visual has become much more prominent. The number of visuals in Aron et al. contrasts dramatically with those in Goodman and Rich. The former has 125 images displayed in eight figures. These visual assemblages consist of various arrangements of bar graphs, photographs at the microscopic scale, and Western blots of genetic components. Over half the images are in color, an enhancement expensive in print and virtually costless on the web. In addition, the web article has an appendix of Supporting Information that consists of 50 additional images packed into four figures.

The visual density of Aron et al. is unusual, to be sure. In the primary texts in our 21st-century selection, the averages for numbers of figures and tables per article are illuminating: In the main text, there are a bit less than 1.5 tables but there are a robust 14 images, about half of which are in color. Moreover, these visuals are more data driven than in previous centuries: Nearly all had at least one graph representing data trends, usually many more than one.

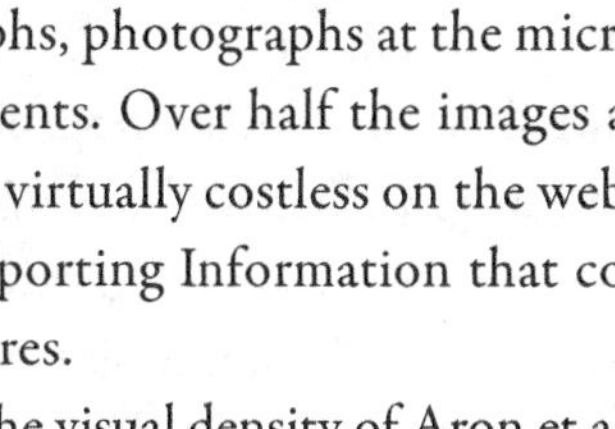

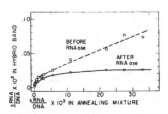

FIG. 3.—The amount of *E. coli* P³² ₈RNA found in the *E. coli* DNA band is plotted as a function of increasing amounts of P³² sRNA in the annealing mixture. All preparations were annealed with 45 γ DNA and varying amounts of P³² sRNA (0.005 to 1.50 γ P³² sRNA, specific activity = 5.6 × 10⁶ cpm/γ). The O.D.₂₆₀ and cpm before and after ribonuclease digestion were measured through the band region as described in *Methods*.

A constant amount of DNA (45 γ) was annealed with varying amounts of sRNA over a 300-fold range in concentration. The dashed curve shows that the amount of attached sRNA in the hybrid band goes up steadily while the solid curve shows that the ribonuclease-resistant part saturates. A plateau appears as a mass ratio of sRNA to DNA of 0.025 per cent. Thus, only a very small portion of the DNA is able to accept an sRNA molecule in hybrid formation. Furthermore, these results show that the preparation does not contain ribosomal RNA, since DNA-ribosomal RNA hybrids contain six times more RNA.[6] If cold ribosomal RNA is added to the annealing mixture, it does not compete with the bonding of sRNA, thereby suggesting that the ribosomal RNA sites are different from the sRNA sites.

The genome in *E. coli* contains a DNA molecular weight equivalent of 4 × 10⁹.[13] Knowing this, and using the molecular weight of *E. coli* sRNA (25,500), we may calculate from the plateau in Figure 3 that there are approximately 40 sRNA sites in the *E. coli* genome. If we assume that there is one site per sRNA molecule, this number provides a direct estimate of the degeneracy of the amino acid code.

FIGURE 2.7 Graph integrated into text in Goodman and Rich (1962) article [H. Goodman and A. Rich, *PNAS* 48 (1962): 2101–2109].

The greatest change in visual presentation in the 21st century concerns the use of color, a rare phenomenon before the 21st century that is now routine: About half the images in our 21st-century selection are in color. In our 20th-century selection of articles, for example, figures in color were so few that they were not worth serious attention. There can be little doubt that the web has ignited a riot of color in the digital scientific article, and its significance is communicative and epistemic, not cosmetic. Among other things, color can improve discrimination among the various components in images and increase their informational density.[41]

The presentation of 21st-century figures on the web also differs markedly from visual representation in earlier centuries. All the journals in our selection, except for the four that do not offer HTML articles, display the images in a thumbnail immediately after their first mention. For each, readers have the option of ignoring it altogether, clicking on a link to view it in a much more easily scrutinized size, copying the figure for use in another electronic document, or viewing and copying the figure as a PowerPoint slide. The last option means that images can be incorporated into an oral presentation for students or colleagues. Several of the sample journals also display all the figures within an article in a separate segment at the article's top or side. For example, *Nature* displays all figures in a horizontal band just after the abstract and before the introduction. With this arrangement, scientists can judge the article's value first by reading the abstract, then by scrolling through all figures in sequence.

While multicomponent figures are rare in earlier centuries, they are rampant in our 21st-century selection. Figure 2.8 is an example (note that original is in color).[42] Meaning emerges as a consequence not only of the interaction between image and text, as in Figure 2.7, but also by means of the interaction among the diverse images within the figure. The article in which Figure 2.8 is embedded reports on a new method for the 3D mapping of "transient interactions with a spatiotemporal resolution of 9 nm and 400 μs"—in other words, biological processes that are incredibly small and incredibly fast. The authors call the method "single-point edge-excitation subdiffraction microscopy" (SPEED). The first image (A) diagrams a key aspect of the research equipment—laser beam path (dark blue)—and compares it with that of two earlier methods: epifluorescence microscopy (light blue) and laser scanning confocal microscopy, or LSCM (cyan). The adjacent diagrams (B) also relate to the research equipment, showing the three different beams striking the object of study, the nuclear pore complex (NPC), in two orientations. Below these images are three sets of three images each (C, D, E), each tied to one of the three analytical techniques. The three interconnected images (C, D, E) each show a picture of the NPC taken by the labeled method and two graphs of its position. The argument behind the visual-verbal assemblage is that

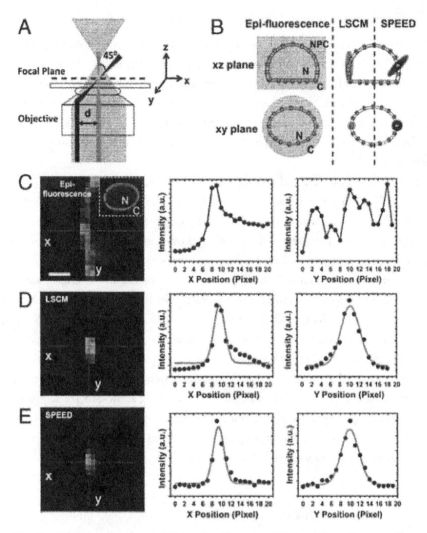

Fig. 1. SPEED microscopy. (A) Optics. The simplified optical diagram illustrates the different excitation beam paths of the SPEED (blue), the LSCM (cyan), and the wide-field epifluorescence (light blue) microscopy. The laser beam in the SPEED microscopy was focused into a diffraction-limited spot in the focal plane (dotted line) from the edge of the objective. An angle of 45° was formed between the iPSFs of the SPEED microscopy and the LSCM when the incident laser beam was shifted 237 μm (d) off the center of the objective (Fig. S2). (B) Illumination volumes in the three microscopes. The diagram demonstrates the NPCs inside (green) and outside (gray) the illumination volume in the xy and xz planes. N, nucleus; C, cytoplasm. (C) Multiple GFP-NPCs were excited using wide-field epifluorescence microscopy. The adopted area is enclosed by the blue box in the image of the entire fluorescent nuclear envelope (Inset). (Scale bar, 1 μm.) (D) GFP-NPCs were illuminated by the LSCM. The fluorescent spot was fit by a Gaussian function in both x and y directions. (E) Only a single GFP-NPC was excited in the illumination volume of the SPEED microscopy.

FIGURE 2.8 Example of multicomponent figure with caption [J. Ma and W. Yang, *PNAS* 107 (2010): 7305–7310].

epifluorescence (C) is not very good as an analytical method; LSCM (D) is much better; SPEED (E) is best. Although such visual assemblages have always been possible, it is hard to imagine their widespread adoption before the invention of the personal computer for their creation and the web for their dissemination. In the Supplemental Information to the article, the authors also include a video showing a biological substance transit from the cytoplasm, through the nuclear pore core, toward the nucleus.

On the basis of our selected articles, however, visuals that are possible only in an online publication are not yet routine: Only six articles had them, a trifling percentage. The prospects would appear to be bright, however, as these images recreate processes or represent changes in data or objects over time in ways not possible with static images. First, interested readers can see what the scientist saw in the laboratory or field, giving an entirely new dimension to "virtual witnessing." Examples drawn from our selection include videos showing the behavior of mice in a laboratory setting[43] and a villager walking through coals before an audience in a Spanish town as part of an annual ritual.[44] Second, readers can watch data as they change over time: In our selection, that includes a set of graphs demonstrating the stabilization over time of the quantum state in a microsystem.[45] Finally, readers can view the shape of objects from different perspectives, rotating a microscopic section of a mouse spleen[46] or a vertebrate limb bud.[47] Our case study in the next section illustrates the intimate connection between generating and communicating knowledge that the development of such visuals embodies.

INTERNET VISUALIZATION AND THE SCIENCE OF SHAPE

Although humans and Neanderthals share a common ancestor, they differ in skull formation. In Neanderthals, the rear of the cranium is characterized by a bun-shaped protrusion, the brows are heavy, the forehead slopes, and no chin is evident. Insofar as these differences are structural, they concern anatomy; insofar as they are functional, they concern physiology. Changes in structure and function, however, also entail changes in shape, patterns of change beyond the disciplinary scope of anatomy or physiology.

Until the second decade of the 20th century, there was no inkling of a science whose task was this subject, the shape of living things as they develop and evolve; until the last half-century, no science existed adequate to the precise analysis of changes in shape incident on the development and evolution of living beings. There was no geometric morphometrics, no happy combination of the mathematical and the visual. That at each stage this evolving science needed to be depicted as well as described gives us our subject, an analysis designed to deepen our understanding of scientific visuals as their practitioners struggle to live within, to exploit, and eventually to overcome the limitations of the printed page in the interest of generating and communicating knowledge.

Birth of a Science of Shape

We begin with D'Arcy Thompson, the first to intuit that evolution and development could be depicted by a fusion of the visual and the mathematical. There is no disagreement among the generations of his followers that the science of shape was inaugurated by *On Growth and Form*,[48] a book so important that it remains in print and is cited to this day, nearly a century after its first publication. This is not because predecessors interested in applied geometry to the living world cannot be unearthed; Georges Cuvier is a brilliant and well-known example. It is because for the first time Thompson provided one visual demonstration after another that dramatized the formidable power of geometry when applied to the changing shapes of developing and evolving creatures. Perhaps the most famous of his images, Figure 2.9, is reproduced in publications by two scientists who later play a role in our story, Julian Huxley[49] and Fred Bookstein.[50] Figure 2.9 superimposes a Cartesian-like grid on the shapes of two fish related by evolution, the porcupine fish *Diodon* and "the closely allied but very different looking" sunfish *Orthagoriscus mola*.[51] In this transformation, the

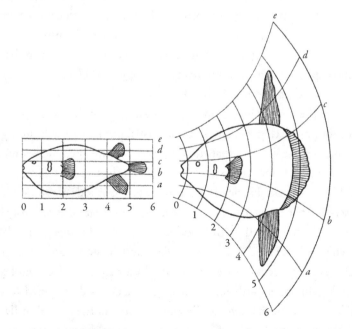

FIGURE 2.9 A Cartesian grid applied successively between *Diodon* and *Orthagoriscus mola* [D'Arcy Thompson, *On Growth and Form* (London: Cambridge University Press, 1917)].

vertical coordinates of *Diodon* have become a system of concentric circles, the horizontal coordinates a system of curves. The transformation allows us to *see* evolution in geometrical terms. In his text, Thompson emphasizes a crucial point about these images: Development and evolution must be represented as integrated networks of change.

Thompson is well aware of the limitations of his method. First, it is not easily quantifiable. He points to

> the simple fact that the developing organism is very far from being homogeneous and isotropic, or, in other words, does not behave like a perfect fluid. But although under such circumstances our coordinate systems may no longer be capable of strict mathematical analysis, they will still indicate *graphically* the relation of the new coordinate system to the old.[52]

He recognizes further that even this result depends on the presence of a pattern of landmarks, a pattern of biologically significant locations he cannot reliably supply, those that fix the degree of change over time. But there is also a limitation Thompson does not recognize: He seriously underestimates the height of the barrier to the next logical step in his research program, the analytical unwieldiness that results when his method of coordinates is applied to actual measurements of networks of growth. Whatever their shortcomings, however, Thompson's images inspired future generations of scientists by posing a problem in the form of a solution, a solution that required a mathematics far more sophisticated than he could muster.

Our story continues with Julian Huxley, who rightly insists that in determining changes in shape only real measurements be employed. His *Problems of Relative Growth* acknowledges the groundbreaking work of Thompson: "the coordinate method [is] of the utmost importance as affording a graphic and immediate proof of the need for postulating regularities in the distribution of growth throughout the body."[53] Moreover, he concurs that the recognition of his own innovation, growth patterns proceeding from centers of growth, is "implicit in his Cartesian transformations."[54] Nevertheless, Huxley feels, Thompson's methods are undermined by a defect so serious that a new beginning is necessary, one that takes seriously into consideration differential growth within bodies over time, "the change in relative proportions with absolute size."[55] Thompson's method "is static rather than dynamic, and substitutes the short cut of a geometrical solution for the more complex realities actually underlying biological transformation." Huxley is determined to map patterns of change of shape mathematically and to represent them graphically.

The differential growth rates of the various organs of the hermit crab are typical in that they are described by the simple formula $y = bx^k$, where y is the length of the differentially growing organ, x is the length of the animal's body, and b and k are constants. The formula can also be written as $\log y = \log b + k \log x$. In this form, the curve that y describes may be plotted as a line graph in which $\log x$ and $\log y$ are the abscissa and ordinate. Figure 2.10, for example, plots the relative growth of the chela or claw of the prawn *Palaemon malcomsoni*.[56] To Huxley, it is this relative growth that has taxonomic and, therefore, evolutionary significance.

In his original publication, Huxley's confidence in his mathematical approach is high. He says of his "law" of growth that "it may (like Boyle's law) prove only to be an approximation, and to be capable of modification in certain circumstances; yet (again like Boyle's law) it may remain fundamental."[57] But in an appendix, first published in 1945, this optimism has proven unjustified. J. B. S. Haldane had pointed out that Huxley's formula could not apply to organs whose parts exhibit differential growth rates,[58] and that Huxley's "assumptions that growth is essentially multiplicative and that changes in the rate of self-multiplication affect all parts of the body

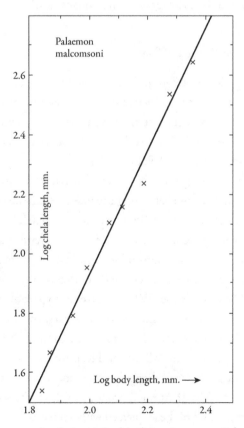

FIGURE 2.10 Relative growth of the chela (claw) in the prawn *Palaemon malcomsoni* [now *Macrobrachium malcomsonii* or Monsoon River prawn]. Logarithmic plotting. [J. Huxley, *Problems of Relative Growth* (New York: Dial Press, 1932)].

equally" could not be supported by the existing evidence.[59] In the end, Huxley had to concede that attempts to add an adjustment factor to his formula had been unsuccessful, and the obstacles encountered were unlikely to be overcome due to "statistical difficulties."[60] To these difficulties may be added those of measurement that Huxley encountered in the absence of firmly established landmarks that would truly make patterns of differential growth exactly comparable. For example, in determining the relative growth of parts of the large claw of the fiddler crab, Huxley speaks of "the impossibility of assigning points along the abscissa-axis to the several joints, since the very fact of their differential growth is causing their centers or ends to shift differentially with increase in absolute size."[61]

The failure of Huxley's program is mirrored in the limitations of the graphs and images he selects to support his case. In the first place, despite his commitment to patterns of growth, his graphs show only relative growth in individual organs and body parts. Furthermore, though in numerous places Huxley acknowledges that growth occurs in three dimensions,[62] he was not able to represent it visually. A new form of visualization that fuses images and their quantification had yet to be created.

The Mathematical Visualization of Shape

It is easy to see why Karl Pearson and G. M. Morant's 1934 *Biometrika* article[63] should have had no immediate influence on the development of the science that would eventually be called geometric morphometrics. The article's eccentric purpose, encapsulated in its title—"The Wilkinson Head of Oliver Cromwell and its Relationship to Busts, Masks, and Painted Portraits"—seals its fate. This general neglect, however, says nothing about the level of insight Pearson and Morant manage to achieve into a science of shape fully capable of mathematization. When the article surfaces again in a 1998 Fred Bookstein review article, it receives the highest praise: "Had Pearson gone on to supplement this splendid analysis with a distribution theory for such comparisons of vectors, instead of merely asserting their identity, he would have invented the entire core of contemporary morphometrics in 1935, and I would be out of a job."[64] This courteous hyperbole signals Bookstein's realization that, despite any appearance to the contrary, the article's purpose is far from eccentric. In fact, Pearson and Morant manage to turn a minor historical puzzle concerning the identity of the Wilkinson Head into a major exploration of the basis required to create a science of shape that fuses the mathematical and the visual.

What is the Wilkinson Head? At the Restoration, Oliver Cromwell's body was disinterred, and decapitated, and his head, pierced with a spike and placed on public view. He was a disgraced regicide. More than 150 years later, in 1815, Josiah Henry Wilkinson purchased what purported to be that very same head (Fig. 2.11a).[65] Preliminary testing yielded encouraging results: Cromwell's hat and helmet could have fit such a head, and an examination of the skull indicated its age as roughly that of Cromwell when he died. But the crucial tests that transformed possibility into probability were comparisons of the Head with Cromwell's many existing portraits, busts, and death masks. Comparison with the portraits, however, posed two insuperable difficulties. First, orienting the Head so that it was in the same position as that with which the painter viewed his subject was more difficult than had been imagined. Second, "if a solid head and a mask or bust are seen from one position to be in corresponding aspects, they will appear to be so from other positions; but this is not so in the case of a flat drawing or portrait."[66] It is for these reasons that the attempts to fit the portraits to the Head were abandoned in favor of a comparison with busts and death masks. The comparison between the Head and the British Museum death mask in Figure 2.11b is visually compelling. Pearson and Morant sum up the results of their qualitative investigation: "we find that even without measurement, but simply by superposition, there exists a very remarkable accordance between the masks and busts of Cromwell and the Wilkinson Head."[67]

It is important to see how well this purely visual accord survives the imposition of actual measurement, lest our eyes deceive us into giving simple coincidence more credence than it deserves. Figure 2.12 shows us eight "points," eight anchors in a network of measurements that will turn the subjective impression of coincidence into its mathematical equivalent, that will transform a pair of 3D objects—the Head and the British Museum death mask—into a pair of objects wholly constituted by mathematics and completely amenable to precise quantification.[68] Each of these eight points is exactly defined. For example:

> *Glabella.* We use this term in a special sense. Let a plane be taken parallel to the Frankfurt horizontal plane and tangential to the upper border of the eyebrows. The point in which the trace of this plane on the forehead meets the "midsagittal" plane will here be termed the *glabella.* The point thus defined is easily determined on full face pictures or photographs.[69]

While these points fall short of homology—while they are not taxonomically or evolutionarily significant landmarks—they give the comparison Pearson and Morant want to make a far firmer base than the measurement-averse grids of Thompson or the single-trait graphs of Huxley. This assertion in no way minimizes the difficulty of pinpointing these "landmarks" with the desired accuracy; indeed, Pearson and Morant rightly prefer to call their "values numerical appreciations rather than measurements."[70] Still, the Pearson and Morant appreciations issue in summary quantitative tables of remarkable coincidences that force us to concur with them that the agreement between the measurements of the "masks and the busts and

FIGURE 2.11 (a) Profile of embalmed Wilkinson Head. (b) Full face of the British Museum wax death mask fitted with the facial outlines of the Wilkinson Head [K. Pearson and G. Morant, *Biometrika* 26 (1934): 1–116].

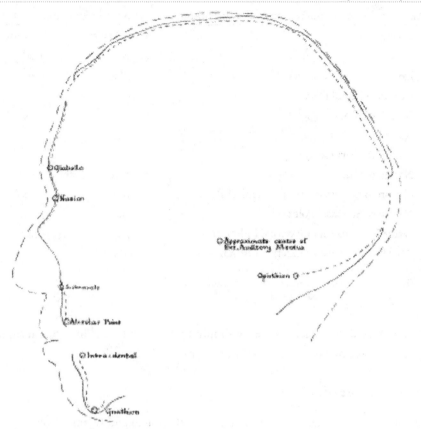

FIGURE 2.12 Profile of Wilkinson Head showing trace of embalmed head (solid line), skull bone (short dashed line), and ordinary flesh allowance (long dashed line) [K. Pearson and G. Morant, *Biometrika* 26 (1934): 1–116].

the Wilkinson Head is astonishing,"[71] a conclusion that leads to the inference that "we appear to have what Bernoulli and Buffon would have termed a 'moral certainty' that the Wilkinson Head is the actual head of Oliver Cromwell"[72] (see example comparison in Table 2.1[73]).

The significant conceptual advance this article represents in the calculation of comparative differences in shape cannot be matched by Pearson and Morant's visual realizations. Although their superimposed images powerfully convey the impression of likeness, they cannot convey its exact degree. Because Pearson and Morant have no way of conveying quantitative similarity visually, they must resort to tables that compare measurements from the Wilkinson Head to those from masks and busts. Additionally, while Pearson and Morant are the first seriously to address the problem that their objects of study are solid, that they exist in three dimensions, the limitations of the printed page force them to represent those dimensions as two: in their case a view of the full face and profile. Nonetheless, theirs is a significant advance,

TABLE 2.1 Example comparison of the Wilkinson Head with masks and busts

Characters	Mean Masks and Busts	Wilkinson Head
External Ocular Distance	98.7	96.6
External Orbital Distance	113.75	112.3
Length of Mouth	58.9	59.5
Nasion to Lip-line	75.2	76.2
Nasion to Wart Centre	28.05	27.2
Nasion to Gnathion	122.3	117.7
Nasion to Lowest Point of "Beardlet" Root	95.9	98.8
Nasion to Subnasal Point	53.8	53.3
Wart Centre to Right External Lid-meet	48.9	49.3
Wart Centre to Right External Orbital Margin	52.4	51.1

From K. Pearson and G. Morant, *Biometrika* 26 (1934): 1–116.

one that lacked immediate influence simply because it appeared in a specialist publication and seemed to focus only on a minor historical puzzle.

Science of Shape and the Internet

Geometric morphometrics, pioneered by Fred Bookstein and F. James Rolf, depends for its development on a mathematical theory of shape. In the words of David Kendall, on whose mathematics Bookstein relied: "if we are not interested in the location, orientation or scale of the resulting configuration, then we find ourselves working with a continuous stochastic [nondeterministic] process describing its change of shape."[74] The application of this theory of shape to biology depends on the location of landmarks, biologically significant features, preferably homologous (that is, of taxonomic and evolutionary significance). It also involves the selection of so-called semi-landmarks, anchored in landmark locations, so that curves, necessarily free of landmarks, such as those on the skull, can be mapped. Changes in relative location of the entire network of landmarks and semi-landmarks track real change—that is, differences where any changes due to orientation, enlargement, reduction, or movement of the object in question have been factored out. Geometric morphometrics is designed to complete the program Thompson initiated: "Differences in shape represented in this fashion are a mathematically rigorous realization of Thompson's idea of transformation grids, where one object is deformed or 'warped' into another."[75] While morphometricians worried about the difficulties and dangers of relying on morphometric analysis to make inferences of taxonomic distance,[76],[77] it was clear that work currently under way represented "a first step toward addressing what is a fundamental problem in morphometrics—the complete modeling of development and evolution."[78]

The first geometric morphometric article with which we shall deal—by Coquerelle, Bookstein, Braga, and Halazonetis—focuses on development. It visualizes "how [humans and chimpanzees] develop a vertical symphysis [joint made of cartilage] during fetal life and how this configuration changes towards a prominent chin in humans but towards an anteriorly inclined symphysis in chimpanzees."[79] The establishment of landmarks makes possible the creation of 3D representations of shape in print. Figure 2.13 consists of three representations of the right half of

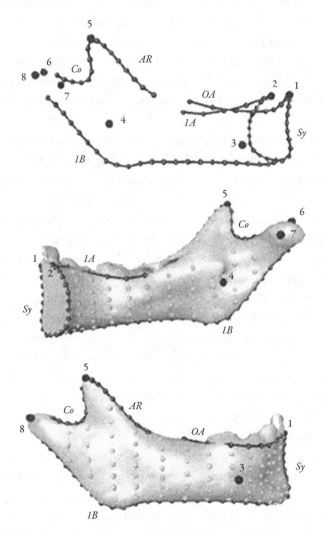

FIGURE 2.13 Three views of a human hemi-mandible, aged one year [M. Coquerelle et al., *Journal of Anatomy* 217 (2010): 507–520].

the one-year-old human mandible with landmarks and semi-landmarks designated over three dimensions.[80] The landmarks are biologically significant locations; the curves are extrapolations from these landmarks. At the top is an outline diagram that displays all of the landmarks and curve semi-landmarks in X-ray view; it is as if a wire were bent in the form of a hemi-mandible. Below this are realistic depictions of the two sides of the hemi-mandible: the middle depiction turns this jaw bone 180 degrees counterclockwise; the bottom depiction turns the middle one 180 degrees further in the same direction.

In these three cases the third dimension is an illusion. In the first case the impression of three dimensions is created by overlapping; in the second and third, by shading and foreshortening. There is an essential point to be made about the limitation of such representations: "Scientific papers are still largely limited to static, two-dimensional pieces of paper or computer screens that make the representation of volumetric changes challenging to say the least. [In these figures,] one can appreciate, but not fully comprehend the volumetric differences being represented."[81] In these representations, moreover, information is omitted or distorted.[82] For example, in the top diagram in Figure 2.13 almost all information of shape is omitted. The middle representation occludes landmark 8; the bottom, landmarks 6 and 7. The middle and bottom representations also distort through foreshortening. Finally, all three representations omit most information concerning the shape and position of the deciduous ("baby") teeth. Adams et al. foresee the eventual solution: "As more journals go online," Adams asserts, "one can anticipate the possibility of interactive publication graphics that would partially address this problem."[83]

In the Supporting Information of their article, Coquerelle et al. solve the problem Adams sets for geometric morphometricians. They produce a series of eight short videos reconstructing the growth of the human and chimpanzee mandible during gestation and up to the formation of the deciduous teeth. The first (screenshot in Fig. 2.14) reconstructs the growth of the human fetus from gestation week 13 to birth. It translates the measurements of landmarks and semi-landmarks into a shape, rotates the shape, and shows its growth over the stated period. In these videos, we can easily see for ourselves that, in the second trimester, "the basilar bone of the mandible maintains a V-shape, while its alveolar process [top segment of mandible with tooth sockets] changes to a shallow U-shape."[84]

Our second example of online geometric morphometrics has evolution as its focus. Maria Ponce de León and Christoph Zollikofer compare the development of Neanderthal and human skulls to demonstrate that the two species belong to distinct lines of descent.[85] In a video accompanying the article online, we see the lengthening and slimming of the human skull in the transformation of *Homo neanderthalensis* to modern *Homo sapiens*, as well as the emergence of the human chin

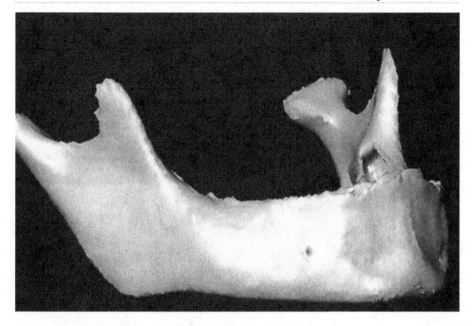

FIGURE 2.14 Screenshot from video of the development of the human mandible, front and side view [M. Coquerelle et al., *Journal of Anatomy* 217 (2010): 507–520]. Video 2.2 [▶]

and the disappearance of the Neanderthal back-of-the-head "bun." The still images in Figure 2.15 hint at the video; they do not do it justice.[86]

The verisimilitude of these 3D representations is a striking realization of Thompson's and Huxley's dream, a visual coincidence between the mathematical and the biological. The achievement is indeed extraordinary, so extraordinary that we have to remind ourselves that these videos are *all* mathematical constructs, constructs hypothesized closely to resemble the real. There is a danger in such vivid virtual reconstructions. In an e-mail, Bookstein makes the point forcefully: "The heightened persuasiveness that often accompanies [their] increased visual clarity is often the scourge of the competent reviewer, whenever the power of the image overrides all the appropriate skepticism that we try to teach our students when facing this unfamiliar semiotics."[87]

In this progress toward the goal of geometric morphometrics, there were two turning points: Thompson's insight that development and evolution could be realized geometrically in a visually striking manner, and the realization by Fred Bookstein that David Kendall's work on the theory of shape, a theory developed in the contexts of astronomy and archaeology, could apply to biology. It is these that led eventually to the intelligent and creative exploitation of the possibilities of representation in 2D and 3D space on the page and on the Internet. While not yet common, virtual visualizations of shape such as these are driving knowledge generation and communication in not only evolutionary biology but other disciplines as

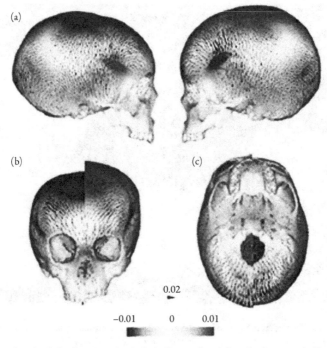

FIGURE 2.15 On the left, the Neanderthal skull; on the right, the human skull. In the online version, red indicates shrinkage, green expansion. [M. Ponce de León and C. Zollikofer, *Nature* 412 (2001): 534–538].

well—for example, intricate 3D interactive chemical structures are now finding their way into the chemical and biochemical literature. See Video 2.3 [⏵].

CONCLUSION

In the words of Paul Ginsparg, founder of the physics preprint archive arXiv,

The transition to article formats and features better suited to modern technology than to print on paper has also been surprisingly slow. Page markup formats, such as PDF, have only grudgingly given way to XML-based ones that support features such as manipulable graphics, dynamic views, linked annotations and semantic markup. Part of this caution is a result of the understandable need to maintain a stable archive of research literature, as provided by paper over centuries.[88]

Our contention here is that there are now substantive differences between the typical printed article in the 20th century and the linked, multimedia article accessible through the websites of current elite scientific journals. These are not merely stylistic or cosmetic; instead, they concern strategies that enrich linear text: enhanced visualization, intertextuality, interactivity, and compartmentalization, techniques designed to accommodate different readers with different interests. Readers not only read but interact with the digital article. The web does not redefine the essence of the scientific article; it has always been a node in a network of knowledge. Rather, the web permits the exploration and exploitation of possibilities inherent in the structure of scientific communication. The article is what it always was, only more intensely, more completely. It is too soon to tell which variations now evident on the web will prove enduring. But while scientific argument remains as rigorous as ever, the means of representing it, providing evidence for it, and accessing it will never be the same. This is why we believe "revolution" is not too strong a word for describing this state of affairs. See Video 2.4 [▶].

We do not foresee the death of the scientific journal but its continued transformation—publishing not only research articles or essays on scientific topics, but also educational materials for students, scientific blogs about original research, comments by peer reviewers and general readers, author interviews, videos about research articles of interest to the public, and virtual reality visuals. Journals might also begin publishing what was once kept private: promising ideas for research projects or the methods and real-time results from research projects in process that might benefit from reader commentary or input. Not only is the scientific article being made anew, but the journal itself.

Now everything indicates that the book in [its]
traditional form is nearing its end.
WALTER BENJAMIN (1928)

3

INTERNET HUMANITIES ESSAYS AND BOOKS

Seeing and Hearing Anew

INTERNET INNOVATION AND THE HUMANITIES ESSAY

Has there been in the 21st-century humanities an Internet transformation similar to that in the sciences? A comparison of online elite journals suggests that the Internet transformation in the humanities is noticeably less far along. This generalization applies to the 10 elite humanities journals identified by Eugene Garfield:[1] *Language* (journal of the Linguistic Society of America), *Journal of Philosophy, American Antiquity, PMLA* (journal of the Modern Language Association), *Linguistic Inquiry, Past & Present, Philosophical Review, American Historical Review, Economic History Review*, and *Journal of Economic History*. Even a journal called *Music, Sound, and the Moving Image* has no music, sound, or moving images. This state of affairs also applies to online journals. Within the past decade, the Open Humanities Press established 17 open-access journals in "response to the crisis in scholarly publishing in the humanities"; tellingly, of these 17, the articles in all but one are in the form of PDF or HTML files with straight text and, typically, few if any links or images. An exception is *Vectors: Journal of Culture and Technology in a Dynamic Vernacular*, which "brings together visionary scholars with cutting-edge designers and technologists to propose a rethinking of the dynamic relation of form to content in academic research."

There is an obvious explanation for this state of digital affairs: the differences between the two cultures. The typical humanities essay is primarily a verbal document composed by a single author, written in a more personal style than that of the scientific article. Typically, it is designed around an argument or narrative that does not easily lend itself to nonsequential reading. One cannot imagine essays by scholars as diverse as Martin Heidegger, Jürgen Habermas, Simone de Beauvoir, Judith Butler, or Martha Nussbaum benefitting in any substantive way from the affordances of the web, aside from easier access to a global readership. In many cases, a simple web-based reproduction of the print version suffices.

Still, the elite humanities journals are not entirely free of Internet innovation. Both *Economic History Review* and *Language* have instituted an "enhanced article (HTML)" that permits inclusion of online supplementary information with videos and audio files. Through the homepage of *Linguistic Inquiry*, you can view numerous podcasts providing discussion among scholars on topics of interest to the journal readership and "snippets," short critical remarks on recently published work. *American Historical Review* has posted several interesting web-only projects, three of which we discuss later in this chapter. Finally, several journals have links to most-cited and most-downloaded articles, and others prominently display comments about published articles and author responses. Searching the web more assiduously, we also found noteworthy exceptions to our generalization about Internet innovation in the humanities, including *Journal of the Society of Architectural Historians, Journal of American History, Music Theory Online, Tout-Fait: The Marcel Duchamp Studies Online Journal*, and *Kairos: A Journal of Rhetoric, Technology, and Pedagogy*. The *Journal of the Society of Architectural Historians*, for example, is open to work in which 3D interactive images advance knowledge. These are not simply supplementary to arguments; they are central to them. The *Journal of American History* offers a small sampling of innovative web-only texts separate from its periodic issues; it also offers an edited transcript of an annual online conversation among select American historians on a given topic. *Music Theory Online* routinely publishes articles that sample recorded performances in support of arguments. The idiosyncratic journal publishing scholarship on the innovative modern artist Marcel Duchamp, *Tout-Fait*, has a multimedia segment that contains animated reconstructions of his art and music created or inspired by him. *Kairos*, a journal similar to *Vectors*, contains "webtexts" that are truly multimedia and in other ways depart radically from the typical humanities article.

The radical web-texts in *Vectors* and *Kairos* prompt a question: Does the Internet provide opportunities not only to enhance academic argument but to remake it, trading a linear for a more dispersive argumentative strategy, one in which readers strongly control the journey through the text, building structures unique to themselves? In the 1990s, philosopher David Kolb addressed the question of whether the Internet should host humanities texts "that may have no fixed beginnings or endings, are hard to explore, may have no conclusions, and may deliberately avoid being caught in any totalizing overview."[2] Kolb reached the heart of the matter when he wondered, "What would thinking mean if it were not providing form and focus, definite claims, critical judgment, beginnings, middles, and ends, and so preventing an indefinite accumulation of words and images? This question remains open." A decade later, Kolb admitted finding not much success in developing nonlinear hypertext: "An overwhelming majority of argumentative and expository texts on the web are either print-like complete essays, or single-step linked mini-essays."[3]

Vectors, published by the Open Humanities Press, is an exception to this general rule. Each issue's "essays" are examples of nonlinear, multimedia hypertext, usually the product of a collaboration among a graphic designer, journal editor, and scholar. There are typically few references other than quotations. No new knowledge claims are made, no definite conclusions reached. "The Virtual Window Interactive" by Anne Friedberg exemplifies the genre.[4] The title captures the project's contents. As amplified by the author in a linked screen, her article is about "windows, their virtual substitutes, and the fractured multiplicity of the multiple 'windowed' screen." According to the editor's accompanying statement, "Friedberg uses the interactive format to construct a . . . 'slit optic,' a form of parallel vision that considers both past and present simultaneously. Through juxtaposition of apertures, contents and avatar-viewers, 'The Virtual Window Interactive' invites us to think critically about the past in light of present sensibilities." According to the project designer, it is a "'playset' in which users . . . experiment with combining elements of a variety of window-mediated viewing experiences."

This *Vectors* web-text places the job of creating meaning in the hands of the viewer. Options abound. In the screen following an introductory screen, the user chooses among

- 56 types of window prevalent from the 13th to the present century—for example, computer screens, stained glass, French doors, television, and picture frame,
- 37 types of content to insert into the frame of the selected window—for example, paintings, photographs, drawings, movie stills, and commercials, and
- 10 types of viewers—for example, man, woman, child, dog, foursome on couch.

By selecting different time periods from a horizontal bar across the screen (say, 14th to 18th centuries), viewers narrow the number of available selections. Having made various selections, they see their creation form on the screen: for instance, a woman watching an Apple iPod commercial in a painting frame. Music from a soundtrack swells. Academic phrases related to windows and apertures dance across the screen. The viewer can click on a phrase and a verbal window appears whose contents expand upon the phrase. See Video 3.1 [▶].

Vectors is also highly unusual among scholarly journals in that it publishes the peer reviewer's comments. The peer reviewer of "Virtual Window Interactive" noted that

> I wonder generally if the basic interactive format in some ways vitiates the force of an ongoing argument, not just in Friedberg's project but in any project presented this way. A book, say, can be randomly accessed but also may have an argumentative spine [as does Friedberg's scholarly printed book on the same topic[5]]. There is certainly a strong spine here, but I find it gets lost in the array of examples and commentary.

We agree.

The innovations we discuss in this chapter—web projects in history, music, and film—are designed to strengthen arguments, to keep the reader focused on their strong spine while exploiting the new communicative possibilities permitted by the Internet, seeing and hearing anew. We will be looking at humanities essays in the form of not only online journal articles, but also e-books and web-only texts.

HISTORIANS SEE ANEW

Photographs as Historical Evidence

When the distinguished historian of France Robert Darnton implemented the Gutenberg-e series of historical monographs with a grant from the Mellon Foundation, he hoped "to develop and test a model for publishing scholarly books through the Internet."[6] He also had had two other aims: "to revitalize the monograph in fields of history where conventional publishing had proved uneconomical and to help beginning scholars launch their careers, despite the difficulties of breaking into print in the conventional manner." The plan was for the American Historical Association to offer a prize of $20,000 to a selection of exemplary doctoral dissertations, an award that would serve as seed money to turn these dissertations into monographs. These would be published electronically—and only electronically—by Columbia University Press. The main source of revenue for the project was to be library subscriptions to the series.

The project got off to a rocky start. At first, there was a dearth of applicants, many having been warned away by dissertation advisors who worried that electronic publication would make the road to tenure more difficult than publication in print. In addition, publication deadlines were unrealistically short, making it impossible for the Press to make good on its promise to institutional subscribers that there would be a steady flow of books. Worse, reviews, the chief indication of disciplinary acceptance, were almost completely absent. With the exception of the *American Historical Review*, no history journal even noticed these publications. In the case of the *American Historical Review*, moreover, electronic publication created a barrier: Some reviewers requested paper copies, forcing the Press to print and bind them at additional expense.

Darnton prudently changed course. He broadened the call for proposals (it originally included only "endangered" areas such as Latin American history), made deadlines more realistic, and encouraged authors to produce straight monographs without the "bells and whistles" that online publication could supply: networks of links, galleries of photographs, and movies. As a result, the project did cross the finish line: 34 titles were "in print." But there could be no real sense of satisfaction on the part of the sponsors, organizers, or participants. Despite their prizes, participants were being awarded tenure at a rate no higher than the disciplinary average.[7] The monographs were still not reviewed in journals other than the *American Historical Review*. Cutting its losses, Columbia abandoned the project, offering the e-books free online and publishing a selection of these in hardcover at $60 apiece. Since none of Darnton's goals was achieved, the Mellon Foundation regarded Gutenberg-e as a failure.[8]

We do not regard it so; we regard it as a first step in the right direction. To make our case, we focus on one of the prize-winning monographs: Helena Pohlandt-McCormick's *"I Saw a Nightmare" ... Doing Violence to Memory: The Soweto Uprising, June 16, 1976*.[9] We have chosen it not because it is typical but because of its quality—it earned its author tenure in the history department of the University of Minnesota—and because its diagnosis tells us something of interest about the use of photographs and official documents as an archive that can supplement, even interrogate the traditional historical archive. Her monograph contains 743 images and reproductions of some 200 written documents in all, a trove hard to imagine in a conventional book. These images and documents are reproduced in an "Archive" in her e-book, and select ones are integrated into the text and hyperlinked to supplementary information.

Key to the book is the black-and-white photograph that appears on the "cover," adjacent to the first paragraph of the Introduction, and in the virtual archive. It shows a young man, Hector Pieterson, who had been killed by the police. He is being carried down the street in the arms of a fellow student, the victim's grieving sister by his side. In the words of Pohlandt-McCormick, this image became an international symbol of resistance to a racist regime: "It became an icon of history . . . It also came to symbolize the violence that runs like a murderous streak through the history of South Africa."[10]

In the introductory paragraph, this image is a portal providing a wealth of additional evidence in support of the claims being made. Clicking on it reveals a set of four links connected to the visual archive ("Soweto," "16 June in Soweto," "Dead and Wounded," and "Children"). These open windows with a selection of relevant images: photographs of the results of vandalism during the uprising, dead and wounded protestors, angry young adults participating in the riots, and pages from police reports giving the official version of the day's bloody events. Another of these images is a photograph of Sam Nzima standing before a large blowup of his famous photograph on display in the Hector Pieterson Museum in Soweto. Clicking on an endnote to the adjacent text produces a quotation from Nzima's testimony before the Truth and Reconciliation Commission, a quotation that provides additional context for the photograph:

> During the shooting I saw a student fall down and another student picked him up and I rushed there to take a picture. I took six sequence shots of that picture of the student, whom we later discovered was Hector Pieterson, and another student . . . picked Hector Pieterson up and Antoinette, the sister . . . was crying hysterically alongside where Makuba was carrying [Hector] Pieterson running towards the direction where our Press car was parked.[11]

Links within the footnote displays the full testimony of Sam Nzima, a link now defunct. A link above the iconic photograph in the Introduction opens yet another window, which displays links to all other places in the book where the image is discussed. In the same place we find text providing further information related to the image, in particular that the first student killed on that day was not the one in the picture but Hastings Ndlovu, who is not much discussed because he was not captured in so dramatic a photograph.

Like the bombing of Hiroshima, the nefarious activities of ordinary German soldiers on the Eastern Front in World War II, and the oppressive Native Peoples policies of the Australian government, Soweto is characterized by a certain argumentative plasticity. To the apartheid government, the events of June 16, 1976, were an outbreak of unreasoned violence on the part of an inferior native people; to the African National Congress, they were a heroic manifestation of the spirit of freedom in a continuing fight against injustice, a manifestation particularly to be noted as its participants were largely children and young adults who took up the fight for equal rights, whereas many of their parents faltered. To the Truth and Reconciliation Commission, Soweto was just one more opportunity to collect victim testimonies.

The story that the apartheid government told is seriously flawed. Clearly, the riots they tried to quell were of their own making, the product of unjust laws enforced by a police state. The particular provocation of Soweto—the mandate to use the hated Afrikaans language as a medium of instruction—was only a last straw, one of many manifestations of a disrespect for native culture. The African National Congress story is equally flawed; it is difficult to understand how arson, vandalism, looting, and violence further the cause of freedom, though it is true that Soweto made available for all to see the injustice of apartheid, vividly demonstrated in the arresting photograph of a young boy shot by the police, cradled in the arms of a man, the boy's grieving sister hurrying beside him. The story of the Truth and Reconciliation Commission is no story at all: Its voluminous legalistic cascade fails to capture the impact and meaning of Soweto.

By means of interactive tables, exemplified by Figure 3.1, Pohlandt-McCormick captures the competing narratives surrounding this historic event. Click on "Police": We learn that the crowds refused to disperse. Click on "Press": We learn that the police could not be heard above the din of the crowd. Click on "Commission": We learn that the police did not have the necessary audio equipment to be heard above the noise.

The hypertext format of Pohlandt-McCormick's e-book, in particular its extensive virtual archives of images and supporting documents, seems particularly well suited for communicating the scholarship behind these Rashomon-like narratives. The supporting information also provides evidence with which readers can even

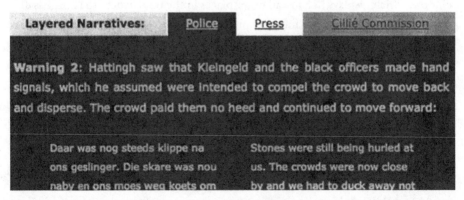

FIGURE 3.1 Table of competing narratives [H. Pohlandt-McCormick, *"I Saw a Nightmare,"* Columbia University Press].

interrogate Pohlandt-McCormick's claims. For example, she speaks of "the meticulous planning of the students."[12] But there is no indication that planning took place other than at a meeting on the previous evening; it does not appear to have been a matter of meticulous planning over weeks and months.[13] This haste helps explain why the posters that might have well been prepared before the march, those that focus on the imposition of Afrikaans, are so crude in execution (Fig. 3.2). Indeed, these posters are evidence of haste.

This haste also explains the fact that the planning did not include an obvious contingency: police interference and how to deal with it. It was at the point when the police reacted with gunfire that the organizers lost control of the crowd. In the words of Zakes Molotsi, one of the organizers:

> the march was organized. But the events after, it was now starting to be a spontaneous anger in response to the killing of Hector and other people who were killed. Because if you remember very well, from that day only, it was a very big number of people killed . . . No it was, as you have heard, this is the end of the world, because everything was just burning, it was smoke throughout Soweto, trains were not working, roads were closed, it was terrible, lot of police.[14]

This quotation appears in an interview of Molotsi by the author, the full transcript of which can be found as supplemental information to a chapter on key riot participants.

FIGURE 3.2 Poster from visual archive: "To hell with Afrikaans" [National Archives and Records Service of South Africa].

Armed confrontation with the police is the point at which the character of the participants altered. According to the police narrative, they ceased to be schoolchildren and became a mob participating in a riot. That narrative is exemplified by the testimony of Police Sergeant Marthinus Johannes Hattingh, reproduced in full by Pohlandt-McCormick as both a photographic image of the official document and a searchable text. Early in that testimony, Hattingh claims that "at this point a large crowd gathered and was made up of schoolchildren and adults." And as Pohlandt-McCormick notes, Hattingh's subsequent language changes in describing the outbreak of violence by the protestors, and he no longer refers to *kinders* (children) but *skare* (crowds).[15] Readers can rapidly check that assertion by an automated search of the text in the archived testimony.

The armed confrontation is also the point at which young women—always very much in the minority in the crowd photographs Pohlandt-McCormick reproduces—ceased to matter significantly in the conduct of events. The photographic and archival absence allows us to rethink Pohlandt-McCormick's statement that "the stories of participants of the uprising also revealed that young women and girls, far from being 'just in the background,' as their male counterparts would have it, were central to the uprising."[16] But it seems likely that primarily grown-ups (*volwassenes*), males who were in their late teens or were young adults, could have caused the widespread damage of that day. Among other images, the overturned truck depicted in Figure 3.3 is evidence for this claim.

Our point here is not to undermine Pohlandt-McCormick's claims but to provide a glimpse into the epistemic and heuristic value of an "open narrative"[17] that includes visual and verbal material that would not have found a place in a typical scholarly narrative.

Art as Historical Evidence

Imaging the French Revolution, edited by Jack Censer and Lynn Hunt,[18] is a work that reimagines the scholarly collection. Its focus is deliberately narrow: 42 images of French Revolutionary crowds. In a special viewer, these can be enlarged and compared; one can even be superimposed on another. The six essays that focus on various aspects of these images were shared among contributors who discussed them in a series of online posts. They revised them based on this discussion. Along with the essays and images, the posts are reproduced on the *American Historical Review* website, both in their original form and in a form edited to focus on eight topics of interest. In a companion article in the *American Historical Review*, Censer and Hunt reflect on the project and direct an audience of historians to it.[19] As a consequence of the interactions the site makes possible—interactions among editors and

FIGURE 3.3 Photo from visual archive: Uncle Tom's Hall truck burned out and flipped [National Archives and Records Service of South Africa].

contributors, interactions of viewers with various aspects of the site—we can judge for ourselves whether the claims the essays make are soundly based on the visual evidence.

In their interaction, contributors treat each other as equals and are open to disagreement within the bounds of civility:

> [T]he on-line format affords a possible solution to one of the greatest problems in using visual imagery produced at the time of the French Revolution. Better analysis and interpretation depends on more information, and only a limited amount of information is likely to emerge from the efforts of any one individual. These essays show the influence of a more interactive exchange, and the construction of links between them will enable readers to join in the debates themselves.[20]

The discussion of Figure 3.4, created by Jean-Louis Prieur depicting an event of July 23, 1789, exemplifies such interaction. The plate shows a mob accompanying a hated government official, Bertier de Sauvigny, as he is being carted away to hang from a lamppost in a public square. Before him, a man carries a pike bearing

FIGURE 3.4 Drawing posted for collaborative analysis in *Imaging the French Revolution*, "Bertier de Sauvignon, Intendant of Paris, is led to his punishment" [J. Censer and L. Hunt, *American Historical Review* 110, no. 1 (2005): 38–45].

the decapitated head of another hated official, his father-in-law, Foulon de Doré, who had suffered the same fate earlier. In his essay on the subject, Warren Roberts uses this image and similar ones to question a previously published socioeconomic analysis by George Rudé,[21] in which he concluded that "revolutionary crowds were made up of artisans, shopkeepers, and petty tradesmen, law abiding people who were neither unemployed nor criminal, but stable and bent upon preserving their traditional rights."[22] Roberts employs Figure 3.4 and other similar images as evidence correcting Rudé's benign portrayal of the revolutionary crowd. Roberts goes further and, it seems to us, makes the essential point about Prieur: "his images . . . add to our understanding of revolutionary crowds in action. As with contemporary textual sources, Prieur's images are evidence that historians can use to reconstruct events that drove the revolution in directions that no one at the time could have predicted."

In a follow-up response, Lynn Hunt seconds that assertion and adds:

So what is truly wonderful about the images is that they often capture, if only inadvertently, the fundamental AMBIVALENCE that many people must have felt about the crowd as something not entirely rational, bent on a form of justice that was not particularly attractive, and yet a fact of revolutionary politics that simply could not be wished away. This ambivalence had been lost in the historiography of the 1960s-1970s . . . that was so concerned to reassert the rationality of the lower classes.

Barbara Day Hickman adds a qualification:

Prieur nevertheless reduces the impact of crowd violence through the elegance of his style, the orderliness of the narrative, and the classical format of his "convoi funèbre" [funeral procession]. I would therefore agree with Lynn [Hunt] that accomplished and pro-revolutionary artists, such as Prieur, muted the threatening nature of crowd violence with both style and intention.

In response, Roberts defends his original position: "Yes, Prieur has brought out the ritualistic dimension of the procession, but not to see Foulon's head stuck on a pike with straw stuffed in its mouth as macabre is to pass over something that seems obvious to me." It is thus that we come to know Figure 3.4 from multiple points of view that converge on agreement.

Can we trust artistic images as historical evidence? We can certainly note the license artists take, and the traditions of practice that influence their work, distorting their reimagining of the past and present. But textual evidence can distort as well. For example, in an autobiography written from a revolutionary prison cell Sylvain Caubert says that he

was born into that most valuable of classes, the People, the class destined most particularly to reap the benefits of the Revolution; son of a worker, a long-time worker himself, always living in the midst of "sans-culottes" he is proud to have learned from them the practice of republican virtues.

In fact, Caubert was a substantial entrepreneur who, it was alleged, referred to the Revolutionary crowd as "scum."[23]

The difference in treatment between the verbal and artistic archives, we believe, comes to this: Historians trust textual archives because, over the centuries, they have learned just how to distrust them. In the case of artistic images outside the discipline of art history, they are just beginning to learn the appropriate skepticism. This is an enterprise the Censer-Hunt collection furthers, a collaborative endeavor feasible only on the Internet. True, the collection falls far short of perfection. Joan Landes speaks eloquently of the limitations of current technology in reproducing images online—limitations to which our reproduction of one of their images bears eloquent testimony.[24] But Wayne Hanley sounds a more positive note. He speaks stoutly of the advantages of collaboration, a view none of the contributors challenges:

> As for the collaborative nature of this particular project, I had a desire, reading through the various contributions, to edit, revise, expand, etc. my own contribution. It is not unlike—for lack of a better term—a virtual conference, where the feedback, criticism, and synergy inspire one to improve one's work (or at least my own work). I think there is a future in that, not only for the contributors but for those who afterward read the various contributions and commentary.[25]

Reinterpreting the Civil War: The Role of Visualization

The subject of William G. Thomas III and Edward L. Ayers's Internet "essay" *The Differences Slavery Made: A Close Analysis of Two American Communities*[26] is the economic status of slavery at the beginning of the American Civil War, an exploration that follows in the long wake of Robert Fogel and Stanley Engerman's groundbreaking monograph *Time on the Cross: The Economics of American Negro Slavery*.[27] Using extensive quantitative data represented in graphs and maps, Fogel and Engerman contended that the Southern slave economy made economic sense. It was an alternative form of modernity. They also contended that slaves were better treated than had been generally thought; after all, contented slaves made better workers. As it turned out, *Time on the Cross* initiated the authors' own time on the cross: Their work was almost universally vilified. But in the two decades that followed, the consensus shifted. In 1993, Fogel won the Nobel Prize in economics "for having renewed research in economic history by applying economic theory and quantitative methods in order to explain economic and institutional change."[28] A new form of history had been created: cliometrics permanently joined to the muse of history. In *Time on the Cross*, however, the visualization of data in the form of graphs and maps was largely segregated in a separate volume. That posed a serious constraint: "anyone interested in 'checking the facts' or the methods of estimation had to go through a process of cross-referencing. That cross-referencing could be done only after one made sense of the condensed presentation in volume II, which itself relied on extensive cross-referencing."[29] In Thomas and Ayers's 2003 web-based essay on the same topic, there is no such constraint. It is an exemplary instance of the use of hypertext in the interest of scholarly argument.

To better understand the genesis of this publication, we need to return to 1992, when Ayers published *The Promise of the New South*, a book that departed from the typical historical narrative "organized in a linear way, either chronologically or in the form of an argument, seeking balance and authority." In its place, this book experimented with an "open narrative"[30] in which Ayers incorporated "material that had not fit into more conventional narratives, combining everything from number crunching to the exegesis of novels." Overall, this scholarly work was well received: It was a National Book Award and Pulitzer Prize finalist. Nonetheless, Ayers felt compelled to write a response to his critics, who had complained of the pernicious influence of several fashionable "isms" within academia: namely, the unholy trinity of poststructuralism, deconstructionism, and Foucaultism. In his response, Ayers explained the method behind his open narrative. Thus it comes as no surprise that Ayers would go on to become one of the leading advocates for and practitioners of online scholarship. *The Difference Slavery Made* is an example.

Thomas and Ayers are social historians who integrate the insights of cliometrics into a broader exploration of how the contrasting social systems of slavery and of a free labor society worked and what sustained them. Their online argument works by "branching and layers and connections rather than operating on one place of exposition."[31] The top layer, the first of five, is an "Overview" under the "Introduction" tab. It establishes their main claim and summarizes the argument behind it and the method by which evidence was generated. Layer two, "Summary of Argument," is a conventionally laid-out précis of the claim organized in nine linked segments, ending with an overall conclusion. While straight text, it does have links that open to supporting visuals, tables, and references. Within these linked segments, Thomas and Ayers make the case that on the eve of the Civil War, North and South faced each other as two viable economies, two sustainable versions of modernity.

Thomas and Ayers focus not on the South or North as a whole but on two neighboring counties in the Shenandoah Valley: Augusta, with a slave economy and just south of the Mason–Dixon line, and Franklin, with an economy based on free labor and just north of the line. There are, of course, differences between the two counties—to feed its slaves and distilleries, the Southern county grew more corn than wheat; it also possessed more minor than major roads, a sign of a more localized way of life. Nevertheless, both had vibrant social and economic structures, ways of life that can truly be called modern, and both sides considered their ways well worth defending. From their analysis of supporting visuals, historical documents, tables, and references, the authors conclude that the War between the States "was the result of two highly mobilized and highly confident regions, each modern in its own way, fighting over the future of slavery in a rapidly expanding United States."[32]

Thomas and Ayers's third layer, "Points of Analysis," is the most innovative and in many ways most important for experts looking to scrutinize the authors' argument. It works by means of multiple visual and verbal comparisons of the two counties. Thomas and Ayers do not simply write about comparisons between the two counties; they consistently visualize these differences in graphic and cartographic form.

Readers do not only read about these differences and similarities; they see them unmistakably and at a glance. Moreover, they see these differences within the rich context of the varied historical evidence. We have not only Thomas and Ayers's analysis of events; we have contemporary newspaper accounts, diaries, and the extended views of other historians. This rich context is not tucked away in a separate volume or appendix; it is only a click away.

For example, under the subheading "[Presidential] Campaign of 1860" in "Points of Analysis" appears a screen with five bulleted items (Fig. 3.5),[33] as might appear on a PowerPoint slide. Adjacent to the top three bullets is a visual icon, a geographic outline of Franklin County; adjacent to the bottom two bullets is a similar icon for Augusta County. Each bulleted item is a statement expressed in a single sentence about the political positions held by different parties concerning slavery. At the end of each sentence is a link, which opens to a screen that repeats the complete sentence

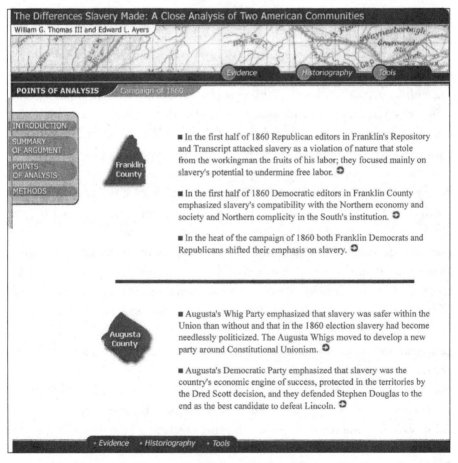

FIGURE 3.5 Five points of analysis on the 1860 presidential campaign in *The Differences Slavery Made* [W. Thomas and E. Ayers, Virginia Center for Digital History at the University of Virginia].

in bold, followed by a paragraph-long amplification, followed again by a list of supporting evidence, followed by a reference list. Each item in the list of supporting evidence has a link that leads to a summary of the document contents, an excerpt from the document, a link to the full text, and a reiteration of the point of interest. The reference list is similarly hyperlinked. These densely linked layers of scholarship can be realized only through the Internet.

Figure 3.5's points of analysis covers the usual documentary evidence for historical research, but Thomas and Ayers also rely upon the sort of visual supporting evidence more common to the scientific article. In their conclusion, they explain the reason behind the focus on details that only quantitative visualization of a representative sample can reveal. First, they define a problem with past historical writing:

> Too often, broad generalizations about the North and the South have been made from the grossest measurements. When historians talk about the South, it is easy to imagine the North as a perfect counterpoint, thoroughly industrialized, urbanized, and full of autonomous people on the move. When we talk about the North, it is easy to imagine the South as rural and fixed, a place virtually without history. When we have bothered to compare the two directly, we have often used the most extreme places—Boston versus Charleston, say, or Massachusetts versus South Carolina—to confirm the dualistic notions we held before we began.[34]

The authors' quantitative analyses gainsay such dualistic notions. The graphs, tables, and maps found in "Supporting Evidence" show that both Franklin and Augusta counties shared a growing prosperity from 1850 to 1860, as did the entire South, North, and United States (Fig. 3.6).[35] When the authors plotted farm size for the two counties in a bar graph (Fig. 3.7),[36] they found an equal distribution to which there is one interesting exception, large farms of 500 acres or more in southern Augusta County. It is a vital difference that marks a distinction between free labor largely confined to small- and middle-sized farms and slave labor, its efficiency particularly noticeable on large farms. A map superimposed with pie charts showing crop percentages (Fig. 3.8) visualizes the mixture in farms across Augusta County.[37] It illustrates the importance of both corn and wheat production, especially on the largest farms. It also illustrates the efficiency of a slave economy. This map serves as linked supporting evidence to the verbal context Thomas and Ayers provide:

> In Augusta the farms in the highest quintile of farm value produced a crop value twice that of the next lowest quintile in both wheat and corn production. This leap was not evident at any other farm value in Augusta or Franklin. Augusta's slaveholders accomplished this jump without a significant expansion

of the amount of land dedicated to a specific crop. These large farms' percentage of total grain in wheat and corn did not differ markedly from the middle and upper quintiles of farms. So, their productivity leap was a function not of crop difference but of large-scale slavery.[38]

A fourth layer in Thomas and Ayers's essay details the authors' methods for acquiring and analyzing their data ("Methods"). Methodological discussions such as this are relatively rare in the humanities, even though, as Borgman rightly claims, "scholarly methods are as deeply seated in the humanities as they are in the sciences."[39]

A fifth layer gathers and organizes supporting information of various types. One is in a section called "Evidence," similar to the "Archive" of Pohlandt-McCormick. That section holds the eight colored graphs, 31 colored maps, and 53 tables that appear as "Supporting Evidence" in the comparisons under "Points of Analysis." There expert readers can focus on the acquired data and take issue with their verbal arguments and claims. Thomas and Ayers also include a section called "Historiography," a collection of all the references cited and of links to further discussion of each reference.

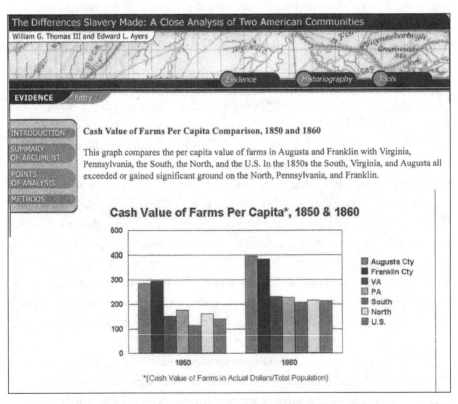

FIGURE 3.6 Supporting evidence in *The Differences Slavery Made*: cash value of farms per capita [W. Thomas and E. Ayers, Virginia Center for Digital History at the University of Virginia].

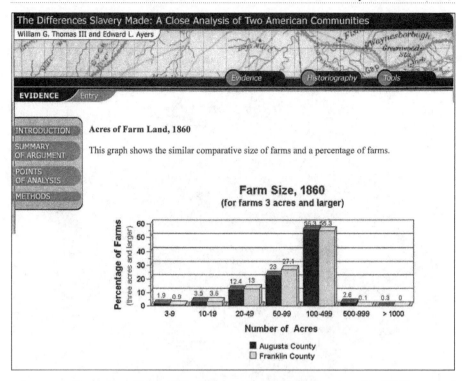

FIGURE 3.7 Supporting evidence in *The Differences Slavery Made*: farm size, 1860 [W. Thomas and E. Ayers, Virginia Center for Digital History at the University of Virginia].

There expert readers can evaluate whether all the relevant literature has been taken into account and get the gist of any references with which they might not be familiar. And finally, under a section called "Tools," readers can view a chart that plots what parts of the overall web text they have consulted.

With so many options for navigating the text, one might ask how scholars can possibly keep everything straight. Indeed, Thomas reported that peer reviewers of the initial draft site complained they could not "track the argument," finding it "almost impossible to read as *an article* because it has no linear structure."[40] Even after the authors had made significant revisions, several readers questioned what had been gained over traditional print articles, but that may be a function of lack of familiarity with evaluating a hyperlinked argument. Thomas also reports that the site had 17,500 visitors in 2005 and 2006, placing it well above the typical most-accessed article in the Public Library of Science journals.

Meeting the Challenge of Urban History: A Multimedia Los Angeles

Lucca, a walled Renaissance city, was tightly bounded; daily life in its markets and churches was constrained by longstanding traditions among succeeding generations

Augusta Country, 1860
Agricultural Production by Precinct

FIGURE 3.8 Supporting evidence in *The Differences Slavery Made*: agricultural production by precinct in Augusta County, 1860 [W. Thomas and E. Ayers, Virginia Center for Digital History at the University of Virginia].

of its citizens. In contrast, Los Angeles is unbounded in time and space. Borders have expanded; dramatic shifts in population have taken place within a generation. It is a dynamism that, it would seem, could never be captured in the medium of print. Unsurprisingly, at the center of Philip Ethington's Internet essay *Los Angeles and the Problem of Urban Historical Knowledge*,[41] a special project associated with a 2000 issue of the *American Historical Review*, are the photograph and the moving image, a city captured on the run. It is by means of the synergy of these that Ethington describes Los Angeles. Its present is represented by such markers of fixity as overlapping political boundaries and such indices of movement as city streets filmed from a passing car. Its past is evoked by maps that make data visible, demonstrating dramatic population shifts over time, and by the juxtaposition of past and present cityscapes and panoramas. In Ethington's interactive map of current political boundaries (Fig. 3.9, original in color), for example,[42] we see dramatized the web of overlapping jurisdictions that make the city difficult to govern: County Supervisor Districts, Municipal Spaces, Congressional Districts, State Senate Districts, State Assembly Districts, and Municipal Court Districts.

We see so little of Los Angeles in place, so much of it only as we move from place to place. In accord with this truth, Robbert Flick, an artist associate of Ethington, filmed long stretches of Los Angeles streets. Afterward, he spliced together frames of these to create substantial painterly displays. In his web essay, Ethington reproduces both the unedited film and the artistic displays produced from it. The unedited film gives us a sense of actually driving through these streets; the artistic displays deliberately unsettle this visual experience, representing the street scene as a "sequential multiplicity of perspectives"[43] within a single rectangular frame, as in Figure 3.10.[44]

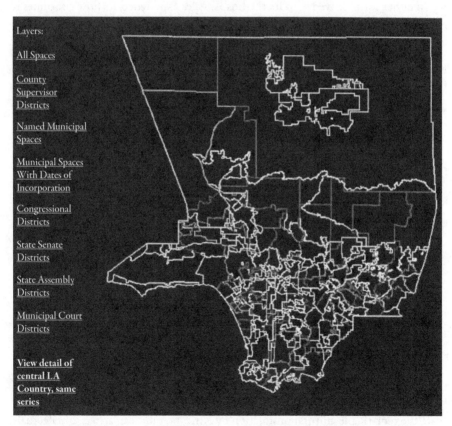

FIGURE 3.9 Interactive map showing complex political boundaries of Los Angeles. Online viewers can choose to see a specific layer by clicking on "layers" on left. [P. Ethington, http://www.usc.edu/dept/LAS/history/historylab/LAPUHK].

FIGURE 3.10 Los Angeles from Robbert Flick's artistic display "Along Central," May 16, 2000. Part of 50-photo photomontage. [P. Ethington, http://www.usc.edu/dept/LAS/history/historylab/ LAPUHK].

In the unedited film we move rapidly from left to right, coincident with the flow of experience. In the artistic display, our movements are unconstrained—left, right, up, down. In whatever direction we choose, we experience disjunction and discontinuity. In either form, as we try to fix the Los Angeles experience, its flow continues to defeat us.

Temporal change is represented by contrast. In maps color-coded to represent the percentage of Hispanic population within a given area, we see its sudden growth from 1970 to 1990 (Fig. 3.11).[45] Via the Internet, we can see such demographic data maps one by one, or in a decade-by-decade animated slideshow, as the Hispanic population grows before our eyes.

In addition to visualizing change over time graphically, Ethington enables us to see it directly. Through the magic of Photoshop, Figure 3.12 show us an existing building on South Central Avenue in Los Angeles covered with display ads from the 1940s and 1990s.[46] As Ethington explains in the accompanying caption:

> The Urban League, a leading civil rights organization, had its offices on the top floor in 1940. Talent agents were busy signing neighborhood actors like Myrtle Anderson (side of building). Real estate agents and physicians served a prosperous, mainly African American middle class. In 1999 "Garcia's Tienda C[entavos] Noventa y Nueve" [99-cent store] filled most of the first floor, catering to a primarily working-class Latino clientele.

Clicking on the image sends the reader to a photomontage illustrating the point that "the remarkable cultural production by African-American artists, intellectuals, and professionals along Central"[47] that existed in the 1940s had been wiped out— partially due to race riots in 1965 and 1992, and partially due to the exodus of African

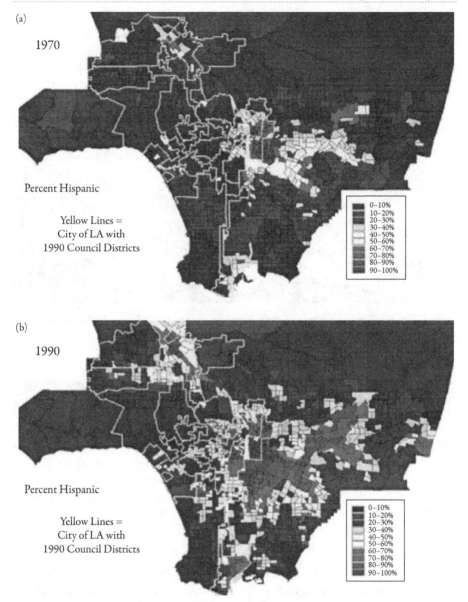

FIGURE 3.11 Maps of Hispanic population in Los Angeles for 1970 (a) and 1990 (b). [P. Ethington, http://www.usc.edu/dept/LAS/history/historylab/LAPUHK]. Video 3.2 [▶]

Americans and their replacement by Hispanics. Viewers can also tour present-day Central Avenue by means of Quicktime movie clips. Overall, by means of digitally altered still images, photomontages, interactive maps, and video clips, they can see for themselves the changes in a Los Angeles neighborhood over time in a way not possible in print.

FIGURE 3.12   Building on 2150 South Central Avenue, altered by Photoshop to display ads from 1940 and 1999 [P. Ethington, http://www.usc.edu/dept/LAS/history/historylab/LAPUHK].

FIGURE 3.13   Panoramas of Seventh and Broadway: 1905 (top) and 2000 (bottom) [P. Ethington. http://www.usc.edu/dept/LAS/history/historylab/LAPUHK]. Video 3.3 [▶]

That is not the end to Ethington's visual innovations in the service of representing historical change over the 20th century in Los Angeles. He also presents us with contrasting panoramas. Figure 3.13 shows sample panoramas taken at the southeast corner of Broadway and Seventh at approximately the same angle and elevation: The first was taken in 1905, the second in 2000.[48] These panoramas are created from photos stitched together to provide a 2D synoptic view. Viewers even have the option of examining these 2D panoramas as 3D virtual reality, simulating the experience of standing at the center of the site and rotating 360 degrees in 1905—when Los Angeles was still a relatively sleepy city of only about one hundred thousand—and in 2000—after the city's transformation into a sprawling metropolis of buildings, parking lots, empty spaces, and the movie and television industry.

It would be presumptuous to say that Ethington's Internet essay with still and moving images solves the problem it addresses. But it would not be presumptuous to say that he forces us to recognize that the problem is best addressed by means of the large toolbox of visual representation the Internet permits. Indeed, his early essay has blossomed into a multimedia book to be published by the University of California Press, *Ghost Metropolis: A Global History of Los Angeles Since 13,000*, a history of the Los Angeles region reaching back 13,000 (sic!) years. In Ethington's own words on the resulting website, now under construction:

> *Ghost Metropolis* attempts to make the ghostly presence of the past visible as a three-dimensional form of mapping. Those three dimensions are: 1) the linear chronological narrative, recounting actions by actors; 2) the visual encounter with the past in photographs, graphic arts, and motion pictures, and 3) the cartographic: visualizing the topography of human action.

In the 40 essays that constitute this digital project, the strong verbal–visual inter-actions made possible by the Internet make "the deep and complex past of a mighty global metropolis knowable, understandable, and visible" in a new way. Viewing the text, photography, graphs, videos, maps, and hyperlinks in Ethington's website, we felt we were seeing a preview of the future of the scholarly book.

Reimagining the Roman Forum: Vision as Hypothesis

In Diane Favro and Christopher Johanson's essay "Death in Motion,"[49] we move from modern Los Angeles to the deep past: We reimagine the ancient Roman Forum. For the first time, these authors have reconstructed "the funerary procession (*pompa funebris*) with specific spaces or in relation to the intricately constructed Roman experience of a funeral."[50] The authors note that past text-based scholar-ship "has favored simplified, static visual representations, which are in many ways antithetical to the experience of events such as ritual processions."[51] To circumvent that past constraint, they have created "interactive, immersive digital models of the Roman Forum that have been specifically designed to represent spatial and urban relationships,"[52] models whose best means of dissemination is the Internet. Favro argues persuasively for the added value of such visual representations for knowledge generation and communication:

> Cities are complex, heady, animated, three-dimensional environments experi-enced by kinetic observers ... Before the advent of digital technology, research-ers could explore only a few aspects of ancient urbanism based on information

presented in static images or small-scale physical models. With computing, the complexity of historical urban environments can be conveyed through the incorporation of myriad fields of inquiry with diverse source materials, and interactive re-creations. For example, [our] models of Rome are linked to a wide range of detailed metadata, including contemporary Latin texts, maps, art, film [and audio] clips, archaeological reports, and photographs.[53]

Readers can view "Death in Motion" in PDF or HTML format, the latter providing considerable added value with regard to its 50 visual representations. First and foremost is a 3D interactive visual that superimposes a simulacrum of the ancient Forum onto the present archaeological site as captured in Google Earth (Fig. 3.14), where the model buildings are reconstructed and situated with the aid of ancient texts and pictorial representations as well as archaeological evidence.[54] By means of the navigation tools on the right, online viewers can conduct a self-guided tour through the streets and byways of the Forum as it existed during a selected time period from roughly 200 BCE to 200 CE. By slowly advancing the time scale in the upper left, they can watch buildings appear and disappear from a

FIGURE 3.14 Interactive model of ancient Roman Forum in "Death in Motion" [D. Favro and C. Johanson, *Journal of the Society of Architectural Historians* 69 (2010): 12–37]. Video 3.4 [▶]

bird's-eye view, as the Forum grows and changes over four centuries when ancient Rome flourished.

From films like *The Hobbit* and *Avatar*, we have become used to 3D representations that seem perfectly to mimic reality. But what constitutes a triumph for cinematic animation constitutes a problem for science and scholarship. We have already met this problem in our chapter on the scientific article. The verisimilitude of the 3D representations with which the chapter concluded was a realization of D'Arcy Thompson's vision, a coincidence between the mathematical and the biological. The achievement is indeed extraordinary, so extraordinary that we have to remind ourselves that these vivid images are mathematical constructs, hypothesized closely to resemble the real. As historians Favro and Johanson wisely caution, their models "are graphical visualizations of textual [and archeological] interpretations fixed into a physical space. They are thought experiments, graphs of ideas."[55] The many images in Favro and Johanson's essay are visual hypotheses, educated guesses whose purpose is to constrain and mark out the cityscape along the route of funeral processions for recently deceased dignitaries in ancient Rome. By viewing the 3D interactive images, readers can simulate traveling those same routes, pausing to inspect the buildings based upon the best available archaeological evidence as they make their way to the sacred place of the funeral oration.

MUSICIANS SEE AND HEAR ANEW

According to philosopher Roger Scruton, "in all traditions, including our own, notation under-determines performance and identifies works of music only when read in the context of a performance tradition."[56] This underdetermination means that

> a person who performs woodenly, unfeelingly or grotesquely may make all the sounds prescribed by the score, but he will show nevertheless that he has understood nothing. Musical understanding is a form of aesthetic understanding: it is manifest in the conscious search for the right phrasing, the right dynamics, the right tempo.[57]

Moreover, according to conductor and pianist Daniel Barenboim, "it must be understood that one cannot explain the nature or the message of music through words . . . [W]hen we try to describe music with words, all we can do is articulate our reactions to it, and not grasp music itself."[58] Because of the nature of the task, musical theory in print must at times fall short of its evidential aim. A debate in the open-access journal *Music Theory Online* over the opening measures of a Beethoven masterpiece, his *Tempest* sonata, exemplifies the problem and illustrates its solution.

Concerning the *Tempest,* William E. Caplin of McGill[59] and James Hepokoski of Yale[60] differ with Janet Schmalfeldt of Tufts over how the sonata realizes its composer's innovative intent, his desire that "from today on I shall take a new path." In this debate, arguments are supported not only by excerpts from the score, as is usual in music analysis, but by excerpts from the music itself. Hepokoski, Schmalfeldt, and Caplin consistently employ this Internet feature. In her prose, Schmalfeldt gets to what is for her—and for us—the heart of the matter:

> I argue that Beethoven's music initiates new stylistic directions whereby, as conventional Classical formal processes become gradually transformed or "deformed," new cases of genuine formal ambiguity increasingly arise. In such cases . . . it is as if the composer invites the performer to play a determinative role in our understanding of the formal process. Thus the alliance between composer and performer—with both of these understood as listeners par excellence, to say the least—grows all the stronger as composers of the early nineteenth century respond to the impact of Beethoven's music. If our exhilarating debate about formal processes in Beethoven's *Tempest* has been warranted, then perhaps Beethoven might occasionally invite the performer to help us settle our differences.[61]

In this debate, we readers are also listeners who can make up our own minds. The journal includes everything we need: musical excerpts in support of arguments, a full score, and a full realization of that score by a master pianist—Malcolm Bilson.

In a previous paragraph we spoke as if the composer's intent were stable. We assumed that we practice and practice and that, as we do, we come closer to what Beethoven had in mind. To think this way, of course, is to exhibit historical blindness; it is to ignore the existence of traditions of performance, preserved in the links between teacher and student over the generations. It is also to ignore the ever-present possibility of performance innovation. In an article in *Music Performance Research* entitled "Baroque Expressiveness and Stylishness in Three Recordings of the D minor Sarabanda for Solo Violin by J. S. Bach,"[62] Dorottya Fabian and Emery Schubert address this issue. Theirs is an experiment to determine whether listeners can differentiate among three approaches to Baroque music performed by three generations of concert violinists: the oldest, represented by Yehudi Menuhin; an older generation represented by Arthur Grumiaux; and a younger, represented by Sergiù Luca. When the experimental subjects heard these violinists play the first few bars of the Sarabanda, the researchers discovered that they were able easily to differentiate among Menuhin's expressive-emotional approach, Grumiaux's modernist-literalist one, and Luca's rhythmically flexible one. Only the last favored detailed articulation and restrained vibrato on period instruments, "Baroque" style. It is this approach that experimental subjects preferred, one they associated with historically informed performance practice. Fabian and Schubert did not only perform their experiment; courtesy of the Internet, they also allowed their readers to become, in effect, experimental subjects. Readers can hear the excerpts the experimental subjects heard; they can make up their own minds. Menuhin, Grumiaux, or Luca? Hear for yourself in Video 3.5 [⏵].

FILM SCHOLARS SEE ANEW

Film studies have traditionally relied upon still photography—a serious limitation, one would think, when the object of study is a moving picture. On the Internet film scholars can now accomplish what film critics as significant as Robert Warshow and James Agee could not: They can incorporate film clips, analytical graphics, and 3D visualizations into their arguments. In this section, we examine the work of four film scholars for whom these visual modes are central: Robert Kolker, Adrian Miles, Stephen Mamber, and Clifford Galiher.

In "The Moving Image Reclaimed,"[63] published in the avant-garde humanities journal *Postmodern Culture* in 1994, Kolker comes to grips with a major problem of film scholarship prior to the Internet—"textual access." While historians could make their points with quotations of primary sources from their archives, film scholars could not fully engage in a parallel enterprise. With the advent of video-capture hardware and software, however, film studies can now claim "a heightened authority" that can go so far as to "correct and advance older methodologies." Kolker exemplifies this new authority by showing us the way visual allusion works. By means of film clips, he demonstrates that Martin Scorsese's *Cape Fear* "quotes" and "transforms" perhaps the most famous sequence in Alfred Hitchcock's *Strangers on a Train*, the one at a tennis match when Guy spots his nemesis, Bruno, staring menacingly from the audience. From this process of creative borrowing, Kolker asserts, we "understand how deeply films grow out of other films."

To exemplify the ability of scholars actually to intervene in the films they criticize, Kolker superimposes a dynamic grid of sightlines on a scene from Orson Welles's *Citizen Kane,* the crucial episode where the young Kane plays for the last time with his sled "Rosebud," a time of happiness that consistently eludes him despite his later success. This technique is a matter of going

beyond quoting images and actually intervening in their structure, inscribing the critical act within the images themselves. This is particularly useful in explaining how a filmmaker articulates narrative structure by framing and moving within a shot. A famous sequence from Welles's Citizen Kane becomes an animated expression of the complex shiftings of narrative point of view as figures change position and dominate or become recessive in the frame.

In *"Singin' in the Rain:* A Hypertextual Reading,"[64] published in *Postmodern Culture* in 1998, Adrian Miles does not focus on the most famous sequence in the film, Gene Kelly's dance to the title number. By means of text accompanied by video clips, he dwells instead on a previous sequence in which Don Lockwood, Kelly's character, confesses his love to Kathy Selden, played by Debbie Reynolds: "Kathy, Kathy, I'm trying to say something to you, but I'm such a ham I guess I'm not able to without the proper setting. Well, come here." With these words, he leads Kathy on to an empty soundstage. She turns to him, saying, "Why, it's just an empty stage." Don responds: "At first glance, yes." But then with the aid of a stepladder, some lighting, and an electric fan, he converts the empty stage into a romantic setting in which he woos Kathy by singing "You Were Meant for Me." After the song, she descends from the stepladder "balcony." They dance together, wordlessly, clearly a couple.

Because Don Lockwood is articulate only in song and dance, this sequence makes a fitting prelude to the famous "Singin' in the Rain" number, a sequence in which being in love is literally embodied in song and dance, epitomizing the central message of the movie musical. These transformations, Miles says, are what the film musical routinely does:

> As they enter from the outside, the spine of light from this huge door partially reveals an interior, but only enough to suggest something immense and as yet unknown. This must be the case, of course, not only for any seduction to be possible, but because this is the future, a realm of possible pathways. It is the future world of film, of what will become the singing cinema. It is yet to be made, and in a very literal manner the film claims it has to be *sung* into being.[65]

This scene does more than advance the plot; it is, more significantly, a scene about the magic of the movies and, more deeply, about how imagination transforms reality. And with the inclusion of the film clip, we are given visual evidence for that transformation.

In *Who Shot Liberty Valance?*[66]—a 3D experiment in "forensic film analysis"—Stephen Mamber compares two versions of the same sequence, the killing of the title character in John Ford's *The Man Who Shot Liberty Valence.* In this fight to the death, Ransom Stoddard, played by James Stewart, a lawyer from the East, represents the new West. In contrast, Tom Donophon, played by John

Wayne, and the title character, played by Lee Marvin, represent the Old West, a land where quarrels are settled with guns, not with laws. In the climactic scene, Ransom faces Liberty in a duel to the death. The episode is told twice. In the first sequence, Ransom guns down Liberty in a fair fight; in a following sequence, told in flashback, Donophon actually ambushes Liberty from a position in the shadows.

Who really killed Liberty Valance? The world believes it was Ransom, a belief that propels him into the U.S. Senate. But in a later scene, Donophon confesses to Ransom that it is he who killed Liberty. In a side-by-side analysis of the two versions of the killing, Mamber demonstrates that this ambiguity is built into the film's structure: We can see from this analysis that the two sequences do not recount exactly the same event. Moreover, a 3D interactive visualization (Fig. 3.15) demonstrates that from his vantage point Ransom would have easily seen Donophon.[67] In his comments on the film's scholarship, included as a hyperlink (Fig. 3.16),[68] Mamber points out that even Ford's controversial decision to photograph in black and white was made to create and "maintain the ambiguity." And in an interview, he persuasively argues for the need for such web-based projects in film studies:

> I think the major sections of the web site offer an analysis that couldn't have been done in any other way; you just need to be able to, for example, juxtapose different sequences in the film and be able to look at them in ways that I couldn't have written about in print.[69]

FIGURE 3.15 Interactive visual for *Who Shot Liberty Valance?* Rance (Stewart), on the left, easily sees Donaphon (Wayne) on the right. [S. Mamber, "Who Shot Liberty Valance?" (Los Angeles: UCLA Department of Film, Television, and Digital Media)].

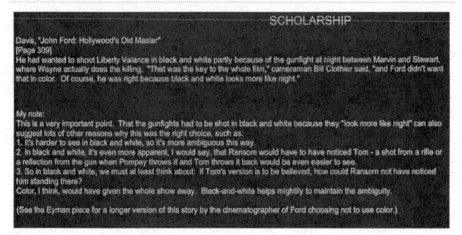

SCHOLARSHIP

Davis, "John Ford: Hollywood's Old Master"
[Page 309]
He had wanted to shoot Liberty Valance in black and white partly because of the gunfight at night between Marvin and Stewart, where Wayne actually does the killing. "That was the key to the whole film," cameraman Bill Clothier said, "and Ford didn't want that in color. Of course, he was right because black and white looks more like night."

My note:
This is a very important point. That the gunfights had to be shot in black and white because they "look more like night" can also suggest lots of other reasons why this was the right choice, such as:
1. It's harder to see in black and white, so it's more ambiguous this way.
2. In black and white, it's even more apparent, I would say, that Ransom would have to have noticed Tom - a shot from a rifle or a reflection from the gun when Pompey throws it and Tom throws it back would be even easier to see.
3. So in black and white, we must at least think about: If Tom's version is to be believed, how could Ransom not have noticed him standing there?
Color, I think, would have given the whole show away. Black-and-white helps mightily to maintain the ambiguity.

(See the Eyman piece for a longer version of this story by the cinematographer of Ford choosing not to use color.)

FIGURE 3.16 Mamber's comment on Davis, emphasizing the importance of Ford's choice of black-and-white [S. Mamber, "Who Shot Liberty Valance?: Scholarship"].

In "Simultaneity and Overlap in Stanley Kubrick's *The Killing*,"[70] another contribution to the 1998 issue of *Postmodern Culture*, Mamber faces a problem that resort to film clips will not solve: representing the whole structure of a complex plot. Mamber's solution is reductive. He sees the plot as a narrative chart and reconstructs a crucial scene in 3D visualizations. Both visualizations demonstrate his point "that narratives may contain implied mappings, a sense that underlying their creation was a mapping that's been hidden from us, so we can be representing, in a sense, what's already there but hidden from us. We may be recreating what an author has worked out yet chosen not to reveal so explicitly."[71] In this chart (Fig. 3.17), the timeline is at the top and each horizontal represents a character's narrative trajectory.[72] The colored rectangles represent narrative sequences. For example, the fourth and last rectangle in the "Nikki the Gunman" horizontal corresponds to the narrator's announcement that "Nikki was dead at 4:23." Mamber also provides us with a 3D visualization of the scene just before Nikki's death: "Nikki waits to shoot Red Lightning," a race horse (Fig. 3.18). In these visualizations, we see at a glance the structure of the complex plot, a series of episodes we experience in real time while watching the film.

Clifford Galiher's video essay, "Three Fates of the Maltese Falcon: Hammett's Novel at Warner Bros.,"[73] is a tribute to what can be accomplished when movie posters, stills, archival materials, and film clips are turned into a multimedia online lecture. Galiher relates the history of three film productions that have their source in Dashiell Hammett's *The Maltese Falcon*; at the same time, he constructs an argument to show that John Huston, the director of the final production, has turned a masterpiece of crime fiction into a film masterpiece.

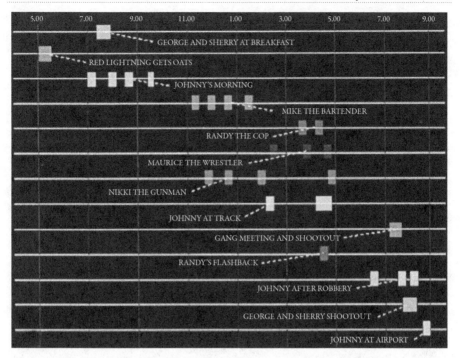

FIGURE 3.17 Chart mapping the structure of narrative in Kubrick's *The Killing* [S. Mamber, *Postmodern Culture*, 8, no. 2 © 1998 Stephen Mamber. Reprinted with permission of Johns Hopkins University Press].

Galiher's display of the three posters (Fig. 3.19) tells us a great deal about the three productions they advertise. The first shows the novel transplanted from the streets to the salon; the second advertises a gritty crime drama turned into a lighthearted spoof. In both cases, the lead actress gets the top credit. While in the first instance she shares the poster with her co-star, in the second she dominates the scene. The third poster presents a stark contrast. Bogart dominates and has star billing. While Bette Davis's gun is merely held, Bogart's is pointed, his finger on the trigger. The pastel colors of the first two posters are gone. The background is the black of night and the red of blood. Above, a falcon hovers.

According to Galiher, an unknown John Huston was told the film could be his if he created a decent script and directed on a tight budget. According to legend, he was advised simply to transcribe the novel. Whatever the case, like the poster featuring Bogart, the film's dialogue is true to the book, as Galiher shows by superimposition (Fig. 3.20). Here, we viewers simultaneously watch the film clip, hear the dialogue spoken, read the accompanying text from Hammett's book, and hear the scholar's commentary—a truly multimedia experience.

FIGURE 3.18 Nikki waits to shoot Red Lightning: 3D representation of *The Killing* [S. Mamber, *Postmodern Culture*, 8, no. 2 © 1998 Stephen Mamber. Reprinted with permission of Johns Hopkins University Press].

FIGURE 3.19 Movie posters for three versions of Dashiell Hammett's *Maltese Falcon* [C. Galiher, *Mediascape: UCLA's Journal of Cinema and Media Studies,* January 27, 2013]. Video 3.6 [▶]

CHAPTER 4: The Black Bird (p. 39)

"This is hopeless, I can't do anything for you. I don't know what you want done. I don't even know if you know what you want."

"You won't go to the police?"

"Go to them!...All I've got to do is stand still and they'll be swarming all over me. Well, I'll tell them what I know and you'll have to take your chances."

FIGURE 3.20 Film clip with superimposed text from *The Maltese Falcon*. The film's dialogue is right from the book [C. Galiher, *Mediascape: UCLA's Journal of Cinema and Media Studies,* January 27, 2013]. Video 3.7 [▶]

FIGURE 3.21 Still frame showing Sydney Greenstreet, shot from a low angle [C. Galiher, *Mediascape: UCLA's Journal of Cinema and Media Studies,* January 27, 2013].

Huston managed to keep within a tight budget by using such unknown contract players as Humphrey Bogart, Peter Lorre, and Sidney Greenstreet and by filming mostly in interiors. He used these scenic restrictions to create a claustrophobic masterpiece in which actors are crowded into scenes and huddled in frames that can barely contain them. Galiher illustrates this point with a series of stills from the movie. In the still above (Fig. 3.21), for example, Sidney Greenstreet, shot from an unusual low angle, dominates the frame; indeed, the frame cannot quite contain him.

CONCLUSION

Our online search of the humanities literature led us to conclude that its innovative exploitation of the Internet has been confined, for the most part, to side-stream venues; mainstream publication has yet to be seriously affected. Nonetheless, our search did uncover numerous individual examples of online humanities essays that show considerable ingenuity in creating an alternative path through argument, linking main text to supporting information, collaborating online to create new knowledge, and incorporating a greater variety of visual and audio representation made possible by the Internet. While it is disturbing that most of these projects have been marginal even in the careers of the scholars who created them, that so many depended on the procurement of federal or private grants, and that all were special projects, not routine activities, we are encouraged that the authors we have featured have made good use of the possibilities of the Internet to produce sound scholarship that can simultaneously impress and inform.

What might the "humanities essay of the future" look like? Based on what already exists, we can make an educated guess. For those disciplines whose published texts have prominently featured the visual for at least several decades—history, music theory, and film studies—one possibility is the information-rich three-pane format. The narrow left pane would be for navigation within the entire essay; the middle pane, for the hyperlinked main text; the right pane, for supplementary information such as scholarly notes, linked bibliographic information, article metrics, translations of the main text or of foreign quotations within it, author biographies, and reader commentary. The right pane could also be used to display any images that can be manipulated in order to highlight a point in the text.

But innovation need not be confined to these disciplines. Even philosophical arguments could be considerably fortified by exploitation of the Internet. A recent example is Bruno Latour's *An Inquiry into Modes of Existence*,[74] a scholarly book in printed form along with a companion web-based version that houses the original text in French and English. And much, much more: The reader accesses the digital book through a homepage that includes a guided tour of the site. In the web-based book, the left pane displays the original text, heavily linked to three adjacent columns: one with definitions of terms and abbreviations, one for supporting scholarly documentation, and one for comment and critique by readers. While the hardcopy has no illustrations, the web version has numerous images, audio files, and videos. The hardcopy was written by a single author and published by Harvard University Press in 2013; the web version is a collaborative work that continued to evolve even after the 2013 publication.

We hope that at this second Gutenberg moment in the history of communication, scholars in the humanities will seriously consider the examples we have featured. We also hope that scholars as forward-thinking as Robert Darnton and journals as forward-looking as the *Journal of the Society of Architectural Historians, Music Theory Online*, and *Postmodern Culture* will continue their efforts to foster institutional change, to turn the marginal into the central.

4

ARCHIVAL WEBSITES IN THE HUMANITIES AND SCIENCES

A SOUTH AFRICAN by birth, white, of German ancestry, fluent in Afrikaans, Helena Pohlandt-McCormick spent six months in her native country in 1993 and a full year in 1994 studying the Soweto uprising. During that time, she assiduously examined the relevant archives but was unable to find any of the posters she knew the marching students carried:

> From the transcripts and correspondence of the Cillié Commission I knew that the Commission had received, from the police, many posters and banners that had been confiscated during various student marches in 1976. None of them would have fit into a traditional archive document box and, though mentioned on the list of evidence associated with the Cillié Commission, they were initially not to be found. I continued to request that archivists search the repositories—without success. Until, one day, perhaps exasperated by my persistence or wanting to finally prove to me that there was nothing to be found in the space associated with K345, the archival designator of my Soweto materials, one of the archivists relented and asked me to accompany her into the vaults in order to help her search for these artifacts of the uprising! To be sure, there were no posters to be found in the shelf space that housed the roughly nine hundred boxes of evidence associated with the Cillié Commission. But then, as my disappointed eyes swept the simultaneously ominous and tantalizing interior of the vault, I saw a piece of board protruding over the topmost edge of the shelf. There, almost 9 feet into the air, in the shadowy space on top of the document shelves, lay a pile of posters and banners.[1]

We can understand Pohlandt-McCormick's mounting sense of excitement. It is not just the discovery itself; it is the sense of being in touch with the past—literally in touch. It is the knowledge that no photograph can do justice to any 3D object, whether it is a collection of posters, a cache of cold fusion memorabilia, or Enrico Fermi's Nobel medal. The point, in fact, is general. While we may live in an age of mechanical reproduction, none of us wants to see behind a museum display case a reproduction of the Magna Carta or the Declaration of Independence: We want to see the real thing. No digital archive can create serendipitous and memorable encounters with the genuine artifacts of the past.[2]

Yet there are obstacles to the study of physical archives, difficult to overcome. Travel to collections can be expensive and time-consuming; facilities for reproduction of books and manuscripts are not always available. Reproduction may not be permitted; when it is, it is almost always expensive. Moreover, in the case of reproduced images, especially color images, inaccuracy can be guaranteed. But without accurate reproductions, how can scholars compare copies that exist in different archival collections? In addition, study of archival materials themselves can be hazardous to the material studied. Although some rare books and manuscripts are remarkably sturdy, others are fragile indeed. None benefits from handling, however carefully. For scholars, these conditions can seriously inhibit scholarship; for graduate students—those learning to become scholars—these conditions are obstacles virtually impossible to overcome unless . . . . unless there exists an archival website whose photographs of manuscripts and rare books are sufficiently accurate for scholarly purposes. If so, what scholar would have a right to complain?

Certainly, no complaint is legitimate in the case of the two archival websites we will examine in detail later in this chapter—those of Walt Whitman and William Blake. These sites, which sensitively and intelligently exploit the possibilities of the Internet, are not simply as good as the materials from which they derive; in many ways, they are better, and in many ways they are superior to in-print scholarly editions of Whitman and Blake. In these and similar digital archives, in fact, the costs of color, so high in print, are trivial; the incorporation of videos or audio is no problem at all. In all of these, moreover, when new material relevant to the archive is discovered or produced, no supplements are needed. New material can simply be slipped in in its proper place. No index is needed; far more powerful search engines and systems of linked pages take their place. In addition, in digital archives time and space have been wholly erased; everything is immediately present to anyone with an Internet connection. No one need wait because someone else is using the rare book or manuscript, or any book or article available on site. In addition, all restrictions to access have been eliminated, so long as the site is not gated. This is the case with the Whitman and Blake archives. What is accessible is accessible equally to senior scholars, junior graduate students, and the average sixth grader. Of course, digital archives have these advantages permanently only so long as they have permanent homes, archival sites that are guaranteed to outlive their creators. Nothing is more frustrating than the dead links that litter the Internet.

The science websites we examine in detail—the Encyclopedia of Life, Tree of Life, Galaxy Zoo, and Protein Data Base—are also superior to their print-era alternatives. Like their humanities counterparts, they are constantly open to revision and amplification, easily incorporate color images and videos, are open access, accommodate multiple users simultaneously, and have the kind of permanence an institutional base provides. Encyclopedia of Life, Tree of Life, and Galaxy Zoo differ from the William Blake and Walt Whitman archives in that they encourage amateur participation. However, other humanities websites, as we shall see, are also open to such participation.

Do these websites exemplify a new genre, as Walt Whitman Archive co-founder Ed Folsom suggests, born in the late 20th century just as the novel was born in the early 18th?[3] When scientists discover a new species, they immediately give it a name to fix it exactly into preexisting taxonomic space. Described in 2012, the carnivorous "harp sponge," *Chondrocladia lyra*, is found off the coast of California at depths between 10,800 and 11,500 feet. *Lyra* is a newly discovered species of a well-established genus. In other words, its relative stability over human, though not over evolutionary, time, is assumed. But the relative stability of humanities and science websites is just what cannot be assumed. These are evolving in form and content as we speak. Eventually, we may be sure, they will be characterized by the stability that the novel or the scientific article has achieved. Then, we can call these websites a "genre"; then, we can say something cogent about similarities shaped by many decades or centuries of history, as we did with the scientific journal article in *Communicating Science.*[4] However different they may be, we have no trouble classifying *Tom Jones, Tristam Shandy*, and *Finnegans Wake* as novels. But of these archival websites, we can say only that they exploit the Internet in ways that are ingenious and commendable.

In our study of these websites, we hope to accomplish two purposes: to give readers a sense of their variety and Protean character and to give them a sense of what it is like to inhabit and employ these sites for scholarly purposes. In the following discussion, we will be using the terms "digital archive" and "digital repository" as shorthand for a website with a search mechanism permitting access to some combination of texts, pictures, audio files, videos, and data. Here, our concern is not just any digital archive or repository, but those specifically designed so that scientists, scholars, or other interested persons can use them to generate new knowledge or deposit information for others to do so. While these hypertext sites are not part of some overarching argument or narrative as in an essay or monograph, they are thematically linked and organized "according to some initial set of design plans that are keyed to the specific materials in the [archive], and to the imagined needs of the users of those materials."[5]

After an extensive search of archival websites in the sciences and humanities, we devised a system of classification to make sense of the diversity that now exists. We divided these sites according to their predominant purpose: to provide resources for scholarship, to store data for scientific research, to store scientific and scholarly papers and related materials, to create new knowledge through volunteer participation, and to codify existing knowledge.

WEBSITES THAT PROVIDE RESOURCES FOR SCHOLARSHIP

There is a wide variety of such sites. Much has been recently written about the "digital humanities," the computer-mediated quantitative analysis of texts. Several sites provide raw material for such studies. The humanities site Corpus of Historical American English is a database comprising 400 million words of American English texts from 1810 to 2009. By means of quantitative analysis, scholars can "see how words, phrases and grammatical constructions have increased or decreased in frequency, how words have changed meaning over time, and how stylistic changes have taken place in the language."[6] Another site, Folger Digital Texts, comprises 13 Shakespeare plays in versions based on the latest editorial scholarship. Texts have been coded to permit sophisticated quantitative analysis of the prose and poetry. Do you want to do a linguistic quantitative analysis of Shakespeare's preoccupation with death and dying in the early and late plays? Such a comparative analysis is possible with this site.

Some sites focus on literary periods. In early English literature, we have Oxford Scholarly Editions Online, a collection of annotated and searchable editions of poems, plays, and prose composed by authors working between 1485 and 1660, including Shakespeare, Christopher Marlowe, John Milton, and John Donne. For those interested in English literature and the visual arts, there is the Victorian Web, a multimedia archive of scholarly resources by and about "eminent and not-so-eminent Victorians." At this site innovative hyperlinking encourages both logical and serendipitous searching of the archive, as one would expect from the site's founder George Landow, an early advocate of the use of hypertext and "networked—i.e., uncentered, nonhierarchical—digital technology."[7]

Digital repositories are also devoted to literary texts in languages other than English. Most impressive of all is Perseus Digital Library, a collection that contains ancient Roman and Greek texts with translations into English, scholarly annotations, and bibliographies. Its ultimate goal is ambitious: "to make the full record of humanity—linguistic sources, physical artifacts, historical spaces—as intellectually accessible as possible to every human being, regardless of linguistic or cultural background."[8] Perseus Digital invites contributions from both students and scholars and makes extensive use of machine-generated knowledge. For example, it maps most frequently mentioned places in a book and provides automated translation of Latin and Greek "to provide reading support where there is no pre-existing human translation." See Video 4.1 [▶]

One feature that is lacking is an audio file with an actor reading the passage in Greek or Latin or English. Anyone interested in how that might work should consult the Princeton Dante Project, which has the usual scholarly materials for such literary sites plus audio recordings of Dante's *Commedia* in English and Italian.

Some sites focus on individual authors. Two exemplary sites are the Walt Whitman Archive—text-based, grounded in his poetry and prose—and the William Blake Archive—instances of verbal–visual interaction between the poet and his other self, the artist of the same name. The Walt Whitman Archive is the creation of two professors, Ed Folsom of the University of Iowa and Kenneth M. Price of the University of Nebraska-Lincoln. Theirs is a multidisciplinary collaboration that involves funding agencies, universities, university libraries, public and private libraries, professors, and computer programmers. Whitman manuscripts have been gathered from near and far, from Amherst, the Boston Public Library, Boston University, Brown, Duke, the Huntington Public Library, Mills College, Ohio Wesleyan, the Pierpont Morgan Library, the Library of Congress, and the Universities of Texas, Tulsa, Virginia, and Yale. In the archive, all of Whitman's books have been made available in their original editions as well as all existing Whitman photographic portraits, a recording of his voice, his correspondence, and a selection of scholarly books and articles on Whitman, limited in scope only by copyright restrictions. Visitors can also read about the history of the project and access its earlier versions. They can read translations of *Leaves of Grass* into Russian, Spanish, German, and Portuguese; they can read the *Brooklyn Eagle*, a daily newspaper Whitman edited for a time.

Visitors can also view all of Whitman's poems published first in periodicals. This means that they can compare "A Child's Reminiscence," first published in the *New-York Saturday Press* with its final version, found in the "Sea Drift" section of *Leaves of Grass*. Its first line starts life as the prosaic "Out of the rocked cradle"; its final form is "Out of the cradle endlessly rocking," a magical transformation whose combined dactyls and trochees imitate a cradle as it rocks in Whitman's memory and in the memory of the human race. Transformations as inspired also begin in Whitman's "Blue Book," a copy of the 1860 edition of *Leaves of Grass* that he annotated over the years. The redacted lines reproduced in Figure 4.1 appear in the poem eventually called "Song of Myself."

The originally prosaic lines are certainly enhanced by Whitman's annotation, two complements ("outlaw'd or suffering") that make the abstract personal. But it is not until the 1871–72 edition that the passage is wholly transformed:

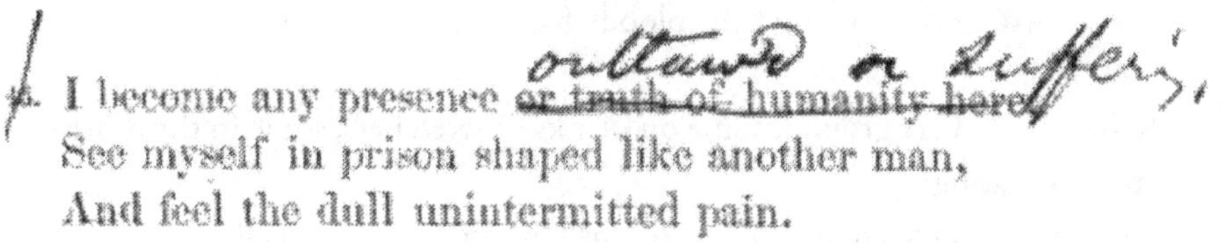

/. I become any presence ~~or truth of humanity here~~ *outlaw'd or suffer'g*,
See myself in prison shaped like another man,
And feel the dull unintermitted pain.

FIGURE 4.1 Proof copy from Walt Whitman's "Song of Myself" [Beinecke Rare Book and Manuscript Library, Yale University].

> You laggards there on guard! look to your arms!
> In at the conquer'd doors they crowd! I am possess'd!
> Embody all presences outlaw'd or suffering,
> See myself in prison shaped like another man,
> And feel the dull unintermitted pain.[9]

In his revision, Whitman has placed us in the midst of a drama heightened by his inspired verbal choices. These create an ascent into empathy, one that turns the wholly unaltered last two lines into an appropriate reaction to the metaphoric turmoil that precedes them.

We also see such transformations when Whitman turns prose into poetry. The manuscript "[scene in the woods on]," physically located in the Library of Congress and virtually present in the Whitman Archive, reads in part:

> battles of the day thereabout—with these it was filled, all varieties, horrible beyond description— _^–the darkness dimly_ lit with candles, lamps, torches, moving about, ~~but dark~~ but plenty of darkness & half darkness.—the crowds of wounded, bloody & pale, the surgeons operating—the yards outside also filled—they lay on the ground _^some on blankets,_ some on stray planks, ~~or~~ —the ~~desp~~ despairing screams & curses of some out of their senses, _the murky darkness, the great gleaming of the torches, the smoke from them too,_ the doctors operating, the scent of chloroform, the glisten of the steel instruments ~~as~~ [as] the flash of lamps fell upon them

Whitman transforms these jottings, a scene at a temporary field hospital related to him by a wounded soldier, into "A March in the Ranks Hard-Prest,"[10] a dramatic poem in which the central character, Whitman himself, comforts a dying soldier:

> Surgeons operating, attendants holding lights, the smell of ether, the odor of blood;

> The crowd, O the crowd of the bloody forms of soldiers—the yard outside
> also fill'd;
> Some on the bare ground, some on planks or stretchers, some in the death-
> spasm sweating;
> An occasional scream or cry, the doctor's shouted orders or calls;
> The glisten of the little steel instruments catching the glint of the torches;
> These I resume as I chant—I see again the forms, I smell the odor;
> Then hear outside the orders given, *Fall in, my men, Fall in*;
> But first I bend to the dying lad, his eyes open, a half-smile gives he me;
> Then the eyes close, calmly close, and I speed forth to the darkness,
> Resuming, marching, ever in darkness marching, on in the ranks,
> The unknown road still marching.

What had then been "horrible beyond description" is now reexperienced as a web of sounds and odors, of light and darkness, a poetic transformation in which "the glisten of the steel instruments as ᵃˢ the flash of lamps fell upon them" becomes "The *glisten* of the little steel instruments catching the *glint* of the torches," nouns in alliteration that turn prose into poetry.

The Archive is not just a compilation; it is a canard to say that it is not scholarship of the highest order. Available manuscripts have not only been reproduced; they have been carefully edited. Moreover, deletions and additions have been color coded. In this way, the Archive gives us privileged access to Whitman's creative process. When we look at the manuscript of "And Yet Not You Alone" (Fig. 4.2),[11] we observe Whitman weaving together isolated words and phrases governed at first only by the vaguest sense of design (online, the colors in the transcription are levels of variants, blue being the first level).

Only after a struggle—a survival of the fittest, if you will—are these threads woven into a single tapestry in which three new key words, "sleep," "birth," and "light," find their proper place.

> And yet not you alone, twilight and burying ebb,
> Nor you, ye lost designs alone—nor failures, aspirations;
> I know, divine deceitful ones, your glamour's seeming;
> Duly by you, from you, the tide and light again—duly the hinges turning,
> Duly the needed discord-parts offsetting, blending,
> Weaving from you, from Sleep, Night, Death itself,
> The rhythmus of Birth eternal.

For anyone who thinks the editorial task was trivial, we reproduce the original note-book page as it appears in the Archive (Fig. 4.3). Scholars wishing to decipher this

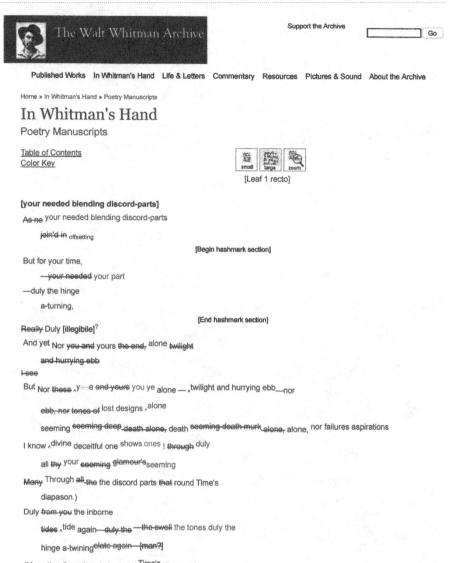

FIGURE 4.2 Coded revisions to poem by Walt Whitman in digital repository [Walt Whitman Archive]. Video 4.2 [▶]

page in the Archive can zoom in or out and scroll up or down in a way not possible in a special collection reading room.

The Blake Archive is also the product of professors—Morris Eaves of the University of Rochester, Robert N. Essick, Emeritus of the University of California–Riverside, and Joseph Viscomi of the University of North Carolina–Chapel Hill. In the 1990s

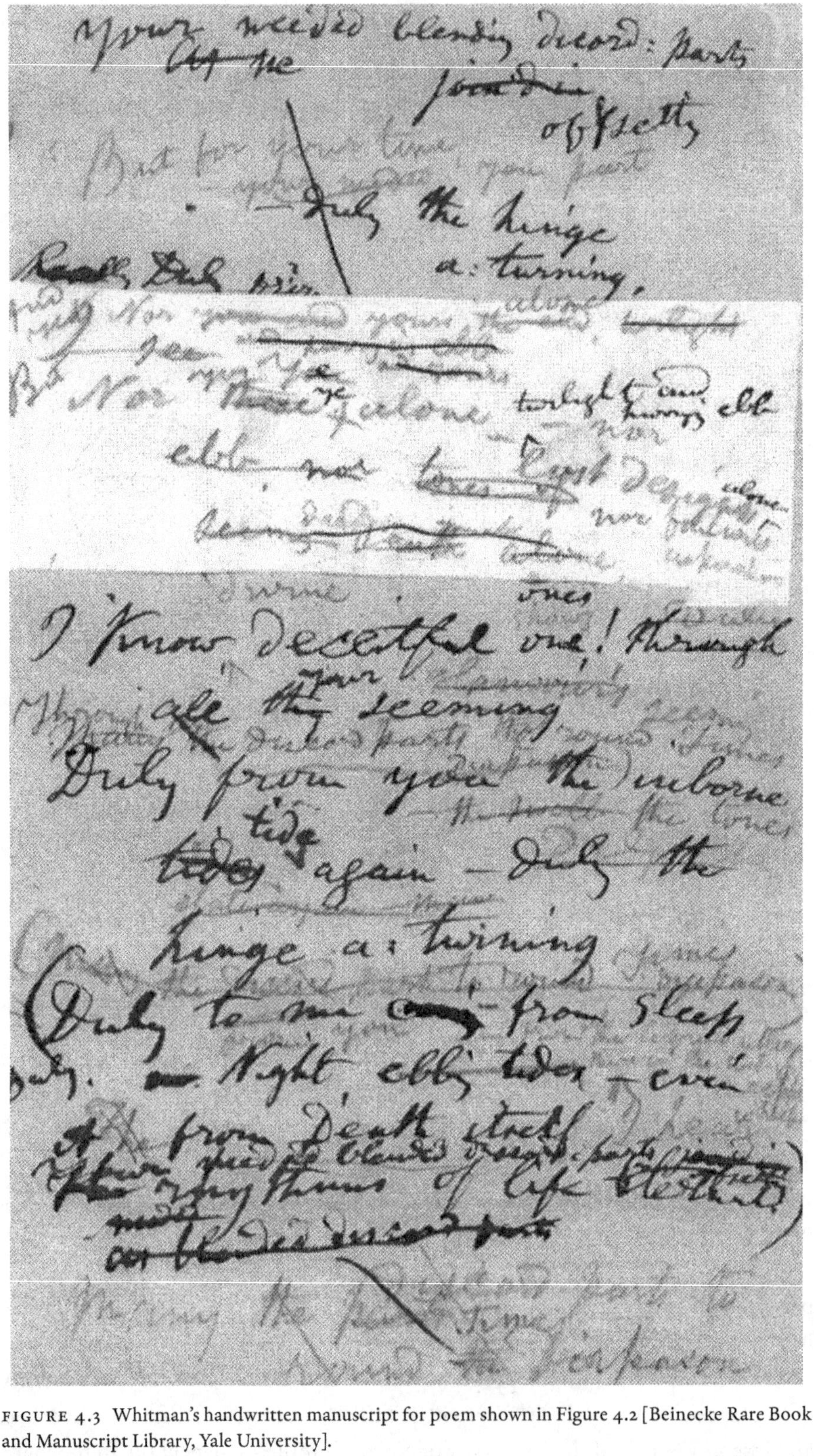

FIGURE 4.3 Whitman's handwritten manuscript for poem shown in Figure 4.2 [Beinecke Rare Book and Manuscript Library, Yale University].

these three distinguished Blake scholars published six volumes of edited facsimiles of Blake's hand-colored books. Their William Blake Archive supersedes these expensive volumes; indeed, "supersedes" is perhaps too mild a word to characterize such a sea change. Their goal was to have online for viewing color-corrected copies of all existing books that had been illustrated by Blake's hand, along with their accurate transcriptions. For those books already posted, every text and image can be searched. Type in the word *angel* in the word search and you get every instance of "angel"; type it in the image search and every image of an angel becomes available. In addition, images can be enlarged and compared, and their components analyzed. Visitors can also access a Blake biography, Blake's letters, and an extensive reference list.

For Blake, each copy of each title represented an individual work, sewn together in a sequence that might well vary. In his *Complete Writings of William Blake*, Geoffrey Keynes reproduces the order of the 1789 copy of *Songs of Innocence* on the grounds that it is "the only one still remaining in its original paper covers as issued by Blake";[12] he reproduces the order of *Songs of Experience* on the basis of later copies in which Blake was more consistent in his ordering.[13] But of the 13 copies of *Songs of Innocence and of Experience* reproduced on the Archive website, only five exhibit a common order. There is no evidence that those who later rebound the poems altered Blake's ordering. Moreover, his consistency is no reason to prefer a later over an earlier version. The point is general. Is the 1850 *Prelude* to be preferred over Wordsworth's 1805 version? What is the proper order of songs in Schubert's *Schwanengesang*? Which version of Bruckner's Fourth Symphony is to be privileged? 1874? 1878? 1880? 1881? 1886? 1887? 1888? Clearly, there is no preferred order of the *Songs of Innocence and of Experience*; Blake just kept changing his mind. The constraints of print forced Sir Geoffrey to choose; the editors of the Blake Archive need not traffic in the fictions that print imposes on editorial choice.

In our examination of verbal–visual interaction in Blake's *Songs of Innocence and Experience*, our goal is to convince our readers that, however fraught with difficulties, no study of Blake can be adequate that does not take seriously into consideration Joseph S. Viscomi's view that

> Blake is author, illustrator, designer, and printer, and his usual technique of relief etching is a pure analog technology that enables him to draw and write in the same space and allow the two acts to literally interact. There is no dividing the author's words by compositors into discrete bits of type, which is then reset into pages and printed by the letterpress printers, with illustrations drawn by artist and executed in copper by engravers and inserted into

the book by yet other hands. You can think of Blake's illuminated plate as a mixed media site, in which poetry, calligraphy, drawing, design, and coloring all come together, invented and executed with the same set of tools. Blake knew that separating his images from their texts was to distort what he was trying to present.[14]

It is this synthesis, this synergy, that the Blake Archive makes evident at every turn.

Blake placed no firewall between his role as a poet and as an artist. *Songs* routinely combines these talents, an invitation to readers to make some connection between his verbal and visual artistry. It is this invitation that we shall take, as such an exploration highlights this website's strengths. While no definitive solution will be offered to the visual–verbal puzzles we encounter in *Songs*, we shall see that all plausible solutions must be constrained by the fact that, as W. T. J. Mitchell says, "Blake sees human life as beginning in this integrated state [that he calls Innocence] and falling into Experience, the world of division where the contraries are at war."[15]

This is not to say that Blake makes the interpretive task easy, that he followed a consistent hermeneutic principle. In *Songs of Experience*, for example, we have his searing comment on city life, "London," a poem that ends:

But most thro' midnight streets I hear
How the youthful Harlot's curse
Blasts the newborn Infant's ear,
And blights with plagues the Marriage hearse.

This bitter view of the underside of urban life is illustrated with two separate images: an old man on crutches being helped by a young boy and a boy warming himself by a roaring outdoor fire. We may be legitimately puzzled by the clash between the poem's meaning and its illustrations.

In *Songs of Innocence* Blake's images are invariably supportive of their accompanying poems. For example, "The Lamb" is accompanied by an image of a boy among a flock of sheep, and "A Cradle Song" by an image of a nurse or mother gazing lovingly at an infant in a cradle. Such reinforcement is not uniformly true in *Songs of Experience*. While "The Poison Tree" is accompanied by an image of a dead man prone beneath a tree, the blighted "London" is accompanied by two positive images; indeed, positive images accompany the majority of poems in this volume. To understand why this is so we need to remind ourselves of the full title of the collection: *Songs of Innocence and of Experience: Shewing the Two Contrary States of the Human Soul*. In *Songs of Experience* these contrasting images reinforce Blake's core belief that in our everyday world these two states exist in an irresolvable tension. Given this tension, it cannot be clear whether optimism or pessimism is the proper attitude toward humanity's future.

The fundamental ambivalence concerning this future is reinforced when we take into consideration the variation in the sequence of poems from copy to copy, a comparison the website makes easy. In copy B (1789), *Songs of Experience* ends with "The Clod and the Pebble":

> Love seeketh not Itself to please,
> Nor for itself hath any care;
> But for another gives its ease,
> And builds a Heaven in Hell's despair.
> So sung a little Clod of Clay,
> Trodden with the cattle's feet;
> But a Pebble of the brook,
> Warbled out these metres meet:
> Love seeketh only self to please,
> To bind another to Its delight,
> Joys in another's loss of ease,
> And builds a Hell in Heaven's despite.

The poem may seem an appropriate climax to a series that deals with contrary states of the human soul continually in tension. The dire effects of this tension, however, are somewhat mitigated by the image accompanying the poem, a placid scene of cows and sheep drinking along with a duck, some frogs, and a worm in a meadow. They are also mitigated by the final image in the copy (Fig. 4.4a), unaccompanied by text.

What is this image of Blake's an image of? Tiepolo's "The Immaculate Conception of the Blessed Virgin Mary" (Fig. 4.4b) helps us understand its iconography, the key to its meaning. In Tiepolo's painting, Mary, the only mortal since the expulsion from Eden born without original sin, ascends to Heaven. (We recognize that Blake's iconographic allusion can be either to the Immaculate Conception or to the Assumption of the Blessed Virgin Mary, two very different Catholic beliefs: the birth of Mary without original sin, and her assumption body and soul into heaven immediately upon her death. As a consequence of the unrepresentability of the Immaculate Conception, the iconography of these two events overlaps.[16])

Blake's iconographic allusion to the class of paintings of which Tiepolo's depiction of Mary is a member is anchored not in Catholic dogma, but in his private theology. The allusion is his reminder that it may be possible for humanity to transcend its dual nature, a sign that Blake chooses to end this particular copy of *Songs of Experience* on a decidedly positive note. This measured optimism contrasts with that shown in the final page of copy V (1821), completed three decades later. Copy V ends with "The Human Abstract," a poem that insists that there exists in the human brain a metaphorical tree whose origin is Cruelty, whose root is Humility, whose fruit is Deceit. The message of "The Human Abstract" is reinforced by its accompanying image, nestled at the bottom of the page: a crouching old man struggling in bondage.

To those who might find the idea of iconographic allusion a tad far-fetched, we refer to no less an authority than W. T. J. Mitchell. We concur with him concerning such allusions in the frontispiece of *Songs of Experience* (to Dürer), in the image accompanying "The Little Black Boy" in *Songs of Innocence* (to Otto van Veen), and in Jerusalem Plate 76 (to Piero della Francesca) and Plate 78 (to Dürer again).[17] To these we would add an allusion Mitchell does not mention, the concluding plate of *Europe*. In this plate (Fig. 4.5a), Blake alludes to the escape of Aeneas from

(a)

FIGURE 4.4 Final image in Blake's *Songs of Experience* followed by Giovanni Battista Tiepolo's *Immaculate Conception* (1767–1769) [Lessing J. Rosenwald Collection, Library of Congress. Copyright © 2015 William Blake Archive]. Video 4.3 [▶]

(b)

FIGURE 4.4 Continued

Troy, his father slung over his shoulder and his son at his side. We see the standard iconography exemplified in the bas relief by Artus Quellinus the Elder, now in the Rijksmuseum (Fig. 4.5b).

At first glance, this allusion seems to leave us with a positive attitude toward the future of Europe: Aeneas is, after all, Virgil's hero. But Blake's attitude toward the *Aeneid* is entirely negative, precisely because of the hero's greatest achievement, the founding of Rome: "Sacred Truth has pronounced that Greece & Rome, as Babylon & Egypt, so far from being parents of Arts & Sciences as they pretend, were destroyers of all Art. . . . Virgil in his Eneid, Book VI, line 848 says 'Let others study Art: Rome has somewhat better to do,' namely War & Dominion."[18] Anthony Blunt makes an analogous point about Blake's penchant for reversing the meaning of traditional iconography. His example is the compasses in the hands of Urizen in the famous frontispiece of Europe. In traditional iconography, they are a "symbol for mathematics and, even more widely, of science and philosophy in general"; in Blake, they become "the reduction of the infinite to the finite and therefore the destruction of the imagination."[19]

Whatever our interpretation of *Songs of Innocence and of Experience*—whatever our interpretation of Blake's illuminated books as a whole—we cannot avoid taking into consideration the fact that copies of the same work may differ markedly, that verbal–visual interaction constitutes their meaning in every case, and that Blake's

FIGURE 4.5 Final page of Blake's *Europe* followed by bas relief by Artus Quellinus the Elder depicting Aeneas's escape from Troy [Lessing J. Rosenwald Collection, Library of Congress. Copyright © 2015 William Blake Archive].

(b)

FIGURE 4.5 Continued

visuals must always be placed within an appropriate iconographic context, one informed by his intensely private theology. Any exploration of these matters is best begun in the William Blake Archive.

The Whitman and Blake archives participate in the reinvention of scholarly editing, a movement that began well before the Internet. *King Lear* was one problem that scholars faced since Shakespeare scholarship began. Both of us had read the play as undergraduates unaware of the difficulty a very young Madeleine Doran had pointed out as early as 1931:[20] The quarto of 1608 looked like a first draft, not like a bad quarto, a mangled version of the play. If this were the case, what were we to make of the considerable differences between the quarto and its folio version, both of which had a claim to legitimacy? The traditional solution had been conflation of the two. But, clearly, the conflated version is an editorial fiction, giving the spurious impression that this is what Shakespeare *really* wrote. In truth, we have two versions of *King Lears*, and no reason to prefer one over the other. Analogously, there can no preferred text of "Song of Myself," no preferred order to *Songs of Innocence and of Experience*.

Traditional editing disguises this fact; these digital archives reveal it. Nearly three decades ago, in his review of *The Division of the Kingdoms*, a set of arguments in favor of two versions of *King Lear*,[21] E. A. J. Honigmann opined that "when the dust has settled, this volume will be seen to mark an important turning point for Shakespeare's editors and critics. For more than thirty years the editors have been overconfident that the new practices of bibliography could detect textual corruption, and have pursued a policy of 'corrective editing' where scholarship too readily merges itself in romance."[22] The Blake, Whitman, and other digital archives could mark a similar turning point in scholarship.

WEBSITES THAT STORE DATA FOR SCIENTIFIC RESEARCH

The sites in this category, for which "database" seems an accurate description, store data, text, and images for scientific research. They are also an important adjunct to journal publication. The stated policy of *Science* is typical:

> As a condition of publication, authors must agree to make available all data necessary to understand and assess the conclusions of the manuscript to any reader of *Science*. Data must be included in the body of the paper or in the supplementary materials, where they can be viewed free of charge by all visitors to the site. Certain types of data must be deposited in an approved online database, including DNA and protein sequences, microarray data, crystal structures, and climate records.[23]

Scientific databases, of course, preceded the Internet. The long history of the Online Mendelian Inheritance in Man (OMNI) is typical of the trajectory of databases that made the transition from print to the digital era. Started in the early 1960s in order to catalog "mendelian traits" (those caused by a gene with simple dominant and recessive forms), it appeared in 12 book editions between 1966 and 1987. An Internet version, released behind a paywall in 1985, was made open access in 1987. OMNI now houses biochemical data on all known mendelian disorders along with over 12,000 genes.

In terms of collecting, organizing, and communicating data, the arrival of the Internet has made a huge difference. Started in 1971, the Protein Data Bank (PDB), one of the most impressive of all "approved online databases," maintains an archive of structural data for about 100,000 macromolecules open to all. Growing at a rate of about 8,000 additional molecules per year, it is a "repository of atomic coordinates and other information describing proteins and other important biological macromolecules,"[24] designed to investigate biology and medicine at the molecular level. The PDB began with structural data on proteins but has since expanded into DNA and has spawned other databanks such as CREDO, which provides data on protein–ligand interactions for drug discovery. The PDB is firmly in the realm of professional science—no citizen "data proteinistas" in sight. It hosts data about biochemical objects and other technical details of interest only to other professionals.[25] Ancillary websites—namely, the Research Collaboratory for Structural Bioinformatics (RCSB PDB, United States), PDBe (Europe), PDBj (Japan), and BMRB (United States)—also serve as portals for downloading new biochemical data and technical details into the central PDB database; for viewing existing data in tabular form, in graphical form, and as 2D and 3D interactive images of the structures; and for reading text about the structures. In the 21st century, two types of communication—journal literature and digital archives—work together to document everything an inquisitive scientist might want to know on a biochemical object of study.

Our example of a PDB molecule is "deoxyhemoglobin S." In 1997, Harrington, Adachi, and Royer determined its structure by X-ray diffraction analysis, which is an extraordinarily important analytical technique in the history of molecular biology: It was Rosalind Franklin's X-ray diffraction image that sparked Watson and Crick's insight that the structure of DNA was a double helix. By applying X-ray diffraction to this protein molecule at a higher resolution than had been attained before (2 angstroms or two ten-billionths of a meter), Harrington, Adachi, and Royer were able to gain further insight into the mechanism behind sickle cell anemia, a disease that the great chemist Linus Pauling and coworkers[26] had first reported as hereditary—caused by a mutation of the hemoglobin protein in blood cells. In May 1997, before journal publication, Harrington and company deposited their diffraction data for the 3D structure of this protein in the PDB. After preliminary evaluation, the data were released to the scientific community in July. In September 1997, the *Journal of Molecular Biology* published the authors' associated scientific article, which not only provided images and other details of the structure but argued for the first time that

> a predominant feature of this crystal form is a double strand of hemoglobin tetramers that has been shown by a variety of techniques to be the fundamental building block of the intracellular sickle cell fiber . . . The new structure reveals some marked differences from the previously refined 3.0 Å [angstrom] resolution structure . . . and may be useful for the structure-based design of therapeutic agents to treat sickle cell disease. [27]

The opening page for this structure on the RCSB PDB website[28] reproduces the abstract of the article (Fig. 4.6).

On the upper right viewers can access a 3D rotatable and interactive image of the structure along with a link to three 2D static views. By themselves, these images do

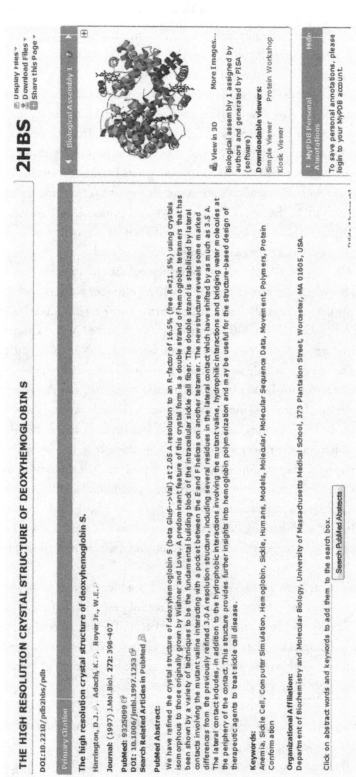

THE HIGH RESOLUTION CRYSTAL STRUCTURE OF DEOXYHEMOGLOBIN S

2HBS

Display Files ˅
Download Files ˅
Share this Page ˅

DOI:10.2210/pdb2hbs/pdb

Primary Citation

The high resolution crystal structure of deoxyhemoglobin S.

Harrington, D.J., Adachi, K., Royer Jr., W.E.

Journal: (1997) J.Mol.Biol. 272: 398-407

PubMed: 9325099
DOI: 10.1006/jmbi.1997.1253
Search Related Articles in PubMed

PubMed Abstract:

We have refined the crystal structure of deoxyhemoglobin S (beta Glu6-->Val) at 2.05 A resolution to an R-factor of 16.5% (free R=21.5%) using crystals isomorphous to those originally grown by Wishner and Love. A predominant feature of this crystal form is a double strand of hemoglobin tetramers that has been shown by a variety of techniques to be the fundamental building block of the intracellular sickle cell fiber. The double strand is stabilized by lateral contacts involving the mutant valine interacting with a pocket between the E and F helices on another tetramer. The new structure reveals some marked differences from the previously refined 3.0 A resolution structure, including several residues in the lateral contact which have shifted by as much as 3.5 A. The lateral contact includes, in addition to the hydrophobic interactions involving the mutant valine, hydrophilic interactions and bridging water molecules at the periphery of the contact. This structure provides further insights into hemoglobin polymerization and may be useful for the structure-based design of therapeutic agents to treat sickle cell disease.

Keywords:

Anemia, Sickle Cell, Computer Simulation, Hemoglobin, Sickle, Humans, Models, Molecular, Molecular Sequence Data, Movement, Polymers, Protein Conformation

Organizational Affiliation:

Department of Biochemistry and Molecular Biology, University of Massachusetts Medical School, 373 Plantation Street, Worcester, MA 01605, USA.

Click on abstract words and keywords to add them to the search box.

Search PubMed Abstracts

◄ Biological Assembly 1 ❔ ⊞

More Images...

View in 3D

Biological assembly 1 assigned by authors and generated by PISA (software)

Downloadable viewers:
Simple Viewer   Protein Workshop
Kiosk Viewer

↑ MyPDB Personal Annotations   Hide

To save personal annotations, please login to your MyPDB account.

FIGURE 4.6 Segment of RCSB PDB page for structure of deoxyhemoglobin S [Protein Data Bank]. Video 4.4 [▶]

not mean much; within the database entry, however, their meaning becomes clear. Scientists consult the posted tabular data for the atomic and molecular components within the structure, view their 3D location in space, and peruse related structural information and extensive details on the X-ray diffraction method used to acquire the data. For those wanting to build upon this research, the extensive structural data and methods in this database supplement the journal article. As recently as 2012, Tyler Clark, Scott Houck, and John Clark made good use of the deoxyhemoglobin S database entry in their study of degenerative processes in aging: "Data sets for the high resolution X-ray diffraction structures of human deoxy-hemoglobin A (PDB:4HHB) and deoxy-hemoglobin S (PDB:2HBS) were obtained from the Protein Data Bank (www.PDB.org)."[29] Further supporting the significance of this molecule is an entry in the digital archive Proteopedia, the equivalent of a highly technical Wikipedia article with rotatable 3D images.[30] The emphasis is on an encyclopedia-like description at the molecular level of the mechanism behind the disease.

In sum, researchers interested in sickle cell disease at the atomic and molecular level have at their disposal the original argument for the currently accepted structure of the defective hemoglobin molecule in the *Journal of Molecular Biology,* the complete X-ray diffraction data and experimental details supporting that structure in the PDB, different visualizations of that data and related information in ancillary websites like the RCSB PBD, and in Proteopedia a technical description of the mechanism behind sickle cell disease accompanied by a 3D rotatable image of the molecule.

We view the PDB as the model for the future, a time when scientists will not only rapidly communicate new knowledge in digital scientific journals or archives, but also routinely deposit their data and other relevant research materials in digital repositories. In turn, that information will be fed into specialized encyclopedic repositories, like RCSB PDB and Proteopedia, linked to scientific articles and databases. As a consequence, bodies of knowledge will acquire a depth and breadth and interconnectedness never before imagined.

WEBSITES THAT STORE SCIENTIFIC OR SCHOLARLY PAPERS

These sites are designed to solve two problems in the communication of new knowledge. One is the inevitable delays associated with peer review and printing. The other is the restriction of access to publications that are behind a paywall. By far the most prominent such digital archive is arXiv. The site founder, Paul Ginsparg, traces its origin to a day in late 1987 when two collaborators and I first included our email addresses along with physical addresses in a preprint, initiating that now-universal trend. When asked at that time, the dedicated librarians maintaining the essential SLAC-Spires [Stanford Linear Accelerator Center-Stanford Public Information Retrieval System] bibliographic database told me they would have loved to maintain online as well a full-text preprint database, but didn't have resources for the additional personnel required to solicit and handle electronic versions of articles.[31]

To meet this need, Ginsparg himself set up a server in 1991 at Los Alamos National Laboratory intended for "about 100 submissions per year from a small subfield of high-energy particle physics." More than two decades later ArXiv now stores about a million pre- and post-review copies of scientific articles uploaded by physicists, mathematicians, and other scientists from around the world and is prospering— with a growth rate of 90,000 articles per year (Fig. 4.7).[32] If you believe sites like ArXiv are repositories of articles unsuited to the elite journals, think again. Within the ArXiv you can find many papers by physics royalty: Stephen Hawking, Steven Weinberg, Edward Witten, Frank Wilczek, Brian Greene, Lisa Randall, Lawrence Krauss, to name a few. In mathematics, a startling success for ArXiv was an article

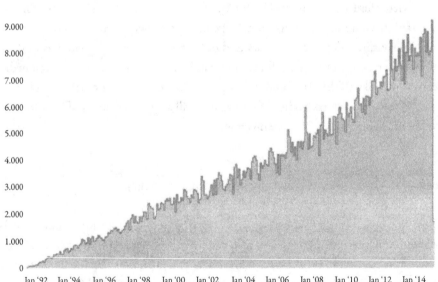

Blue: Number of new submissions received during each month since August 1991.
Hover over the graph to see the exact count for a given month.

Total number of submissions shown in graph as of April 8th, 2015 (after 23.7 years) = 1,025,468

FIGURE 4.7 ArXiv monthly submission rates [ArXiv].

posted by Grigoriy Perelman in 2002 proving the Poincaré Conjecture, a particularly knotty problem in topology.[33] Perelman never felt the need to publish this article in a peer-reviewed journal article. Nevertheless, the proof won Perelman the Fields Medal, the Nobel Prize of mathematics. It was a prize he refused because, he felt, proper credit was not given to another mathematician.[34] Paradoxically, this made his achievement even more memorable.

Originally limited to research articles in physics, ArXiv has expanded into various specialties within mathematics, quantitative biology, computer science, and finance. Biologists were initially reluctant to participate. Ginsparg tries to explain this reluctance:

> You sometimes hear from biologists, "If I present materials before they're published and someone else quickly reproduces the results and publishes first, they get full credit and I get no credit at all." To physicists, this attitude has always been non sequitur . . . That's one reason why physicists were so eager to adopt ArXiv, because it permitted staking intellectual property rights for an idea, and it was time-stamped so nobody could dispute it. That should be obvious to people in the life sciences—and maybe it is, increasingly so—but I still hear mention of this concern that results are not properly credited until formal publication.[35]

The future for digital repositories like ArXiv seems bright, an idea with revolutionary implications for science and scholarship:

> If scholarly infrastructure can be upgraded to encourage maximal spontaneous participation, then we can expect not only increasingly automated interoperability among databases and increasing availability of materials online for algorithmic harvesting—articles, datasets, lecture notes, multimedia, and software—but also qualitatively new forms of academic effort. Expertise-intensive tags, links, comments, corrections, contributions to ontologies, and linkages, all actively curated, will become increasingly important, acting to glue databases and texts together into a more powerful knowledge structure. Such work will need to be credited as scholarly achievement, along with the future analog of conventional journal publication.[36]

Various self-archiving repositories have followed in arXiv's large footsteps. For example, the Social Science Research Network (SSRN) posts abstracts and full papers in a wide range of research areas loosely connected with the social sciences, which include such diverse topics as accounting practices, cognitive science, economics, law, political science, and rhetoric and communication. The total number of abstracts and papers in SSRN has exceeded a million. And a new kid on the block, Figshare, is designed to make available the whole panoply of documents related to scientific research, not just journal articles or abstracts. Included are images, datasets, multimedia, posters, presentations, even computer code. In January 2013, Figshare announced an alliance with the Public Library of Science (PLOS), by which Figshare postings are now being integrated into PLOS journal articles.[37]

Not all self-archiving sites have met with rousing success. Cogprints posts papers in a wide range of disciplines loosely connected with the cognitive sciences, which includes philosophy, psychology, and linguistics. Posts per year have yet to exceed several hundred.

WEBSITES THAT CREATE KNOWLEDGE THROUGH VOLUNTEER PARTICIPATION

These sites are designed to persuade geographically dispersed individuals, professionals and nonprofessionals alike, to volunteer "their time, experience, wisdom, and creativity to form new . . . knowledge."[38] Throughout the history of science, research projects have sporadically relied upon such enthusiasts. Charles Darwin gathered much observational data about various species by corresponding with a "huge network of amateur botanists and ornithologists and rural vicars and pigeon fanciers."[39] The Internet has taken such citizen participation to an altogether other level. One such site, Planet Hunters, asks volunteers to examine astronomical images from the NASA Kepler Space Mission, findings then analyzed by professional scientists. Their goal is the discovery of new planets. To date, sifting through the data has resulted in identification of 34 new candidate planets, and the site includes a page of resulting publications. Volunteers to Planet Hunters are rewarded for their efforts by seeing their names appear on a webpage in the site.

A more challenging type of citizen science site, Foldit, is structured as a game (see Foldit video[40]). Its purpose is the unraveling of the structures of complex proteins. In this case, problem solving requires not simple visual recognition of specific shapes as in Planet Hunters, but genuine creativity in spatial visualization. Participants simultaneously win points as in a video game and solve molecular problems in the real world. The site lists seven scientific articles to which Foldit contributed, including one in *Nature* called "Predicting Protein Structures with a Multiplayer Online Game."[41]

Arguably, the most successful such site to date is Galaxy Zoo. At Galaxy Zoo—a repository linked to millions of astronomical images taken by the Sloan Digital Sky Survey and Hubble Space Telescope—visitors seduced by the website's appeal can participate in an astronomical research project within a matter of minutes. Galaxy

Zoo is founded on the presumption that humans en masse are better at pattern recognition than computers. At this site, hundreds of thousands of volunteers have contributed to furthering our understanding of the universe.

Its homepage is dominated by the black of outer space. Foregrounded in the black background is a picture of a spiral galaxy, the primary object of study. Immediately above that is a marketing pitch to potential contributors, in large white letters meant to immediately grab attention: "Few have witnessed what you're about to see. Experience a privileged glimpse of the distant universe, observed by the Sloan Digital Sky Survey and Hubble Space Telescope." For this "privileged glimpse" all one has to do is "Classify Galaxies" as explained in the textbox adjacent to the spiral galaxy. Within the textbox is a lime green button marked "Begin Classifying" that echoes the similarly highlighted Galaxy Zoo name at the top. Clicking the button sends registered viewers to a screen that looks like Figure 4.8. By this means anyone can immediately classify the shapes of galaxies, where "If you're quick, you may even be the first person to see the galaxies you're asked to classify." Owing to effective visual presentation, website visitors know immediately where they are, what the screen is about, and how to contribute. According to the Galaxy Zoo website, "In the end, more than 50 million classifications were received by the project during its first year [2007–2008], contributed by more than 150,000 people."[42]

Because of the inclusion of an online discussion forum at the Galaxy Zoo site, "zooites" need not limit their participation to viewing, classifying, and clicking; they can engage in collaborative problem solving around classification issues. For example, on September 27, 2012, zooite Graham Silsby posted the following comment for forum readers: "Need another identification option or two: *Object is at the limit of resolution, object is beyond the limit of resolution.* Some of the objects are most

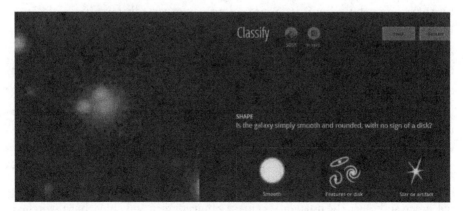

FIGURE 4.8 Screen for user input to Galaxy Zoo Project. Viewer matches shape in astronomical image on left with drawn shapes on right, bottom. (Having met its original objectives, Galaxy Zoo creators have started a new research project, Galaxy Zoo 2.) [Galaxy Zoo Project]

likely to be galaxies but are so pixelated that no further information can be deduced. This would tag those objects for longer exposure in the future if someone cared" [our emphasis].[43]

The first reply to that comment recommended that he just do his best at classification, however poor the image resolution: "These objects are probably half way across the universe. We'll mop them up by Galaxy Zoo 42 (We're on 4 just now). In the meantime, just classify it as best you can." But that was not good enough for other industrious zooites, who on their own initiative digitally altered poor-quality images to clarify the shapes within, and posted their results and technique on the forum. As Tom Zolotor commented: "Altered image may take up much time to do because these 'FHB' or Faint Hubble Blob galaxies are downloaded to the computer before the astronomers on the science team see them; however, it seems like a good idea to try to make them clearer as possible. It would make sense to make them easier to classify."[44]

One of the earliest and most successful examples of this collaborative process dates to within weeks of the opening of Galaxy Zoo in July 2007. On August 13, 2007, at 11:16:40 a.m., a 25-year-old Dutch schoolteacher, Hanny Van Arkel, asked, "What's the blue stuff below [see Fig. 4.9]? Anyone?"[45]

Many replies to Hanny's post poured in the same day. The first came a mere three minutes after the initial post: "looks like a cloud." While that was not especially insightful, the second zooite's reply immediately recognized the blue smudge's potential significance, "This is very weird, I've never seen anything like this in SDSS [image bank for Sloan Digital Sky Survey]. You should try to bring the expert's attention here, Edd or one of the Zookeepers for example." Indeed, a short while later on the same day Galaxy Zoo administrator Edd responded: "Well, my best guess, and the best guess of someone else I pulled in from the next office, is either some irregular galaxy or a nebula, but it is a weird colour—unexpectedly faint in r[esolution]. I'll give zookeepers another poke towards it." But soon thereafter another Galaxy Zoo administrator, Kevin, posted that it might only be a "camera defect." Edd countered with a very brief and technical explanation of why not: "uiz image here (rather than gri). I think there's a maybe a detection in the blue (u) and definitely part of it in the i (green), so I'm not convinced it's something in the g only. I may be imagining it though." Hanny sensibly replied, "Thanks guys, I really don't know what you're talking about [Edd]. But we agree on one thing: it's weird."

Subsequently, Edd explained further, with a short tutorial on astronomical image generation: "SDSS sees in five colours (u,g,r,i and z) and computer monitors only do red, green and blue. The usual images make g blue, r green and i blue, but I switched some round to see the u and z instead, making u blue, i green and z red. The weird thing about this object is that the detection was pretty much only in the g band,

FIGURE 4.9   Galaxy Zoo image with "blue stuff" below spiral galaxy IC 2497 at center [Sloan Digital Sky Survey, http://www.sdss.org].

rendered blue in your original image, but I thought there might be more hints in the others—and I think you can see a faint blue triangle there. So I suspect it's real, but I don't really have a good idea what it actually is." After much discussion that day but no further headway, at 8:14:45 p.m., Hanny signed off: "I want to name it 'Unidentified Bluey Stuff.' But I'm really going to bed now . . . have to work tomorrow so . . . "

Chatter about the "unidentified bluey stuff" continued in the following days. Ten days later [August 23] the doubting Kevin had changed his mind: "Whatever it is, it's got huge errors on its photometry, its measured brightness [Fig. 4.10], but it looks like it's real. It's also a fairly powerful radio source . . . Intriguing."

At this point the bluely stuff became an unsolved scientific problem to which professionals applied further astronomical observations and analyses. After many months, the professional consensus was that the object did exist, and that no one had seen anything like it before. Two years later, in 2009, Chris Lintott, a University of Oxford astrophysicist and leading member of the main Galaxy Zoo team, along with 19 co-authors posted a scientific article on the arXiv digital repository in which they

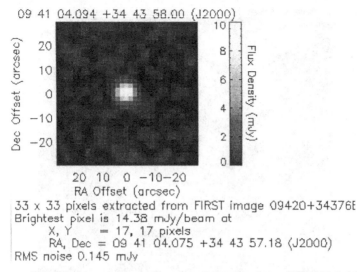

FIGURE 4.10 Radio photometry image of previous Galaxy Zoo image [Sloan Digital Sky Survey, http://www.sdss.org].

gave the bluey stuff an official name, "Hanny's Voorwerp" (the discoverer's name followed by the Dutch word for "object"), and proposed a plausible scientific explanation for its existence, "a quasar light echo."[46] What the voorwerp actually is, however, is yet to be confirmed. Fittingly, the byline to the scientific article, immediately below its title, lists zooite Hanny van Arkel as an author, and a footnote to the title on the first page reads "This publication has been made possible by the participation of more than 100,000 volunteers in the Galaxy Zoo project. Their contributions are individually acknowledged at http://www.galaxyzoo.org/Volunteers.aspx."

As of 2015 the zooite data have been a factor in about 59 scientific publications. Given the scientific and social success of Galaxy Zoo and similar projects that preceded and followed, we agree with Michael Nielsen that "It's not too much of a leap to imagine Galaxy Zoo becoming an institution crucial to the whole field of astronomy, and perhaps to other fields"[47] where hordes of enthusiastic amateurs—clickmeisters—can make a real contribution to scientific knowledge.

The humanities are also making use of websites for creating new knowledge. The Ancient Lives Project invites the general public to help decipher much-damaged papyrus fragments that had been stored in Oxford University. Viewers are asked to match Greek letters in ancient manuscripts, displayed on the screen, with Greek letters on a keyboard—no knowledge of Greek required. This Internet project is the logical continuation of a century-long research project by classical scholars to decipher "the random waste-paper of seven centuries of Graeco-Egyptian life." Its final product will be the publication of these papyri, "as owned and overseen by the Egypt

Exploration Society, in the Society's Greco-Roman Memoirs series in the volumes entitled *The Oxyrhynchus Papyri.*" Since 1898, the Society has published 77 volumes, with at least 40 more volumes planned.

Also worth noting here is the recent launch of Tolstoy:ru with the assistance of some 3,000 volunteers from around the world. These citizen volunteers proofread digitally scanned pages from the 90 volumes (46,800 pages) of the Russian literary master's collected works, which will form the cornerstone of a massive scholarly website with all his published and unpublished writings, as well as interactive maps, photographs, videos, and audio recordings. Volunteers compared a PDF of the original Russian text with a version scanned by an optical reader, and corrected any discrepancies. They completed this job in a mere two weeks—another shining example of the considerable power of crowdsourcing. After proofing numerous pages from a children's book, letters, diaries, *War and Peace*, and *Anna Karenina*, one Muscovite participant noted "I spent all my free time 'in conversation with' Tolstoy. Proofreading was engrossing. You couldn't predict what a new set of pages would be about, and this element of surprise made me want to read more."[48]

WEBSITES THAT CODIFY EXISTING KNOWLEDGE

Our final category codifies knowledge, displaying what we know on a topic in a manner that can be used for scholarly or scientific purposes. In the humanities, Rome Reborn is an important representative of the future of scholarly visualization. Its goal is an archive of "3D digital models illustrating the urban development of ancient Rome from the first settlement in the late Bronze Age (ca. 1000 B.C.) to the depopulation of the city in the early Middle Ages (ca. A.D. 550)." A sizable international effort centered at the University of Virginia, this Internet project has involved not only historians and classicists but 3D modelers and scanners as well as web designers. These researchers have established a multimedia model of ancient Rome in 320 AD, the peak of its population; others have been invited to create and add their own models, the goal being an online archive covering about 1,500 years of Roman history. Just as scientists can study 3D interactive models of molecular structures, humanists can study multimedia models of important historical periods.

In the more traditional vein, there is the online Stanford Encyclopedia of Philosophy, a "scholarly dynamic reference work" presenting peer-reviewed academic essays on philosophical topics from abduction and Aristotle through Zeno and zombie. Its index lists both topics that have been covered and those that await completion by scholarly volunteers from the philosophy community.

The encyclopedic type can not only organize and consolidate existing knowledge on a select topic but also provide a framework for adding new knowledge with some specific goal in mind. Our primary example of such a site in the sciences is the Encyclopedia of Life (EOL), whose inspiration can be traced to a 2003 article by visionary scientist E. O. Wilson:

> Imagine an electronic page for each species of organism on Earth, available everywhere by single access on command. The page contains the scientific name of the species, a pictorial or genomic presentation of the primary type specimen on which its name is based, and a summary of its diagnostic traits. The page . . . comprises a summary of everything known about the species' genome, proteome [set of proteins expressed by entire genome], geographical distribution, phylogenetic position, habitat, ecological relationships and, not least, its practical importance for humanity. . . . All the pages together form an encyclopedia, the content of which is the totality of comparative biology.[49]

Five years later Wilson's dream became partial virtual reality when the EOL launched. In a marketing video, the site acknowledges Wilson's inspiration.[50] Now, a mere seven years after startup, EOL has over three million pages on one million species contributed by life scientists, educators, students, and nature enthusiasts. Its ultimate goal is "to document all 1.9 million named species of animals, plants and other forms" (estimates of the number of unnamed species run from 10 million to 100 million).

The EOL website has a fairly simple homepage, its center of visual attention a string of six images across the top. These are photographs of different species, each of which changes every 30 seconds. Hold the cursor over an image and the species name (Latin and common) appears. Click the image and the acquired knowledge about it appears in several layers (Fig. 4.11), providing access to more images of the selected organism, a world map showing its geographic distribution, a schematic showing its taxonomic line of descent, a comprehensive verbal description, acquired data, and links to references and related reading.

While EOL has a strong pedagogical thrust, as one would expect from any encyclopedia, it is also a valuable tool for biological researchers in generating and communicating new knowledge. According to doctoral student Tristy Vick Majors,

> I recently used EOL to help with describing the taxonomy of eukaryotic gene sequences discovered in a survey of lake water samples. I typically work with bacteria and archaea rather than eukaryl microbes, and found EOL to be quite helpful in "putting a face to the name" of the organisms that I was finding.[51]

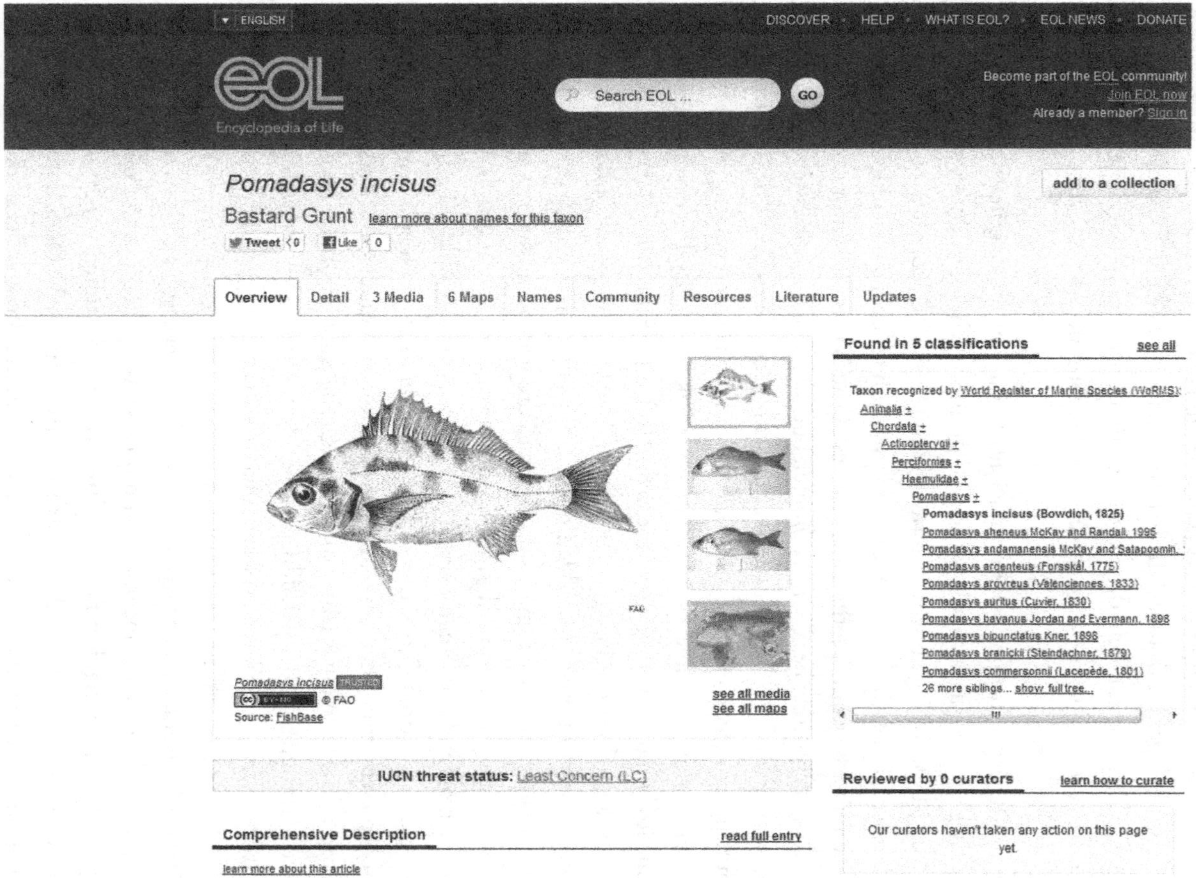

FIGURE 4.11 Snapshot of EOL contents page for *Pomadasys incisus*. Different layers of information accessible through tabs at top. [Encyclopedia of Life]. Video 4.5 [▲]

And zoologist Kate MacNeale reported that

> I work with datasets relating to communities of freshwater macroinvertebrates, and I often use EOL to double check spellings, see any pictures that might be available, and most importantly to check or find out their position within their group's phylogeny. It is especially helpful when I'm trying to compare various datasets that have different degrees of taxonomic resolution—e.g. I use EOL to check that I'm comparing my apples to apples, or subclass to subclass.

The EOL depends upon volunteer scientists for contributing new content and evaluating content submitted by others. Typical of such a distinguished contributor is C. Michael Hogan, who describes himself as a "[t]heoretical physicist who has devoted his last three decades to biophysics and modeling of ecological systems. I would rather be exploring the inner reaches of the Namib Desert or the glaciers of Antarctica than sitting beside my computer, but, alas, I end up splitting my time 50/50 between the two."[52] The site credits him with adding an astounding 545 articles, submitting 3,344 comments, commenting on 2,145 taxa, and curating no less than 3,289 submissions. Comments tend to be Tweet-like in brevity. For example, Hogan commented on information about the taxon Tofieldia (False Asphodel) specified in Tropicos, a database originally created by the Missouri Botanical Garden for internal use by botanists and later added to EOL for public access. This corrects EOL, which had previously been "misleading in that European occurring taxa are ignored." Because of many such devoted professional contributors like Hogan, as well as science educators and nature enthusiasts, EOL has grown with Wikipedia-like rapidity.

The recently started Open Tree of Life also intends to produce a comprehensive visual representation of the evolutionary relationships among the Earth's species. One promising form of visualization that might be employed is the interactive fractal tree diagram recently created by biodiversity theorist James Rosindell and available at the website OneZoom. As explained in *PLOS Biology*, current visualizations of large amounts of data in general, and the phylogenic tree diagram in particular, do not "take full advantage of the freedom that a computer display gives us over printed sheets; we read and write documents and browse web pages that are constrained to be optimal for printing, but fail to realize that such documents are unlikely to be optimal for visualization on a digital device."[53] By contrast, the OneZoom visual representation of the tree of life can accommodate an infinite number of branches and works by zooming in or out in a way similar to Google Maps (Fig. 4.12). OneZoom has posted an example fractal tree diagram covering tetrapods (all four-legged animals), a diagram derived from existing evolutionary data. It is much more intuitive than the traditional tree diagrams employed in evolutionary biology. We anticipate

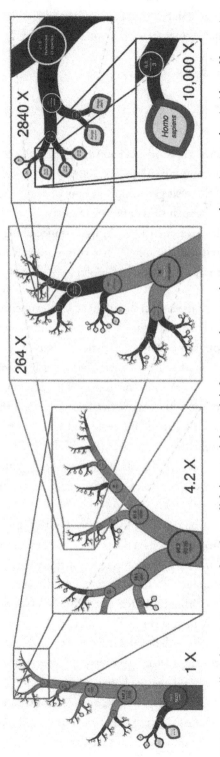

FIGURE 4.12 Drilling down in OneZoom fractal tree of life (moving left to right): from animals to vertebrates to mammals to primates to hominoidea to *Homo sapiens* [OneZoom].

that most encyclopedic and database websites will one day be linked to similar sorts of innovative digital visualization optimized not only for searching but for analyzing the information in new ways.

CONCLUSION

One can easily imagine the sorts of specialized digital archives we have described growing enormously in importance in the 21st century. What must happen for them to become a genre that "the next generation of humanists [and scientists] will take for granted"[54] ? How might such sites enter the mainstream in the lives of scientists and scholars, and one day take their place in importance alongside the traditional journal article or research monograph? What communicative norms beyond the usual stylistic and structural ones must they evolve?

- First, the content must meet disciplinary needs. To explicitly make that case, some sites incorporate a disciplinary justification statement into an "About" or equivalent section, some include statistical data on site usage, and some include a bibliography of journal articles resulting from site usage. In the sciences, for example, Galaxy Zoo has a page with disciplinary justification called "Astronomers"; another page with site usage data, "The Story So Far"; and another page with a list of site-generated journal articles, "Published Papers." From the humanities, the Victorian Web has a page called "What Is the *Victorian Web*?" It includes site usage statistics (1.5 million page views per month!), acknowledges funding sources, and makes the case for filling an important disciplinary niche.

- Second, viewers must be sure that the content of the site is trustworthy— that it has been subjected to some regime of expert evaluation. Most current scientific and scholarly sites use some form of traditional peer review, but other innovative evaluation methods can be found. Galaxy Zoo establishes data reliability by requiring that each astronomical body be classified by at least 40 volunteers. It then subjects those data to a statistical evaluation to determine accuracy. Before deposited data are released in the PDB, an algorithm checks for accuracy of the "geometry, chemistry of the polymer and ligands, nomenclature, and the likely biological assembly." Also, "structure factors and NMR [nuclear magnetic resonance] constraint files" are automatically checked against existing experimental data. ChemSpider has in place a human and computerized content check "for error correction and data cleansing at deposition time,"[55] and it recruits human evaluators from past successful volunteer depositors.

- Third, viewers also need to be assured that the websites have an institutional base, that URLs will always work. Some of the digital archives are maintained by a small group of individuals. What will happen to them when those individuals retire or decide to pursue other interests? Many of the sites we examined do have strong institutional support.

- Fourth, the finding system must be so designed that readers easily locate specific information, and also discover other, not immediately apparent connections among the raw materials and stored data and images. Among all current digital archives, the PDB now has one of the most sophisticated finding systems. From the search box at the top, visitors can search by author, macromolecule name, amino acid sequence of the macromolecule, and name of a ligand or component within the structure. A high-level linked index with eight main entries appears at the homepage center. From there visitors can drill down by protein-bearing organism (e.g., *Homo sapiens, E. coli*), taxonomy (e.g., bacteria, viruses), experimental methods used to determine the structure (e.g., X-ray diffraction, nuclear magnetic resonance), release date, and four other categories. Furthermore, researchers can draw a simple chemical structure and search for all structures in which it appears. In the humanities, Victorian Web has the usual verbal search box plus an innovative visual design that encourages productive browsing for scholarly purposes.

Finally, a matter not genre specific. There must be a built-in motivation for scientists and scholars to contribute to such sites. For nonprofessionals, attribution somewhere on the site or just the fun of contributing anonymously may be enough. For professional scientists and scholars, attribution or fun will not be enough. Managing a site and contributing to it must attain an appropriate level of institutional recognition and reward, a subject we address in the final chapter.

5

EVALUATION BEFORE PUBLICATION

Opening up Peer Review

IN THE MIDST of the controversy over the Nemesis affair—over whether a hidden star was the cause of periodic extinctions on Earth—David Raup and Jack Sepkoski were faced with a dilemma peer review had deliberately created:

> The Tremaine analysis was technically hearsay, because it did not exist in the conventional sense of a scientific publication. To be sure, he sent us a copy of the manuscript shortly before submitting it for publication in a special volume based on the Tucson meeting. We were working on a response but could not say anything substantive about it publically, for fear of having our own paper on the subject disqualified by prior publication in the press. Besides, we had nothing to rebut until Tremaine's paper was reviewed, revised, and finally published.[1]

Precisely: Only peer review followed by publication gave them something to rebut. A survivor after a half-century of criticism concerning its efficacy, peer review remains the best guarantee that published manuscripts and funded grant proposals conform closely to community standards. Moreover, in both the sciences and the humanities, the review criteria are the same: originality, significance to the discipline, argumentative competence, and clarity of expression. When we examine the ways the Internet is transforming peer review, we will see that the transparency and interactivity of the new medium make possible sounder judgments according to these criteria.

Interactivity gives practitioners a firmer sense of the disciplinary-specific meanings of the standards on which their judgments are based; transparency broadcasts this firmer sense to the discipline as a whole. Under any form of peer review, knowledge is what it has always been, an agonistic system in flux, the site of a constant struggle for survival in the realm of ideas. But it is a system that cannot function properly unless each component—each bundle of claims, evidence, and argument—exhibits provisional stability. To confer this stability is the task of peer review. For the system of knowledge generation to function, scientists and scholars must embody a sentiment attributed to Martin Luther at the Diet of Worms: "*Hier stehe ich. Ich kann nicht anders. Gott helfe mir.* (Here I stand. I cannot do otherwise. May God help me.)" They can declare this of their work only if what they set before their public represents a confluence of two independent judgments of worth: their own and that of their community. It is this confluence that works the necessary magic: It changes the knowledge status of a paper or a book manuscript. Before peer review, they were private documents, immune from public criticism in the scientific and scholarly literature; after peer review, they are public documents, open to such criticism.

In this chapter, we review the extensive literature for and against peer review, examine how Dan Sperber's theory of epistemic vigilance combined with Jürgen Habermas's theory of the ideal speech situation (ISS) applies to the peer-review process, and finally, illustrate how Habermas's communicative ideal is being approached by open online peer and community review. The case is made that a shift to full transparency via the Internet is far more likely than continued secrecy to improve knowledge evaluation in both cultures, the sciences and the humanities.

THE CASE FOR AND AGAINST PEER REVIEW

Peer review has been defined broadly as "the systematic use of judges to assess the acceptability of manuscripts submitted for publication."[2] This practice is "the primary avenue of quality assessment and control in the academic world."[3] Scholars have traced the sporadic and rudimentary implementation of peer review to shortly after the origin of the first scientific journals, but it was not until 1752 that the first major scientific journal, *Philosophical Transactions of the Royal Society of London*, formed a committee to read and select articles for publication on the basis of "the importance and singularity of the subjects, and the advantageous method of treating them." And it was not until well into the 20th century,[4] after the widespread professionalization of science and the flowering of the research university, that this self-regulating selection mechanism became standard practice in both the sciences and the humanities.

In the last several decades, the Internet has transformed the process of peer review. E-mail has sped up the process of soliciting peer reviewers, sending them manuscripts, and managing their reports. Web-based systems for managing that entire workflow are available. The Open Journal Systems (OJS) of the Public Knowledge Project is notable in this regard:

> OJS assists with every stage of the refereed publishing process, from submissions through to online publication and indexing. Through its management systems, its finely grained indexing of research, and the context it provides for research, OJS seeks to improve both the scholarly and public quality of refereed research. OJS is open source software made freely available to journals worldwide for the purpose of making open access publishing a viable option for more journals, as open access can increase a journal's readership as well as its contribution to the public good on a global scale.[5]

Without the Internet, the largest peer-reviewed journal in existence, *PLOS One*, would never have been able to publish more than 33,000 articles in 2014. In the same year, "readers worldwide viewed approximately 11.6 million PLOS articles each month, published by authors from more than 200 countries with the assistance of nearly 7,000 academic editors and 90,000 reviewers."[6] That's crowdsourcing on a grand scale.

Today, peer review in the sciences and humanities is exceedingly robust, an institution reproduced, essentially unchanged, every time a new journal is founded, or a new foundation decides to award grants. Moreover, as befits so vigorous an institution, the literature on peer review is extensive. True, it almost entirely concerns the sciences, especially biomedicine: Where the stakes are high, the scrutiny is bound to be intense. Lutz Bornmann, perhaps its most avid student, has shown that the judgments of peer review are a good predictor of future citation success,[7] and that rejected papers that escape significant criticism concerning their design and relevance do well on resubmission to another high-impact journal.[8]

But the evidence for efficacy is not entirely positive. Studies have also found that peer review does a poor job of detecting plagiarism and fraud. Nor is it clear that rejection always correlates with low quality. A survey of leading economists, many of them Nobel Prize recipients, contains a parade of anecdotes concerning rejected papers that were later published and became citation classics.[9] Furthermore, in one notorious study, Peters and Ceci[10] resubmitted papers to journals that had *already* published them, changing only the names and institutional affiliations, making the former unknown and the latter far less prestigious. Only three out of these 12 papers were detected as previously published; only one in the remaining nine was eventually accepted for publication. Stephen Cole[11] suggests that the same result may well have been achieved had the names and affiliations remained unchanged. Cole makes a good point. These studies suggest that peer review does a poor job of detecting quality.

What is true for journal peer review is true also for the review of grant proposals.[12] Unsurprisingly, only those applicants who benefit from the process feel that it works well. Moreover, three out of 10 think there is a bias that favors the elite universities from which a majority of the panelists come, four out of 10 feel that the panels are controlled by "old boy's" networks, and six out of 10 feel there is a systematic bias against innovative research.[13] Finally, the proposal review process is bedeviled by a lack of grant funding, forcing panelists to make discriminations "down to the third decimal,"[14] distinctions so fine no one could possibly make them in defensible manner. One panelist muses:

> As a member of the ACS [American Cancer Society] study section, I am saddened by the decisions we must make. There are many fine proposals but funds are so scarce that we must eliminate two-thirds of the truly outstanding proposals. The survivors are just lucky. Often they have a convincing respected reviewer on the study section.[15]

In her study of multidisciplinary granting panels in the humanities, Michèle Lamont[16] is more positive. Still, in the competitions she analyzed, panelists considered criteria having nothing to do with academic excellence, the presumed gold standard for acceptance: geographic location, disciplinary affiliation, the inferred moral qualities of the applicants, their sex, and their inferred ethnicity. Moreover, because of time constraints, differences were sometimes settled not by the better argument, but by negotiation and compromise; because panelists did not always budget their time well, there was sometimes a rush to judgment toward the end of sessions. Furthermore, the more interdisciplinary the proposal, the worse its chances, as "older, more established disciplines continue to define the rules of the game."[17] One panelist reflects on the poor job he and his fellows did in targeting excellence: "Every panel kind of gets its own rhythm going and there is a kind of randomness having to do with who got picked to be on the panel, and the results could be different on another day."[18]

This deeply flawed process is also costly. No figures are given for the cost of panels from such grant agencies as the National Institutes of Health, the National Science Foundation, or the American Council of Learned Societies. A look at the labor involved is nevertheless instructive. Scientists and humanists spend hundreds of hours writing proposals, many of which will not obtain funding. Agency program officers are hired to select and manage the panels. Academic screeners must filter the proposals prior to panel review, eliminating those they judge unworthy of the more senior panelists' attention. Panelists themselves must review at home and in detail the many proposals that survive the initial screening. After this review, senior panelists are flown to the foundation site for two or three days of meetings. In addition to the actual expenses of this process—plane fares, hotel rooms—there is the time devoted to the process, lost time that might have been devoted to science or scholarship.

In the case of journal review, we can roughly calculate costs. We assume an average of two reviewers and an average review time of three hours each.[19,20] One estimate is $1,500 for the professional time that needs to be devoted to each submitted paper.[21] This of course will vary, depending on whether the reviewer is an affluent thoracic surgeon or an impecunious classicist. One estimate of editorial costs—for screening and correspondence with authors and reviewers—is in the range of $120 to $420.[22] Given the avalanche of submissions experienced by high-impact journals, the costs of peer review can be high indeed. In 2006–2007, *Nature* had 9,847 submissions, accepting only 837 for publication.[23] If the peer-review cost for a *Nature* article per submission were $1,750, then the annual peer-review cost would be about $17 million and the cost per published article about $21,000. If we assume that 60% of submissions are rejected after an initial editorial screening and not sent out for peer review—a figure available for *Science,* but not for *Nature*—then the cost is about $7 million, or about $8,000 per published article. Given the high cost combined with the associated delay in publication date and a host of quality-control issues, some have questioned whether the return on investment is worth it.[24]

ARGUMENT THEORY AND PEER REVIEW

Whatever its flaws or shortcomings, peer review is doing the job it is designed to do. It allocates scarce financial resources in the form of grants and contracts; it allocates articles and books among journals and presses of varying prestige. It does not always get its allocations right, any more than the justice system always gets its verdicts right. At its heart, as at the heart of the justice system, is the making of arguments embedded in a set of procedural norms. It is unfortunate, therefore, that the most impressive theory of argumentation we know, that of Mercier and Sperber,[25,26] seems at first glance to undermine the likelihood of ever getting these allocations right. According to them, skilled arguers . . . are not after the truth but after arguments supporting their views. This explains the notorious confirmation bias [ignoring evidence inconvenient for the case they want to make]. This bias is apparent not only when people are actually arguing, but also when they are reasoning proactively from the perspective of having to defend their opinions.[27]

This tendency toward persuasion over truth in creating arguments would seem to make the case against peer review in any form. However, this implication is only apparent. Mercier and Sperber also argue that this all-too-human tendency can be mitigated if participants exert "epistemic vigilance," that is to say "share an interest in discovering the right answer."[28] This is what the scientific and scholarly community tries to do: "contrary to common bleak assessments of human reasoning abilities, people are quite capable of reasoning in an unbiased manner, at least when they are evaluating arguments rather than producing them, and when they are after the truth rather than trying to win a debate." Indeed, Mercier and Sperber aver that "the whole scientific enterprise has always been structured around [such] groups, from the Lincean Academy down to the Large Hadron Collider." Peer review is one of several social mechanisms used in the sciences and the humanities for institutionalizing epistemic vigilance.[29]

Still, Mercier and Sperber's theory seems to mean that rational consensus is not the product of argumentation, but its accidental byproduct. This is the case if we assume that participants are always self-interested agents. But Amartya Sen reminds us it is a mistake to assume that "a person is given *one* preference ordering, and as and when the need arises this is supposed to reflect his interests, represent his welfare, summarize his idea of what should be done, and describe his actual choices and behavior. Can one preference ordering do all these things?"[30] Sen's answer is a resounding "no," and we think Mercier and Sperber would agree. We feel we are paraphrasing them accurately when we say that an arguer's preference ordering varies with argumentative context, and that in some contexts self-interest may well be held in abeyance. While peer reviewing, participants will tend to exercise epistemic vigilance, evaluating claims and arguments in the interest of the truth. Reviewers will be all the more inclined to do so because they will be forced publicly to justify their positions.[31] True, in traditional peer review that public consists only of editors and fellow reviewers. But to us this limitation suggests that, in the open review the Internet makes possible, reviewers will improve the quality of arguments in their evaluations, and candidate knowledge will enter the public sphere on a more secure footing.

This link between peer review and the possibility of rational consensus justifies, we feel, our use of Habermas's ISS to characterize this process.[32–34] This theoretical formulation, derived from speech act theory, consists of a set of pre-suppositions that is required for the creation of a rational consensus based on mutual understanding achieved by undistorted communication among partici-pants:[35] In the ISS, interlocutors must reveal themselves, they must have every opportunity to initiate communication and to make assertions, and they must have equal power over the exchange. In the pursuit of rational consensus under these conditions, bias is revealed, countered, neutralized. While the ISS priv-ileges consensus, it is also comfortable with the dissensus that often prevails. Because ISS defines rationality as a process, it is not embarrassed by seemingly wide differences, such as the diverse referee judgments that routinely character-ize peer review. If rationality is a process, we are wedded not to the truth of par-ticular claims, but to communicative actions whose goal is rationally motivated consensus, an agreement in science concerning our best account of the products of nature, an agreement in scholarship concerning our best account of the prod-ucts of culture.

Habermas's ISS does not enunciate a set of utopian conditions designed to gauge the rationality of any actual interchange. Neither is it a generalization from actual communicative practices, nor a set of rules designed to control events, like those that manage traffic flow. Rather, it is a rational reconstruction of the criteria that make a certain kind of experience possible, namely, in the case of science and scholarship, the rationally motivated agreement that must be the foundation of knowledge. Whether its conditions are realized in a particular communicative exchange is irrel-evant to the robustness of its theoretical status: Together, these form "the constitu-tive condition of rational speech."[36]

For ISS to apply to peer review, there must be consensus concerning the crite-ria by which quality will be judged. From an analysis of rejected scientific papers, Chubin and Hackett derive a wide-ranging list of reasons for rejection: from defec-tive methodology, to poor writing style, to ignorance of the relevant literature, to poor argumentation, to misunderstanding the data, to lack of novelty, to naïveté.[37] In her analysis of the proposal-review process, Lamont seems to offer us no more help than Chubin and Hackett in making unity out of diversity. She warns us that different disciplines favor different styles for creating knowledge. For economics, an empirical discipline, knowledge is objective, to be discovered by established methods. For English literature, an interpretive discipline, knowledge is intrinsically subjective: The world is a text to be understood. Even among those disciplines that favor an interpretive orientation—English literature and cultural anthropology, let us say—there will be profound differences of approach. Nevertheless, this diversity does not preclude the existence of central tendencies: "among the respondents, sig-nificance and originality stand out as the most important of the formal criteria used, followed by clarity and methods."[38] One of Lamont's informants defines the relationship among these terms, formulated as a set of questions to be asked:

> Is research based on some rigorous testing, in terms of the way in which it's collected, the ideas behind [it], the methodologies that are used to follow up the conceptualization of a project. Clarity of thought, having very clear ways for interpreting why [it is] important and what it means, and what relevance it has to a particular field of knowledge. Explaining what contribution it's going to make, and making some important contributions along the lines of originality, along the lines of ... building on ... the work of others in very significant ways, perhaps branching out, expanding other important work.[39]

From these studies, we derive a unified set of criteria for knowledge evaluation: originality, argumentative competence, significance to the field, and clarity of expression. It may seem that the sciences and the "hard" social sciences differ in that, unlike the humanities, their work routinely includes a methods section. But it is a mistake to equate the lack of a methods section with a lack of method in the humanities: In every case, argumentative competence includes the use of appropriate methods.

THEORY APPLICATION

To apply ISS to real-world examples, we first turn to the sciences. Our source is a large cache of e-mails released in the wake of the "Climategate" controversy. In November 2009, a hacker breached the Climate Research Unit at the University of East Anglia, copied thousands of personal e-mails sent by the scientists at that institution, then distributed them worldwide through the Internet. Some of these e-mails contained vituperative remarks about the research of those who questioned the link between global warming and human activities; passages extracted from the released e-mails provided fodder for arguments by those who believe, as one polemical website puts it, "anthropogenic global warming, history's biggest scam." But that much-discussed brouhaha is not our concern.

Instead, we are interested in the fact that embedded within these missives were peer-review reports not intended for public release, a trove offering a behind-the-scenes glimpse into traditional peer review, where the e-mailed reports normally remain private. Because these e-mails were released without the permission of either the senders or the recipients, we have altered all identifying data and do not reference any quotations from them. The identity of the hacker remains unknown.

In these reviews, lack of originality, our first criterion, is a serious flaw, meriting manuscript rejection. Employing this criterion, a reviewer of a proposal says that, even though the authors are "good people" and some of the work is "worthy," he cannot recommend funding. In particular,

> Neither [proposed] idea can be considered original. For an example see Heinrichs et al. in Boreas (2005) pages 192–206 or Lotter et al. in Palaeoclimatology (1997) pages 395–420, or Heiri et al. (2003) in Palaeo pages 35–53, or Seppa and Birks (2002) in Quaternary Research pages 191–199.

Argumentative competence, in which the reviewer points to perceived logical flaws in the argument, is our second criterion. Of one scientific paper, a reviewer writes that the issues raised are "worthy of discussion in the literature, and JGR [journal] is an appropriate venue. The authors, as is typical, have done a careful job with their analysis, and it appears sound, as do the primary conclusions, although I have some specific reservations." One of those is that

> there is a potential "straw man" argument being introduced here. Precisely which "annual temperature" reconstructions are being referred to here? The statement made could arguably apply to Crowley and Lowery (2000), which is based on scaling a composite of largely extratropical (and mostly summer-sensitive) proxy records against the annual mean Northern Hemisphere mean instrumental series. It is far more difficult, however, to argue that the authors' statements fairly characterize the Mann et al (1998; 1999) annual mean temperature reconstruction.

Significance to the field, our third criterion, represents the reviewer's educated guess concerning the potential impact of the published article, as measured eventually by such metrics as citation counts after publication. Concerning this criterion, a reviewer says that "this paper addresses a very important problem in contemporary climate record analysis. It points out that several recent reconstructions of NH [Northern Hemisphere] climate over the last thousand years might have some biases . . . It can be published." Alternately, a paper may be significant, but not significant enough to publish in a specific journal. Of a submission to *Nature*, a journal with an impact factor that is off the charts—36.1 where 3 to 5 is more than acceptable for a specialized journal—a reviewer writes to an editor:

> Things have been very hectic for me and I am sorry it has taken some time to do this. I have really had to study it and several associated papers before coming

to this conclusion. My overall opinion is reject. There is little I believe that is significant here, and a lot of implied significance and absence of clear interpretation of the results. There is also a "new" approach to processing data hidden in the supplementary material but this is not relevant to the substance of the paper as the later processing negates the need to use it in the end anyway.

The paper was eventually published in a journal with an impact factor of 3.8. It was important, but not important enough for *Nature*.

It is also true that a paper may be significant enough to publish in the journal to which it was submitted but still need increased clarity if that significance is to be apparent. A reviewer writes to a journal editor on this point: "I agree with you that this is an important and interesting piece of work, that should definitely be published. I was actually pretty disappointed that it was written up rather badly, so that it needed some major revision." But clarity in presentation is significant only because it reveals the other three qualities with a minimum of effort. It is not per se a measure of quality:

> Though this paper is one if the best-written papers I have received for review lately, I must recommend that this paper NOT be accepted for the following reasons: The data in the paper do not support the authors' conclusion that the mixed scaling "replicates GCM data better", there is no attempt at cross-validation, there is no physical basis for the curve-fit, and in fact it is logically inconsistent, and finally, the metrics of goodness-of-fit given here are weak.

By and large, the manuscript evaluations in the Climategate e-mails show the reviewers attempting to employ "epistemic vigilance" in judging the worth of the submitted proposals or articles. Do the most deserving applicants obtain grants? Do the right papers always end up in the right journals? These are the wrong questions to ask. The concern must always be that, as with the justice system, the correct review procedure has been followed, a procedure that is a real-world approximation of the ISS. Even so—even in the presence of a wise judge, strong and fair advocates on both sides, alert and intelligent jurors—justice can go awry. The centrality of procedure makes its violation a legitimate source of outrage, as this comment makes clear:

> I strongly agree that this is an abuse of his position as IPCC [Intergovernmental Panel on Climate Change] reviewer! . . . Hartley could of course submit a comment after your paper was published if he wished to criticize certain aspects, and that is the route he should have followed. He tried to stop publication of a paper that I was a co-author on, Gosford et al. (2005), by contacting the editor

of J. Climate with various criticisms. Fortunately the editor told him firmly that the route to take was to submit a comment after publication. However, in our case the paper was already in press. In your case, with the editor's decision still to be made, there is clearly more scope for Hartley to influence the decision in your case—and this certainly should not happen.

But even in the best of circumstances, traditional peer review's deviations from the ISS are considerable. Its first principle permits each interlocutor an equal opportunity to initiate speech acts, equal power over the exchange. In an obvious way, a review cycle deviates from this principle: After their initial request for manuscript evaluation, authors never initiate speech acts, but only respond to those of the referees or the editors. In addition, there is usually only one round of referee critique, editorial mediation, and authorial response, hardly enough to ensure the mutual understanding that must precede rational consensus. Moreover, because interaction between referee and author is generally out of the question, authors are forced to respond without benefit of interactive clarification. They must reply to every question and respond to every criticism, despite the fact that, were interaction possible, some questions might not have been asked, nor some criticisms made.

Still, it is possible for an editor to overcome these restrictions in the interest of salvaging for publication a flawed but worthy effort. Toward the end of June 2002, an author submitted a paper to a climatology journal. There was considerable delay in getting it reviewed:

The problem has been referees. I sent it out to two, one of which sent back a very cursory "seems ok to me" response by email and the other who consistently has not responded to requests for an update (though admittedly left too long before pushing). The paper was therefore only recently sent to another two referees who were asked to respond quickly. I will hassle these more strongly. It is very likely, unless some real problem is found, that this will be published—but I need at least one positive response from one of the new referees.

In fact, it was not until the following June that the reviews were in, a year after the original submittal. Despite the editor's optimism, the consensus was negative, and the paper would have to be revised yet again if it were to be published:

You will see that all of [the reviewers] agree that the paper should not be published in its present form. The recent added delay has been while I then went through the paper and all reviews carefully myself to give what I believe is an objective opinion of my own. I too feel that I cannot justify acceptance in the present form but I note that neither of the original reviewers recommend rejection. The normal procedure at this stage would though be a polite rejection on the grounds of pressure of space and the apparent requirement for significant new work. I certainly will not recommend this course of action and instead request that you and your co-authors look over these opinions and let me know whether you think it possible to deal adequately with them. I would be happy to consider a revision.

In this response, the editor signals his reluctance to reject and thus discards "normal procedure." Clearly, he wants to publish the paper, but his professional judgment is that it is still not fit to print, in accord with the reviewers' responses. The paper was rewritten again, passed muster, and was published in the journal.

A second principle of ISS is that all interlocutors have the opportunity to reveal their "inner natures," to allow their discourse to become transparent to their full subjectivity. Of course, there are limits to this openness in any exchange that aspires to civility. In peer reviews, given their general anonymity, such strong negative emotions as annoyance, anger, and contempt are bound to surface on occasion. When they do, however, they threaten to derail any claim to rationality. Because of this persistent danger, a mechanism must be in place capable of repair, of reaffirming the imperative that peer-review discourse must be civil. If emotional neutrality and politeness are temporarily set aside, as in this review of a submission to the *International Journal of Climate*, it is invariably referees who are the first offenders. In the case in question, a referee is contemptuously dismissive, accusing the authors of "trying to rediscover the wheel." The referee goes on to say that the manuscript has "major flaws" and is "well below the standard acceptable in IJC or any other refereed journals." The manuscript does not contribute to the area of research, the reviewer opines, and the methodology used for comparison is "naïve" and "unacceptable in scientific publications."

Understandably, reviewer contempt fuels authorial anger directed at an editor so naïve as to heed comments so clearly biased. His pride wounded, the author fired back:

> The two reviewers have not realized the novelty of this paper. The WG [Weather Generator model] is fairly new and we are certainly not re-inventing the wheel! . . . You've missed a good paper for IJC [journal abbreviation] here! Your reviewers have not read it carefully enough, nor understood what it was about. You can ignore this email if you want. I won't be submitting this paper to IJC again.

This was not the end of the story. The editor was apologetic, saying that he had little choice but to heed the judgment of the referees, even though he is "very conscious of the fact that you [the author] personally have given wonderful service to IJC and I would hope that this incident does not damage the long term relationship you have with the journal." He suggested a third referee, and the author agreed. We do not know the outcome of that review, but we assume the paper was finally rejected. It was eventually published in a journal with half the impact factor of the journal of first submission.

There are two additional criteria of ISS: All interlocutors must be free to use any civil speech act, and they must have equal power over the exchange. But, clearly, in traditional peer review, authors are prohibited from issuing commands and inhibited from asking critical questions, while editors and referees do both freely. This difference is an index of the power of the latter and the relative powerlessness of the former. Further, the general rule of referee anonymity forces authors to frame a reply in ignorance of their interlocutors. Of course, to balance matters, authors may also be anonymous, but genuine author anonymity, in the sciences at least, may be an ineffectual charade: Any worthwhile research program leaves an intellectual fingerprint. Finally, since multiple submission is seen as unethical, authors are forced to endure delays beyond their control, delays that may cause them, but not their editors or referees, considerable anxiety and that may reduce the value of their submission as a contribution to ongoing scientific or scholarly debate.

Aside from deviations from the ISS criteria, the lack of reliability among referee and editor judgments may seem to count against the alleged rationality of the consensus. Though we may concur that referee global judgments are reliable in the sense that two scientists or scholars acting independently will generally agree about the approximate value of a paper they are refereeing,[40] their reasons often differ markedly. Still, insisting on this level of agreement cannot be a general rule: Referees may disagree for the very good reason that they bring different sorts of expertise to the table.

In any case, the full realization of the ISS is necessarily limited. This limit stems from a compromise, always more or less uneasy, between principles that cannot coexist in their more extreme forms. ISS cannot be viewed as a goal toward which we gradually move, because such a construal involves us in a paradox. We must suppose that rational consensus is a good we can pursue without regard to its possibly undesirable effects on other, equally desirable goods, such as the timely production of new science and scholarship. In other words, we must subscribe to the view that all good things are compatible, that in an ideal world all good things will form an integrated whole:[41] We must subscribe to an Enlightenment myth. The heedless pursuit of rational consensus would have an unavoidable, and undesirable, cost. The ISS cannot be fully realized without devaluing professional time and progressively undermining peer review's central purpose: the timely initial certification of new science and scholarship. But, as we shall see, Internet peer review contrasts with its traditional counterpart in its ability more effectively to realize the conditions of the ISS within existing institutional settings.

OPEN INTERNET PEER REVIEW IN THE SCIENCES

In 2006, *Nature* ran a trial of open review. After passing an initial editorial screening, authors were given the option of subjecting their manuscript to open community commentary. Out of more than a thousand papers, authors of only 71 (5%) agreed to open review. Of these 71 papers, only about half received public comments during the trial period, few of which were substantive.[42] Understandably, *Nature* declared this trial a failure. Nevertheless, it left the door open to future experimentation:

> This was not a controlled experiment, so in no sense does it disprove the hypothesis that open peer review could one day become accepted practice. But this experience, along with informal discussions with researchers, suggests that most of them are too busy, and lack sufficient career incentive, to venture onto a venue such as *Nature*'s Website and post public, critical assessments of their peers' work.[43]

We agree that routine reliance on volunteer commentary will not work as a dependable means of open manuscript evaluation. Still, other journals incorporating some form of open review have demonstrated that researchers granted anonymity will most certainly "post public, critical assessments of their peers' work."[44] These journals include the *BMJ Open, Biology Direct*, and one of the journals in the *Nature* publishing group, *The EMBO Journal* of the European Molecular Biology Organization. But the first major scientific publisher to implement open peer review that comes closest to realization of Habermas's ISS is the European Geosciences Union (EGU). Over an eight-week period, manuscripts submitted to EGU journals are subjected to simultaneous open online review by both designated referees and members of the discourse community at large.

Begun in 2001, as of 2015 this venture consists of 16 peer-reviewed journals. All but two employ open peer review, and all are open access. All have respectable impact factors for specialty journals; they are a clear mark of success, matching or exceeding more conventional journals in climate science, some with far longer histories. Do the EGU journals have a citation advantage the others do not? While some might allege that their impact factor is inflated by the two-stage review process that all employ—publishing and archiving both revised papers and their original versions—Bornmann et al.[45] have shown that this is not the case.

We focus on two of the EGU journals, the founding journals *Atmospheric Chemistry and Physics* and *Climate of the Past*. We target the first because its peer-review process has been subjected to extensive scholarly analysis, the second because one of its articles, the one we will examine, is embedded in the same intensely fought controversy over global warming as that of the peer-review documents we have already analyzed. Both of these cases of open peer review exemplify a closer approximation to the ISS than traditional peer review. Both are more nearly a realization of the conditions of rational debate. Both give full voice to all interested parties in the evaluation of a paper's clarity, argumentative competence, originality, and significance. Both allow all interested readers to evaluate the original and revised versions of submitted manuscripts as well as reader comments and author responses. Both post a preprint for all to read shortly after manuscript submittal and complete their reviews in a timely fashion.

In *Atmospheric Chemistry and Physics*, Ulrich Pöschl and his collaborators set up a peer-review system with three distinct stages.[46] In the first, an editorial screening eliminates papers that are inappropriately submitted or obviously inept. In stage two, the papers remaining in the pool are assigned to an academic sub-editor and are, simultaneously, posted online for eight weeks. During this period, they are reviewed by referees chosen by the sub-editor and are commented on by any interested readers. Throughout, the judgment of referees and commentators is guided by explicit criteria. These are, not coincidentally, parallel to our own: "scientific quality," "scientific significance," and "presentation quality." A follow-up question focuses on originality as a factor in determining significance: "Does the paper present novel concepts, tools, or data?" During this second stage, the discussion paper has the professional status of a publication in a proceedings: It has not yet passed the more rigorous review of senior representatives of the relevant scientific community. Referees chosen from this community and self-chosen commentators accomplish this purpose. These can elect to be named or they can choose to remain anonymous. Online commentators must identify themselves, presumably in the interest of encouraging responsible responses. Light monitoring by the sub-editor suffices to eliminate the inappropriate and the unsubstantiated. Upon completion of the second stage, we enter into the final one, which is closed to the public: Here a decision to accept or reject is made, either by sub-editors themselves or, in difficult cases, with the help of additional, anonymous referees. If the decision is positive, the original paper, its revised counterparts, the referee reports of the open discussion stage, and all public commentary are permanently archived.

In a comprehensive research project conducted by Bornmann et al., Internet open peer review was found to be generally predictive of success, as measured by a paper's citation counts.[47] It is a sign of this accuracy in prediction that rejected *Atmospheric Chemistry and Physics* papers published elsewhere have, on the whole, lower citation counts. While the rejection rate of *Atmospheric Chemistry and Physics* is low, this suggests not low standards, but the high quality of initial submissions: The journal's impact factor is high for a specialized journal. Predictable validity is high as well—that is, referees generally make excellent guesses concerning the impact of the papers they judge acceptable as measured by eventual citation counts.

This may well be due in part to the quality of the referee reports. Bornmann et al. found that *Atmospheric Chemistry and Physics* reports were four times as long as those in a comparable journal employing conventional review and were far more detailed than their conventional counterparts. This suggests an increased desire to be thorough and to try to effect whatever improvements are possible. That these comments are public may be partly responsible for this increased diligence. A rise in quality is also inferable from the language of the peer-review exchanges.[48] *Atmospheric Chemistry and Physics* referee reports and public comments used more hedges (words such as *maybe* and *probably*), suggesting a more nuanced approach to judgments. There were also more pronouns in the second person, *you*, suggesting a simulation of face-to-face communication, a situation in which the norms of civility fall naturally into place, a condition that may well hold polemic in check. Furthermore, the number of emotional words was low, suggesting a preference for rational debate. Bornmann et al. sum up in a manner compatible to the conditions of ISS:

> the language patterns indicate that PPR [public peer review] and ACP SC [comments by the scientific community] adds a new quality to the peer review process. In our study, the language use in PPR was characterized by a more open and tentative as well as cognitively elaborated style as compared to CPR [closed peer review]. This might be due to the fact that the reviews are open to the interested audience and thus themselves subject to evaluation. This might lead to a more careful and elaborated peer review process.

After traditional peer review, claims that have been vigorously disputed in camera and revised as a consequence are turned again toward the world; also after traditional peer review, its machinery disappears from sight. Publication performs this task; it frees the scientific report and the scholarly article from the doubts that peer review generates, those that had shifted its status from knowledge about nature or about culture to knowledge about referee consensus. In other words, publication after traditional peer review obliterates all traces of the procedure by which the knowledge it asserts is certified. As a consequence of this obliteration, publication misrepresents the status of the knowledge it makes public. The archiving of Internet peer-review documents preserves the true knowledge status of the paper in flux, permanently embedded in the debate over whether it is original enough, significant enough, competently argued enough, well composed enough to have been published. These real-life approximations of ISS remain permanently open to scientists and scholars interested in the subject under debate, and to those scholars, like Bornmann, interested in the debate itself. Open peer review, by definition, makes the machinery behind peer review visible to any interested party.

To exemplify the application of open peer review in the sciences, we turn to a specific paper, one from a sister journal to *Atmospheric Chemistry and Physics, Climate of the Past*, a contribution to the global warming controversy. Both sides in this controversy generally agree that the 20th- and 21st-century Earth is becoming significantly warmer. They disagree, however, on whether this warming is part of a normal cycle or is an anomalous spike, a manmade creation. Because scientists do not have global temperature records stretching back thousands of years, they must settle this controversy by employing proxies sensitive to climate change, such as tree ring measurements. They must then feed these proxies into elaborate climate change models. The choice of proxies can be legitimately criticized, as can the models scientists choose to employ to derive predictions from these proxies. Despite persistent debate, however, a consensus among climatologists has emerged that manmade global warming is a reality, a problem governments—and humankind— must address. That there is a consensus, of course, does not mean that scientists or others who disagree are mistaken. The slightest knowledge of the history of science demonstrates that those displaced to the margins of science are sometimes proved to have been correct; the example of Alfred Wegener springs to mind. Given the assumptions of early 20th-century geophysics, and the defects of Wegener's model, who could believe that something so counterintuitive as continental drift could take place?[49]

The Internet peer-reviewed paper we shall examine, along with the online interactive discussion (Fig. 5.1), is "Millennial Temperature Reconstruction Intercomparison and Evaluation."[50] It has eight authors and is the product of an international collaboration involving England, Switzerland, the United States, Sweden, and the Netherlands. The main claim to new knowledge has to do with global temperature change back to the year 1000. The open review process, which lasted from September 26, 2006, to April 18, 2007, consisted of exchanges among the sub-editor, the authors, one referee, and three science community commentators. The subsequent closed review involved three more reviewers and lasted almost six

1/26/13 CPD - Interactive Discussion - Millennial temperature reconstruction intercomparison and evaluation

Volumes and Issues Contents of Issue !

Clim. Past Discuss., 2, 1001-1049, 2006
www.clim-past-discuss.net/2/1001/2006/
doi:10.5194/cpd-2-1001-2006
© Author(s) 2006. This work is licensed
under a Creative Commons License.

Millennial temperature reconstruction intercomparison and evaluation

M. N. Juckes, M. R. Allen, K. R. Briffa, J. Esper, G. C. Hegerl, A. Moberg, T. J. Osborn, S. L. Weber, and E. Zorita

Abstract Discussion Paper (PDF, 907 KB) Supplement (1609 KB) Final Revised Paper (CP)

Interactive Discussion **Status: Clos**

AC: Author Comment | **RC**: Referee Comment | **SC**: Short Comment | **EC**: Editor Comment
- Printer-friendly Version S - Supplement

AC S516: 'Correction', Martin Juckes, 02 Nov 2006

AC S535: 'Clarification', Martin Juckes, 03 Nov 2006

SC S536: 'Transparency', Willis Eschenbach, 04 Nov 2006
AC S602: 'Transparency', Martin Juckes, 21 Nov 2006
SC S715: 'Multidisciplinary Comments 1', Willis Eschenbach, 20 Dec 2006
AC S924: 'Response', Martin Juckes, 06 Mar 2007
SC S720: 'Multidisciplinary Comments 2', Willis Eschenbach, 20 Dec 2006
AC S925: 'Response', Martin Juckes, 06 Mar 2007
SC S724: 'Multidisciplinary Comments 3', Willis Eschenbach, 20 Dec 2006
AC S916: 'Response to Eschenbach', Martin Juckes, 06 Mar 2007

SC S587: 'What good is this board?', Willis Eschenbach, 15 Nov 2006

RC S689: 'Anonymous reviewer', Anonymous Referee #1, 15 Dec 2006
AC S914: 'Response to anonymous reviewer', Martin Juckes, 06 Mar 2007
EC S964: 'Comments on the response to Referee 1', Hugues Goosse, 18 Apr 2007

SC S697: 'Comments - M&M Issues', Stephen McIntyre, 19 Dec 2006

FIGURE 5.1 Interactive discussion page for *Climate of the Past* [M. Juckes et al., *Climate of the Past* 3 (2007): 591–609].

more months, until October 5, 2007, when the final paper was published. While the referees were all anonymous, as in traditional peer review, here we can name at least some names since the process was partially open. The sub-editor was Hugues Goosse, a professor at Louvain; the public commentators were Willis Eschenbach, Stephen McIntyre, and Mark Rostron. McIntyre is the best known of the group, a strong advocate for the position that anthropogenic global warming is a myth, a position regularly defended on his blog "Climate Audit." Although the three science commentators may have been amateurs in the field, Eschenbach and McIntyre were in no way amateurish. Both had published articles in respected journals critical of previously published articles supportive of global warming model calculations: McIntyre in *Geophysical Research Letters* and *Energy and Environment*, Eschenbach in *Nature*. Rostron is otherwise unknown to us.

This amount of prepublication scrutiny this publication received is highly unusual. Most Internet peer-reviewed papers receive no comments outside of invited reviewers, a phenomenon noted as a flaw in *Nature*'s assessment of its open peer-review trial. This criticism misses the point: What *Nature* calls a flaw is merely a feature we would expect in any real-life instantiation of ISS. It is common sense that most papers do not motivate commentary, unless commentators are solicited for that purpose (see Chapter 2 with regard to the paucity of online commentary to articles after publication). Papers others find useful are simply cited; papers found irrelevant to research interests are simply ignored; papers that raise interesting issues simply lead to other papers. Only controversial papers, such as the one we examine here, generate extensive and intense commentary. This general neglect is entirely salutary; it means that the system is free of a burdensome superfluity that wastes everyone's time.

Together, the *Climate of the Past* peer-review documents available to us form a rich object for analysis, one generally supportive of Bornmann et al.'s conclusions concerning *Atmospheric Chemistry and Physics*.[51] The referee report is over four times the size of the traditional referee reports Bornmann et al. analyzed. While Rostron's commentary merely matches those closed reports in length, McIntyre's and Eschenbach's commentaries are about 14 times as long. There is also a tendency to address interlocutors directly. Four commentaries make use of "you" and "your," two are in the form of personal letters, two of Eschenbach's commentaries are signed "w," an abbreviation of his first name, and the sub-editor's final decision, although not in letter form, is "signed" with his full name, "Hughes Goosse." Still, as we might expect in so heated a controversy, civility does not always prevail, and authors and commentators can be summarily dismissive. McIntyre and Eschenbach's remarks periodically erupt in negative words and phrases. Eschenbach insists that there is "a fundamental flaw in the argument" and that the paper should be rejected as it is only "a minor variation on existing reconstructions."[52] McIntyre finds the paper to be scientifically and morally defective, establishing academic credibility on false pretenses:

> Juckes et al have already withdrawn a false allegation that we had failed to archive our source code and, after the above admission, should also have withdrawn these further false allegations concerning supposed "errors." In making these allegations, Juckes et al also perpetuated prior "academic check-kiting" by Wahl and Ammann.[53]

Of the paper itself, McIntyre is dismissive: "Given the already crowded controversy in this field, I see little purpose in reviving an issue in peer-reviewed literature that is not actually in controversy and which has negligible impact on any result."[54] Unlike McIntyre and Eschenbach, the corresponding author, Martin Juckes, maintains civility in his replies to criticisms. In his relatively brief responses to individual comments, he adopts an even tone that sends a message: The accusations of Eschenbach and McIntyre have not changed his convictions or disturbed his equanimity. At one point, however, Juckes does become exasperated. McIntyre ends his final commentary with a reference to his blog: "There has been extensive discussion of various aspects of Juckes et al at www.climateaudit.org—see http://www.climate-audit.org/?cat=36."[55] Juckes responds dismissively, "Extensive and ill-informed."[56]

This is not to say that McIntyre and Eschenbach's criticisms are without foundation, that they do not exercise epistemic vigilance. The question is not whether they are annoyed or angry, but whether their anger and annoyance are justified. Despite their polemical edge, their remarks contribute to the paper's considerable improvement from its first to its final draft. Indeed, their focus on the originality, argumentative competence, and significance of the target paper is seconded in the responses of the one referee who participated in the open review process. Although that referee says "the introduction is quite interesting and gives a nice overview"—faint praise indeed—the referee feels that the paper "does not provide much new results," and that "the choice of [methods] is arbitrary."[57] In keeping with the rules of the game, Juckes et al. feel obliged to respond to all allegations point for point, providing countervailing evidence when necessary. They also acknowledge and agree to correct at least some of the errors McIntyre and Eschenbach allege, as in the case of their initial geographic proxy locations. Furthermore, they make some changes based on McIntyre and Eschenbach's criticism of their proxy selection. In response to the criticisms of the anonymous referee and of McIntyre and Eschenbach, the authors are forced to defend their choice of methods. These two communal commentators, however, do not address clarity of presentation. It is the anonymous referee who finds that certain aspects of the paper are "not clear"; it is the sub-editor who finds the paper "difficult to follow." In his final decision letter to the authors, Goosse also dwells on clarity, saying: "if you follow these suggestions, the paper would be more focused and easier to read."[58]

In response to these criticisms, Juckes et al. extensively revised their draft. One section of the paper was shortened so as not to try the reader's patience; another was lengthened so as to bolster the paper's central claim with additional arguments. In response to McIntyre's criticisms, Juckes et al. renamed and rewrote a whole section dealing with papers critical of the "consensus on millennial temperatures," including four co-authored by McIntyre. In response to various reviewers' methodological criticisms, the number of proxies used in their models was reduced from 18 to 13, and their results were recalculated. Finally, the claim was narrowed so as to include only the Northern Hemisphere instead of the whole Earth. Nevertheless, the core finding of the paper is essentially untouched from first to last, and its prose is for the most part unrevised. Most important, the abstract and conclusion of the revised paper are virtually the same as the original, with some minor adjustments designed to moderate its degree of assertiveness. The revision reads: "There are fewer concerns related to the ability of the proxy records to capture more rapid changes on a 10 to 50 year time scale, such as we have experienced in recent decades." This is less assertive than the original's "There does not appear to be any doubt." The revision reads: "We have also reviewed and, in some cases, tested with new analysis, papers (in particular Soon and Baliunas, 2003, MM2003 and MM2005b) which claim to refute that IPCC 2001 conclusion and found that those claims were not well supported." This is less derogatory than the original's "found to contain serious flaws."

The revision was successful enough for the paper to enter the literature without difficulty. By 2015 it had been cited a respectable 59 times. Although most of these citing articles were published in specialized journals and collections with limited audiences, one was in *Nature*, another in *Proceedings of the National Academy of Sciences*. The former has garnered 113 citations, the latter 368.

It is a tribute to the public character of Internet peer review that all of the critics of this paper, solicited and unsolicited, tempered or vociferous, have been given a voice; that those dissenting opinions are part of the official record; and that the authors of the original paper took all of their criticisms to heart. This is not to say that either McIntyre or Eschenbach was satisfied with his treatment. Having posted a comment and not seen a response from Juckes after eleven days, an impatient Eschenbach vented his frustration in an ironic mode:

> I had made the foolish assumption that this discussion board was an opportunity to discuss the paper with the authors. However, they seem to be curiously unwilling to respond to my questions. If they are not willing to answer questions . . . what is the point of having a discussion forum at all?[59]

After peer review and days before the article's publication, McIntyre wrote a long posting in his blog "Climate Audit" in which he repeated his criticisms verbatim, followed by Juckes's responses, followed by his criticisms that these responses are "completely unresponsive." McIntyre also sent an e-mail to Martin Claussens, co-editor in chief of *Climate of the Past*, which he published on his blog:

> Juckes' replies to these Review Comments were evasive and unresponsive. I have attached an Appendix comparing my Review Comments with Juckes'

Replies, and inserted some comments. You can immediately verify Juckes' total unresponsiveness and even insolence, which editor Goosse did not repudiate . . .[60]

In Claussen's response, also published on "Climate Audit," we get an insight into the *Climate of the Past*'s review process:

During the discussion phase of the paper in question, there was only one reviewer who delivered his/her comments in time. And there were the (unsolicited) short comments by you and Willis Eschenbach and Mark Rostron. Unfortunately, the discussion phase with only one reviewer passed, and it was closed automatically . . In this situation, the editor reacted responsibly, and he approached 3 more reviewers. I read these reviews, and without interfering with the integrity of the (then anonymous) review process I can state that 2 reviewers were positive about the paper, one, rather negative. The authors submitted a revised version until the third reviewer was fully satisfied. The editor based his decision on the 4 reviews (not the short comments by you and others), the revised paper and the re-review. At the end, he submitted an editorial comment to explain his final decision.[61]

At first glance, this seems to misconstrue and to devalue science community commentary: The community commentary to which Claussen refers is far from "short" ("short comment" is the somewhat unfortunate term used by the journal to describe community comments whatever the length). Moreover, to ignore such commentary in decision making clearly defeats its purpose. But Claussen cannot mean that these comments were ignored—indeed, the authors responded to them to varying degrees. He can only be referring to Eschenbach's judgment that Juckes et al.'s manuscript was fatally flawed and McIntyre's that it falls well below the publishable threshold. It is these judgments that were not taken seriously into consideration in the final decision. Surely Claussen was correct if he concluded that Eschenbach and McIntyre would not find acceptable any article that made the claim about global warming of Juckes et al.

Claussen's letter does not mean that he was satisfied with this case of *Climate of the Past*'s peer review. In a parenthetical remark, he says: "By the way, automatic closing of the discussion phase with only one review and without comment by the editor is not possible any more." It is difficult to overemphasize how extraordinary this parenthesis is. For Claussen and his associates, Internet peer review is an emergent phenomenon, subject to correction from the experience of *all* interested parties. It is difficult also to overemphasize the importance of the other differences Internet peer review makes. Its inclusiveness means that judgments are ratified on the basis of input by whole communities, including strong dissenters. Its transparency means that most of the process is open to public view, and therefore to criticism. It means also that the process is open to graduate students who can learn from the comments how to be scientists and to scientists who can learn from them how to be better scientists. Especially important in this process of constant fine-tuning is the work of scholars such as Bornmann, who can now study these peer-review documents without the usual restrictions to access, teaching us more about science and science more about itself.

OPEN INTERNET PEER REVIEW IN THE HUMANITIES

Open Internet peer review remains a rarity in the sciences—none of the science journals mentioned in Chapter 2 has yet replaced traditional with open peer review. The humanities have been even more wary—there is no equivalent to the EGU journals. The first and only significant humanities journal to attempt some form of open peer review has been the *Shakespeare Quarterly*. To date, this journal has published three special issues generated by peer review—2010, 2011, and 2012. Their process begins with a closed review during which an editorial team decides whether to accept the essay for continued evaluation. This stage is followed by a period of open commentary involving solicited and unsolicited reviewers. After open commentary, authors revise, and the editorial team makes a final decision behind closed doors. The guest editor of the first special issue notes that "this experiment should properly be called a 'partially open peer review process' rather than an 'open' peer review process, since it includes two phases of traditional editorial oversight." The Shakespeare community's response to this experiment appears to have been enthusiastic, in contrast to the similar trial by *Nature*: Each of the 26 essays for the three *Shakespeare Quarterly* issues received comments, from as few as three to as many as 80, and many of the comments were substantive.

In the visual display of original text, reader comments, and author responses, *Shakespeare Quarterly* takes full advantage of MediaCommons Press's Internet-based platform for open discussion of displayed texts. Prospective reviewers see a screen divided in two. The larger left pane shows the draft text with the paragraphs numbered; the right pane displays links that open to display reviewer comments and author responses applicable to the numbered paragraph. This visual arrangement is much more suitable to the give-and-take of a truly open forum than the separate posting of comments used by *Climate of the Past* and other science journals (compare Figs. 5.1 and 5.2).

FIGURE 5.2 Screenshot of open commentary page for *Shakespeare Quarterly* [*Shakespeare Quarterly Open Review*, "Shakespeare and New Media"]. Video 5.1 [▶]

In many respects, *Shakespeare Quarterly*'s open commentary conforms to Habermas's ISS. Participants are identified by name. All have equal opportunity to make an assertion or respond to one. And civility prevails—exchanges between reviewers and authors have the character of friendly conversations among colleagues. Thus, Andrew Murphy, a professor at the University of St. Andrews, responds cordially to an essay by Alan Galey, a professor of information at the University of Toronto:

> Isn't the war context crucial, Alan? Hinman and Bowers were both ex-military intelligence & it was, of course, analysing aerial photographs that brought Hinman to developing his collator. There's a very useful article on this by Steven Smith in *Studies in Bibliography* 53.[62]

Galey's response is equally cordial:

> Thanks, Andy—I had missed the Smith piece, but will be sure to respond to it in my revisions. Agreed about the wartime context![63]

These typical comments show that a key element is absent from this process, one essential in the review of Juckes et al.: The *Shakespeare Quarterly* reviewers are most assuredly not expressing their opinions on whether the manuscripts ought to be rejected, accepted provisionally, or accepted without reservations. As the editor to the second special issue diplomatically advised potential reviewers: "Both praise for strengths and helpful criticism to correct weaknesses will be appreciated."[64] In effect, the editorial team had made a provisional "accept" decision before the open commentary, and the reviewers were being asked to improve papers destined for publication, papers that were, in most cases, close to publishable form. We suspect this partial open review had the effect of heavily weighting the resulting comments toward clarity and argumentative competence, and away from questions about originality or disciplinary significance. That is to say, reviewers assumed that, since the manuscripts had already been filtered to a select few by an editorial team, they had passed muster as original and possibly significant contributions to Shakespeare scholarship. Of course, commenting intelligently on the first two evaluative criteria is not an unimportant task. Only argumentative competence can certify the veracity of any original and significant claims, and only clarity can convey this competence effectively to others.

It is also important to note that, while the sciences and the humanities share the same four evaluative criteria, their views of these criteria markedly differ.[65] In the sciences, articles are judged significant to the degree with which they advance a research front. What is significant in Shakespeare studies? One answer must be discarded immediately: A scholarly article in *Shakespeare Quarterly* is significant to the degree that it accounts for the literary quality of the work in question. The Shakespeare scholars in our sample do not try to explain or to justify the Bard's literary status; they assume it. For the most part, what interests them are the socio-political, cultural, and historical issues the plays and their performances presuppose or engage. It is this frame of reference that largely determines what counts as significant work. Shakespeare studies must tell us something notable about the playwright in the context of cultural or historical forces. What does it mean to categorize the plays as histories, comedies, or tragedies, Hope and Witmore's subject?[66] What can we say about the reception of *Merchant of Venice* in post-Holocaust West Germany, Ackermann's subject?[67] How have the new computer media changed the marketing of Shakespeare by the Shakespeare industry, Rumbold's subject?[68]

Moreover, while argumentative competence is always a criterion, there is nothing like the uniformity exhibited in experimental articles, a rigor that instantiates an idealization of the scientific method (see Chapter 2). In science generally, questions of argumentative competence hinge on whether the methods employed and results obtained justify the claims being made, a subject the form of the article tends to mirror. By contrast, the argumentative structure of each humanities article is unique, constituting for its author a problem to be solved. For example, while Todd A. Borlik, a professor of English at Bloomsburg University, is sympathetic with the aims of Robert Tierney's essay on an early Japanese production of *Othello*, and highly compliments the erudition of its author, he is severely critical of the essay's argumentative structure:

> the article's greatest asset (its expertly etched vignettes of Meiji Japan's attitudes toward gender, its emergent anthropology of racial difference, and the nation's geopolitical ambitions that sparked the Sino-Japanese war) may also be its principal liability. That is, the essay at times threatens to fragment into three different essays, as the transitions between the various topics could be articulated more seamlessly. The section on "Imperial Performance and the 'House of Peoples'" does a superb and dexterous job of inter-weaving the various narrative threads. But gender, race, and imperialism are 3 hefty balls to be juggling simultaneously. To its credit, the essay manages this feat with surprising poise ... the essay does recognize these inter-sections but could—via a few choice revisions—announce its intent to chart them more clearly upfront. The final two sentences are golden—my main suggestion is merely that the paper foreshadow this conclusion sooner.[69]

Tierney took this criticism seriously. His revisions were so extensive that his essay did not appear in the special issue on Shakespeare and performance, but in the following, regular issue of the journal. Taking Borlik's advice, he virtually eliminates a long digression on gender and creates an introduction that makes clear right from the start the relationship among *Othello*, race, and empire. The last sentence of his draft, virtually unaltered in the published version, summarizes this relationship with admirable conciseness:

> Ultimately, the play *Osero* [Japanese for Othello] shows that the fashioning of a Japanese empire was inseparable from the subordination of subaltern groups to the cynical *realpolitik* of the modern state. While the government acted to mobilize these groups for service within the Japanese empire, it also treated them as disposable and callously discarded them once their services were no longer required.[70]

Many of the *Shakespeare Quarterly* open review comments concern clarity. Between the sciences and humanities, however, these norms differ dramatically. Scientists routinely speak not of writing, but of "writing up," of writing that does not call attention to itself but to its subject matter. In his *Shakespeare Quarterly* essay, Alan Galey discusses the work of Claude Shannon, especially his famous paper "A Mathematical Theory of Communication," which appeared in a 1948 issue of the *Bell System Technical Journal*. Shannon's prose easily meets this scientific standard:

> The fundamental problem of communication is that of reproducing at one point either exactly or approximately a message selected at another point. Frequently the messages have *meaning*; that is they refer to or are correlated according to some system with certain physical or conceptual entities. These semantic aspects of communication are irrelevant to the engineering problem. The significant aspect is that the actual message is one *selected from* a *set* of possible messages. The system must be designed to operate for each possible selection, not just the one which will actually be chosen since this is unknown at the time of design.[71]

In contrast, in the conclusion to an essay defending computer-mediated analyses in Shakespeare studies, Galey's prose deliberately calls attention to itself. In an exercise of stylistic agility, he leaps from W. H. Auden to "cyberinfrastructure" and back to Auden:

> "[T]hou shalt not sit/ With statisticians nor commit/ A social science" was W. H. Auden's caustic response to the humanities' postwar displacement by the sciences, part of a "Hermetic Decalogue" which includes

another commandment regularly ignored by digital humanists today (myself included): "Thou shalt not worship projects." Yet the message that computing brings an inevitable turn toward a positivist form of quantitative research—and, implicitly, away from other approaches favoring history, materiality, gender, ideology, and performance—is simply not true. Its promulgation within sectors of the digital humanities is less about recognizing the computer's essential nature, and more about a disciplinary sleight-of-hand by which post-structuralist and materialist influences are displaced by an empiricism more amenable to the cyberinfrastructure model of big science and an administered world . . . The optimism that usually attends new media can lead us to forget that our everyday acts of individual communication, supported by mobile devices and social networks, are governed by master narratives which cannot go unquestioned. Digital encryption, for example, has become so ubiquitous as to seem mundane . . . In this light, even the most mundane of digital interactions fulfills Auden's fears by deepening the militarization of all human communication.[72]

In Galey's paragraph, somewhat far-fetched literary allusions receive a warm welcome; specialized terminology from wildly differing fields is freely dispensed; and sentences are as complex (if not as elegant) as those of historian Edward Gibbon. We know these are not aberrant personal predilections but disciplinary norms because no reviewer questioned the clarity of this passage, though it was revised significantly in the final version. Moreover, Galey is capable of writing far more direct prose. He responds as follows to the open peer review comment by Martin Mueller that some texts are allographic—that is, that, like the Braille *Othello* and Norton *Othello*, they remain essentially the same despite radical differences in medium:

I understand and appreciate your second point, about allographic texts, but can't entirely agree with you. Your thought experiment is a good one, but I'd answer with one of my own. Imagine if our example wasn't Sophocles or Milton or Beethoven, but a Raymond Chandler detective story published in a cheap pulp magazine in the 1930s, surrounded by ads and other lurid paratexts. Then imagine the same Chandler story gets canonized and reprinted in a Norton anthology, on high-quality paper (well, imagine a Norton with high-quality paper . . .) and without ads or the lurid pulp-fiction cover. The sequence of letters might be exactly the same in both versions, but I think they would be different texts because I take "text" to mean more than the letters and language. That doesn't mean one can't reprint the Chandler story in a Norton anthology, but it does require us to be alive to what's lost and gained in transmission.[73]

It would be misleading to say that Galey and Shannon, or Galey the commentator versus Galey the essayist, are engaged in different enterprises. In each case, they are conforming to disciplinary norms.

Not only has the *Shakespeare Quarterly* open peer review improved essays that are on their way from drafts to publication, but the scholarly conversation that Internet peer review encouraged sometimes raised larger issues, ones that need to be addressed in the broader context of disciplinary practice. Such was the case in the special issue devoted to computer-mediated and web-based Shakespeare studies. In this issue, authors and commentators raised methodological questions. For example, Galey complained about Hope and Witmore's use of an outdated Shakespeare edition in their work of data mining—the so-called Globe edition (more than 100 years old and, therefore, in the public domain):

> Andrew [Murphy] and Jonathan [Hope], your comments here represent the crux of what I think is a huge question for digital humanities generally, not just Shakespeareans: can we take texts and corpora that are just "good enough" and call them our data set? Lots of data-mining projects in the humanities are doing exactly that, and have been for decades. I come in on the "no" side—certainly in the case of the Moby [Globe 1887 edition]—but what's more interesting about the question is that both sides of the argument make points that can't be ignored.[74]

Murphy's review of open-access Shakespeare sites in the same issue firmly criticizes the use of this text:

> Are the shortcomings of the Globe wholly fatal to the Open Source Shakespeare [OSS]? Sadly, for scholars and serious students, the answer is likely to be "yes" . . . The trouble is that the concordancing tools—which are, after all, one of the central new resources offered by OSS—are the element of the package likely to be of most interest to scholars, and no scholar could really contemplate using these tools for serious research, when the dataset they are being applied to is almost 150 years out of date.[75]

It is of no consequence that this legitimate criticism is ignored by Hope and Witmore in the context of peer review. No one could expect them to withdraw their paper, or redo it entirely, based on these comments. It would be of consequence, however, if Hope and Witmore continued to ignore these criticisms in future work, or, worse, if the profession continued to ignore them.

Peer review as practiced by *Shakespeare Quarterly* and *Climate of the Past* is similar to traditional peer review and differs from ISS in that it privileges the journal editors and invited reviewers over authors, calls a halt to further discussion after a specified period, and still keeps some portion of the process closed to the public. But it is consistent with ISS and differs from traditional peer review in two important respects: It is far more transparent and it makes members of the discourse community part of the process. Equally important, it makes a provisional version of the article or book available to readers shortly after submittal. It is thus disheartening to find *Shakespeare Quarterly* has not repeated open peer review since the 2012 issue, nor has any other significant humanities journal adopted it. Longstanding institutional practices die hard.

PEER SOURCING: THE WAVE OF THE FUTURE?

In *Planned Obsolescence*, Kathleen Fitzpatrick argues for a radically different system of open review for scholarly books and articles.[76] In Fitzpatrick's view, the problem with traditional peer review is that "small groups of the like-minded reinforce one another's biases and produce unspoken social pressures toward conformity with what appears to be majority opinion."[77] Her solution to overcoming this corruption of the system is "peer-to-peer review," which involves eliminating assigned reviewers and editors and replacing them with communal reviewers. In Fitzpatrick's new form of knowledge evaluation, authors first publish online without the benefit of any outside reviews. It is at this point that community review begins, a process open to all and without a specific end point. The volunteer reviewers judge the worth of what has already been made public.

Fitzpatrick feels that genuine peer-to-peer review would require "one's contributions to reviewing being considered as important as, if not more important than, one's individual [writing] projects."[78] With that in mind, as an incentive to comment, she recommends authors only gain the privilege "to publish [books and essays] in these new electronic publishing networks by actively serving as reviewers," say, by a requirement to review three articles to be able to publish one. Moreover, she recommends reviewers' judgments themselves be subject to judgment, a shift in the target of epistemic vigilance: "In a peer-to-peer reviewing system, 'reputation' will be determined not simply through an assessment of the scholar's own production but through an assessment of her reviewing practices."[79] Peer-to-peer review is a process that the Internet seems born to support. Absent the Internet, its implementation is inconceivable.

One might object that the open review system proposed by Fitzpatrick places a heavy burden on professional time and undermines the timely certification of knowledge, the central concern of traditional peer review. In a footnote to the manuscript, Fitzpatrick raises the first objection, then counters it:

> A brief note to acknowledge another difficulty in the system I am proposing: it will require a phenomenal amount of labor on the part of all scholars as readers and discussants of one another's work. That having been said, it might also be worth pointing out that such labor is already being done, arguably in a less-equitably distributed fashion; review is certainly a function within which we'd do well to draw upon the "wisdom of the crowds," particularly as there are far more potential readers for any given text than two or three select reviewers, and as such crowd-sourced review will enable us to see how critical opinion of a text develops over time.[80]

But the review work "already being done" by two or three assigned reviewers implies the feasibility of the current system. However imperfect, it works. By contrast, the development of a scientific or scholarly reward system that requires researchers to volunteer to critique the work of others "on behalf of the community" would require a major cultural shift. This seems unlikely, however attractive it might sound at first glance. It is also worth noting that labor under the current system does not go unrewarded. The request to review, couched as a favor, is rightly perceived as a compliment that defers to the potential reviewer's expertise. Moreover, it is labor that will eventually be reciprocated when reviewers themselves submit a manuscript for review. A gift that is given will later be received; fairness is operative.

Fitzpatrick does not mention another problem with the system she suggests. Because peer-to-peer review is never over, documents under this regime would never achieve the stability—and therefore the epistemological status—of knowledge that it is legitimate to employ or to criticize in the public sphere. Our initial anecdote concerning David Raup's experience is pertinent in this connection.

Aptly, Fitzpatrick was not content merely to recommend an alternative; hers was an experiment designed to test and exemplify a limited version of it. A MediaCommons Press site she hosts—the same platform on which *Shakespeare Quarterly* launched its experiment in open review—consists of the manuscript of her book, *Planned Obsolescence*, along with 259 comments by 44 commentators.[81] The above quotation in a footnote to her book was a response to reader commentary. That aside, nearly all the comments concern minor adjustments in a text that was, to begin with, close to its published version—that is, the process mirrors the *Shakespeare Quarterly* trial. Two years after the initiation of communal review, in 2011, New York University

Press published a hardcopy and electronic version of her book. While the decision to publish was based on traditional closed peer review, in the final version she did take into account the comments from the communal review.

CONCLUSION

We cannot say that any journal in the sciences or the humanities would be mistaken in refusing to jettison closed peer review and to replace it with some form of open review based on the successful models of the EGU or *Shakespeare Quarterly*. While the examples in this chapter suggest that open peer review is a better realization of Habermas's communicative vision than traditional peer review, there is no clear case that widespread adoption of open forums would guarantee that all potentially worthwhile research results would always be shared with appropriate peers. But while the evidence in favor of open peer review is sparse in the sciences, and absent entirely in the humanities, the evidence against its implementation is nonexistent. In the experiments so far, there are no horror stories, no examples of vituperation drowning out rational debate, even with regard to controversial claims on global warming. When Internet peer review has been studied, the results have been positive. Our chapter suggests that manuscripts that pass through the process seem to be more clearly written and more rigorously argued.

High-impact journals like *Nature* do have special problems with any form of open peer review. Surely, they cannot be expected to subject every one of their 10,000 annual submissions to an open process! But the challenges for high-impact journals are hardly insurmountable. A sizable submission fee—say $500—would reduce submissions markedly as well as ease the burden on editorial costs: Scientists would think twice whether their paper *really* was front-page news. In any case, for high-impact journals, Internet peer review would become operative only when, after intensive editorial screening, the number of submissions became manageable. These are in any case very special problems, existing only at the margins of academic publishing. Most journals in the sciences and the humanities have submission rates low enough to be easily manageable under the conditions of Internet peer review. These journals could transform themselves now, adopting one of the existing successful models. But they might do more than imitate; they might exhibit some of the inventive brilliance of an Ulrich Pöschl, the architect of the model adopted by the EGU, recreating peer review to serve new and useful academic purposes.

Another stumbling block for subscription-based journals like *Nature* is that they do not want to grant free access even to drafts of articles they might one day publish in revised form, a practice that might diminish their number of paying customers.

A partial way around that problem would be for subscription journals to conduct a closed online discussion with the authors, assigned referees, and editors, then make that review public to subscribers and open to their comment after acceptance of a submission—as in *The EMBO Journal* of the European Molecular Biology Organization. In addition, following the *Shakespeare Quarterly* model, select articles or even whole issues might be periodically subjected to open review by both assigned and volunteer reviewers. The point is that no one model of open peer review need fit all circumstances.

Our examples of Internet peer and communal review make the current system more transparent and participatory; they recognize that the Internet is a vehicle ideally suited to realizing these goals. None of these suggestions assumes, absurdly, that the humanities and the sciences share common goals concerning what knowledge is or how it should be generated. We assume only that the humanities and the sciences share common communicative goals—to publish articles or approve research proposals that are judged by experts to be clearly written, argumentatively sound, and original and significant contributions in their fields. It is this assumption that makes the literature on peer review and the successful experiments in open peer review relevant across the board.

6

EVALUATION AFTER PUBLICATION

Setting the Record Straight

JUST HOW MUCH confidence should we place in published research findings, even if peer reviewed? What should we ignore, reject, modify, incorporate, pursue? To answer these questions, the sciences and the humanities must be continually in the business of keeping the record of knowledge straight at the edge, an enterprise the Internet can fruitfully enhance. Accordingly, this chapter looks at some Internet-based possibilities concerning this postpublication process: watchdog blogs in the sciences, blogs and discussion forums in the sciences and humanities, and book and article reviews in the humanities. For these activities, as for peer review, Habermas's ideal speech situation provides a useful theoretical framework. The goal is the same: the achievement of rational consensus concerning the originality, significance, argumentative competence, and clarity of expression of the work in question.

WATCHDOG BLOGS IN THE SCIENCES

After reading Chaucer's *Canterbury Tales*—after the sweeping "Prologue," the dramatic "Pardoner's Tale," the raucous "Miller's Tale," the sermon that is the "Parson's Tale"—readers come upon what may well be the world's first "Retraction Notice":

> Now I pray to all who hear or read this little treatise, that if there is anything in it that they like, they thank our Lord Jesus Christ for it, from whom proceeds

all wisdom and goodness. And if there is anything that displeases them, I pray also that they attribute it to inadvertence rather than intent. I would have done better if I could. For the Bible says, "All that is written is written to support the teaching our faith" and that is what I wish to do. Therefore I beseech you meekly, for the mercy of God, that you pray for me that Christ have mercy on me and forgive my sins, especially my translations and works of worldly vanity, which I revoke in my retractions.[1]

In acknowledging error, some editors of science journals lack the poet's candor. One minced no words, responding to a request from the editors of the blog "Retraction Watch"—Adam Marcus and Ivan Oransky—for reasons that a paper was retracted with the following terse comment: "It's none of your damn business."[2] This reluctance to admit error with candor and dispatch can have serious consequences. When Pei-Suen Tsou and his coworkers published an article on the effect of oxidative stress, they found useful a much-cited article in the *Journal of Biological Chemistry* by two Japanese researchers, Naohito Aoki and Tsukasa Matsuda, published 12 years before. Their discussion contains a paragraph in which a conclusion of this earlier article is incorporated into their argument by means of endnote 42, a reference to PTP1B, an enzyme. We can safely ignore the details of their argument, paying attention only to the fact that one of Aoki and Matsuda's conclusions has become part of it, as revealed by our italics:

> We examined the expression and function of PTP1B, which has been reported to be a negative regulator of receptor tyrosine kinases such as PDGFR (30,31). The association between PTP1B and PDGFR is further supported by a study using PTP1B-knockout mice (38). In addition to the PDGFR pathway, PTP1B appears to be a negative regulator in both insulin and leptin signaling pathways (39,40). *Epidermal growth factor receptor (41) and tyrosine-phosphorylated proteins such as STAT-5 (42) have also been shown to be targets of PTP1B.* Although the expression of PTP1B was similar in normal dermal fibroblasts and SSc dermal fibroblasts (Figure 4B), the activity of PTP1B was significantly lower in SSc fibroblasts, suggesting that only a portion of the expressed PTP1B is active in SSc fibroblasts.[3]

Were reference 42 eliminated the article's case would not fail, though it would be weakened. As it turns out, it must be weakened, for in March of the previous year, the Japanese paper had been retracted: "This article has been withdrawn by the authors" was all that was said. This omission provoked only consternation on the part of the two editors of "Retraction Watch":

Whoa there! TMI! [too much information] Don't share so much!

Alas, that's all [the editor] wrote. In fact, neither the abstract nor the article itself is marked as retracted, so it's worse than useless.[4]

It would be a serious mistake to say that Marcus and Oransky are just reporting; they are deeply engaged in the politics of change, a politics with important consequences for what counts as knowledge. True, they are merely publicizing error, not detecting it. Nevertheless, they are not merely participants, but leaders in the process of scientific self-correction.

What is "Retraction Watch"? Begun by two medical journalists in August 2000, it is a blog with a difference. It was hosting about 100,000 page views a month shortly after its launch and by mid-2014 claimed 33,490 followers, a testimony to its importance as an influence in setting the record of science straight. In an entry called "What People Are Saying about Retraction Watch,"[5] the site posts prominent endorsements of its mission. One such is from the former editor-in-chief of *BMJ*, Richard Smith: "Retraction Watch is one of the best innovations in science in recent years. The wit enhances the message. Tune in." In a Twitter feed, John Rennie, former editor-in-chief of *Scientific American*, concurs that the blog is "one of the most important recent developments in science journalism." In *Columbia Journalism Review*, Craig Silverman calls "Retraction Watch" "a new blog that should be required reading for anyone interested in scientific journalism or the issue of accuracy."[6] Ben Goldacre of the *Guardian* concludes: "Ivan Oransky and Adam Marcus are two geeks who set up a web site called Retraction Watch because it was clear that retractions are often handled badly."[7] An editorial in a Canadian newspaper asserts:

> Fortunately, there are some people in the world of science who think more attention should be paid to retractions. Two of them have started a popular blog, Retraction Watch, which has shed light on about 200 retractions since its inception a year ago. The authors, both medical journalists, hope to "open a window onto the world of scientific publishing, and, by implication, science itself." If scientific publishers cared more about transparency than damage control, that window would be easier to pry open, and science would be better for it.[8]

We will also be discussing "Abnormal Science," a German blog started in 2011 and written by Joerg Zwirner, a former university science professor. It is defunct now, reportedly because of the editor's health problems.[9] Unlike "Retraction Watch," "Abnormal Science" was devoted first to revealing and then to publicizing error, plagiarism, and fraud. Like "Retraction Watch" it was a blog deeply implicated in the politics of change, the process of setting the record of science straight. According to Zwirner:

> With this blog I hope to contribute to a critique of the absence of transparency and of the secretive machinations of German universities when it comes to scientific misconduct. The public review of cases in the news illustrates serious flaws in the process of revealing misconduct. The behavior of the German Ombudsman is a notorious example.[10]

WHAT WATCHDOG BLOGS REVEAL

What is revealed in these watchdog blogs need not be the consequence of scientific misconduct. On January 7, 2011, "Retraction Watch" reported that an article had been retracted because researchers mistakenly used the wrong mice, the result of a misreading of a confusing catalog entry.[11] On January 19, an article that appeared in the *Journal of the National Cancer Institute* was quickly withdrawn by its authors: A conceptual error had been made. Of the latter case, "Retraction Watch" commented: "no misconduct involved—just good old-fashioned self-correcting science. So we applaud Baker, Simon, their co-authors, and the JNCI."[12]

Nevertheless, retractions very often involve plagiarism and fraud. For plagiarism, the rule is this: The ideas that scientists present to their public should be entirely original, except where a citation is provided; their prose should also be wholly theirs, except where quotation marks are present. When Reginald Smith published two overlapping papers in two journals, he clearly violated this principle. A paper published in the *European Respiratory Journal* was retracted by editorial fiat for the same reason:

> Although the two papers were not exactly identical, there were overlaps between the two papers, and more importantly, the authors have failed to mention the existence of a closely related paper, using the same cohort of patients, and being submitted to another journal. We do not say whether this was intentional or simply due to a misunderstanding of our journal's policy, but the fact that the authors have failed to report (either to us or to the chief editor of *Respiratory Medicine*) of this almost concomitant submission of two very closely related papers was real and undisputable.[13]

However defined, plagiarism is an offense against, and only against, the social community that is science; it does not affect the community's knowledge base.

It has no consequences for the realm of scientific knowledge. It is its effect on scientific knowledge that makes fraud the far graver offense. The case of Silvia Bulfone-Paus's group, a case we reconstruct from "Retraction Watch" and "Abnormal Science," reveals the importance of the Internet and its blogs in ferreting out fraud, pursuing the truth relentlessly despite considerable institutional opposition. Marcus, Oransky, and Zwirner provide us with a window into institutional resistance to detecting and correcting fraud and in punishing offenders.

What is symptomatic of an article in need of retraction on account of fraud? In general, it is published in journals with a relatively high impact factor, reflecting the ambition of its first authors; it frequently has a relatively large number of co-authors, a tactic that obscures responsibility; it is very often one of a series, a repetition indicating a pattern of deception; and, finally, the delay between publication and retraction is typically long, resulting in large part from the authors' reluctance to admit fault.[14] The Silvia Bulfone-Paus case exhibits all of these characteristics.[15–18] Twelve of her group's papers were retracted after an extended period of delay, clearly marked by resistance on her part as manager of the group. On average these papers had nearly eight authors. Their impact factor averaged 5.813, over double the average for journals in immunology, Bulfone-Paus's field.

The first hint of difficulty with Bulfone-Paus's laboratory's work surfaced in November 2009, when Karin Wiebauer, a Ph.D. working in her laboratory at the German Research Center Borstel, alerted her to the possibility that some papers published by her research team may contain manipulated images. Far from acting at once, Bulfone-Paus waited until February 29, 2010, to inform her superiors of the possibility. Only in May was an internal investigation initiated. Apparently as a result of this investigation—its report was never released—in July 2010 an external investigation began, headed by Werner Seeger of the University of Giessen.

In the meantime, the Internet had not been silent on this matter. In his private blog, Martin Frost, a pseudonym for a person unknown to any of the parties in the investigation, openly accused Bulfone-Paus of fraud. The first reaction of the scientific community was severely critical of an interference that it regarded as gratuitous and unwarranted. In September, a *Nature* editorial accused Frost of carrying out a "trial-by-Internet" and threatening "the impartiality of misconduct inquiries."[19] Two reader comments appended to the *Nature* article reflected the conflicting emotions within the scientific community about this case at the time. The first, by Anurag Chaurasia, read:

> Editor is right that being an educated person we should behave with dignity in the charges of scientific misconduct. Such cases should be kept secret, confidential till the enquiry is over.

The second comment, by Eugenie Samuel Reich, read:

> Without knowing who is right in the case discussed, I feel this editorial sends
> the wrong message. In many cases, public allegations are the only way to get the
> truth out to other members of the scientific community, and the public who
> fund the work or decision-makers who base policy on it. *Nature* has itself made
> [similar] serious allegations public [in other cases].

In October, Frost received a letter from a Hamburg law firm, presumably initiated by Bulfone-Paus, asking him to remove his allegedly libelous comments. He
did not comply. In November–December 2010, the report of the external committee was made public. It concluded that two postdoctoral students, co-authors
Elena Bulanova and Vadim Budagian, were responsible for image manipulation;
however, there was no falsification of data "in the sense that anything was made up."
There was no doubt, however, that "fundamental responsibility" for any scientific
misconduct had to rest on the senior author, also Director of Immunology and Cell
Biology. Despite this finding, there was no reason for wholesale retraction because
there was no indication, the report asserted, that the "core findings" of these papers
were in any way undermined by the fraudulent images. In November, pending the
public release of this report, Bulfone-Paus was asked to resign as Director. She did
not comply.

In December, an e-mail from Karin Wiebauer appeared on Martin Frost's blog.
This appearance represented the turning of the tide against Bulfone-Paus's group. In
less-than-perfect and often boldfaced English, Wiebauer detailed the difficulties she
had in getting a hearing for her warnings, and, later, her accusations of fraud, accusations that pointed directly at Bulfone-Paus's group:

> Incidentally, in the long year, that followed my email to Silvia on 4th November
> 2009, I took great pains to stay on the "legal" route for whistleblowers, trying
> to keep this case within the limits of the scientific community and, most nota-
> bly, acting always under my full name.
>
> Did it lead me anywhere? It didn't. Instead, I had to endure the mind-
> boggling lies and/or excuses of all parties involved in this case of scientific
> misconduct, starting with **Prof. Bulfone-Paus** and including the poor co-
> worker condemned to reproduce non-existing data, the **Editors-in-Chief of**
> *Journal of Immunology* and *Molecular and Cellular Biology*, **the speakers
> of ombudsman**, and other committees, and—last not least—the "**Deutsche
> Forschungsgemeinschaft**" (DFG) [German Research Society]: This organi-
> zation provided most of the money that enabled Prof. Bulfone-Paus to publish

a series of science fiction articles for the past 10 years (SFB 506/C5, SFB 415/A10). It also approved the establishment of SFB 877 (the successor of SFB 415) that contains a proposal by Prof. Bulfone-Paus, which was based in part on publications that were purportedly under investigation.[20]

These accusations were accompanied by a visual series that made the degree of image manipulation abundantly clear. Figure 6.1 shows one of Wiebauer's mashups. It is hard to believe in the innocence of Bulfone-Paus's group when we see Figure 5D transformed by Photoshop to Figure 3B.

Now the story approached its climax. On March 16, Research Center Borstel received an open letter, signed by 24 researchers from America, England, Sweden, Germany, Italy, and Israel, a stout defense of Bulfone-Paus as a researcher above reproach. It was clear testimony to the high regard for her genuine achievements within the relevant scientific community. On April 6, the Board of Directors of the Research Center Borstel responded, defending its case against Bulfone-Paus.[21] They pointed to "Silvia Bulfone-Paus's prolonged failure to be completely up-front about the nature and extent of the fraud occurring in her lab." They added that "Silvia Bulfone-Paus received repeated warnings (in writing) from her former co-worker Dr. Karin Wiebauer as early as January 2004." They dismissed those who would trivialize the consequences of her misconduct:

> It has been stated that, since many of the incriminated manipulations "only" concern Western Blots showing loading controls, the main results reported in the papers appeared not to be affected by the manipulations. The data supporting this contention, however, have not yet been examined by independent referees from the respective Journals.

Finally, they stated unequivocally that "the principal investigator bears full responsibility for any faulted data in publications." As a consequence of their brief, Bulfone-Paus was demoted: She would no longer be Director.

What was the motivation for Bulfone-Paus's misconduct? Why did this competent and talented researcher become implicated in fraud due to image manipulation in her lab? According to Robert Merton, there are five shared norms essential to the proper conduct of science—originality, communalism, universalism, disinterestedness, and organized skepticism.[22] These do not describe the way all scientists behave; they describe the way all scientists ought to behave. Science editors whose retraction notices lack candor violate the norm of communalism; plagiarists violate the norm of originality; fraudsters, like those in the Bulfone-Paus case, violate the norms of disinterestedness, universalism, and organized skepticism. Why?

(a)

Multi-Step Duplication

Although this example of an image manipulation does not belong to the "Death deflected...." article, I included it, because it is quite an artful and the most interesting example of the duplication techniques shown so far.

Method:
Non-linear "cut and paste" technique

The Westernblot row in Fig. 5D, supposedly showing PLCγ1, was extended vertically, rotated 180° and five out of the six lanes were used for the presentation of IL-2Rγ in Fig. 3B.

Please note: In this method, it is of paramount importance not to forget "the pencilling-in of [the correct] two molecular weight size markers afterwards"! This does not always happen.

It is also not easy to spot: I missed it in my very first analysis of the Bulanova et al. (2001) JI article...

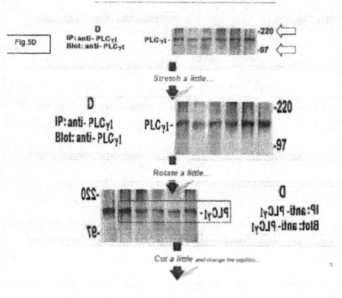

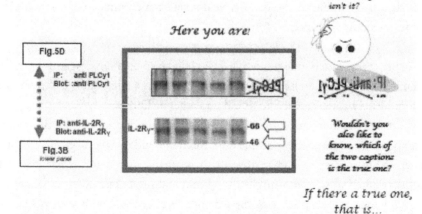

FIGURE 6.1 Mashup illustrating image manipulation in a 1999 retracted article by S. Bulfone-Paus et al. ["Frost's Meditations," now defunct].

They do so because there is a problem with these norms. Behaving well may be a necessary condition for a successful scientific career, but it is never sufficient. Adherence determines only membership in good standing; it does not determine relative status, the size of one's share in the rewards one's fellows can offer. This size is a consequence of the significance of scientists' work to their peers, its impact on their particular community and on science as a whole. While it is possible to increase one's status without deviating from any community norms, it is also possible to achieve the same result more swiftly simply by violating them. In a healthy community, there is consensus that the benefits from adherence will exceed those of violation, that crime does not pay. But if this consensus does not obtain routinely—if adherence is perceived by some as a path to failure in the competition for status—a state of anomie may well arise. For some at least, the norms cease to be compelling. As more and more norm violations succeed, as they lead to an increase in status for more and more members of the community, radical indifference deepens and spreads; as it does, deviant behavior spreads. If the infection becomes general, the community becomes pathological: Deviant behavior becomes a serious problem rather than an aberration. Scientists can no longer be fully trusted to do trustworthy science.

The temptation to which the Bulfone-Paus group succumbed is not theirs alone; it is a problem within the biomedical community of which they are a part, a community that suffers from increasing anomie, a state of affairs in which the norms of originality, communality, universalism, disinterestedness, and organized skepticism are in constant peril. Too often, in biomedical articles recommendations and conclusions are not supported by data; too often their significance is exaggerated.[23-26] Too often, conclusions are biased by financial ties to sponsoring pharmaceutical companies.[27-30] Too often, there is a lack of transparency: Protocols are not presented and vital methodological information is missing.[31,32] Too often, industry-supported studies in medical journals are more likely to report positive findings, regardless of the evidence, and to support new and off-label treatments over standard ones.[33-36] Despite the heavy involvement of industry in funding research, a survey established that only 26% of North American medical journals required disclosure of any conflict of interest that might arise from drug company subsidies.[37]

As a consequence of these trends, we might infer that the number of candidates for retraction exceeds by far the number of articles actually retracted: Bulfone-Paus and her fellows, exposed by "Retraction Watch," are the tip of the iceberg. This is indeed the case. On the basis of one count, between 1995 and 2004, there were 328 retractions out of 5,041,587 articles listed in PubMed.[38] This is an absurdly small number (33 per year or 0.0065%), given the articles likely in need of retraction. A survey of over 3,000 researchers funded by the National Institutes of Health (NIH) reported that one-third of the respondents admitted to "a range of questionable practices that are striking in their breadth and prevalence."[39] Owning up to falsifying results was rare (0.3%), though still significantly higher than the number of papers actually retracted. If 0.3% of about five million papers published in a decade are fraudulent, then about 15,000 are; that is about 1,500 a year.

The NIH study also provides evidence of undue influence. A substantial number of respondents acknowledged changing important aspects of a study owing to pressure from the funding source. Also alarming was the fact that nearly a third of respondents self-reported sloppy recordkeeping, a practice that makes extremely difficult the assessment of human error, experimental replicability, or fraud. In addition, the results of this survey may be an underestimation because, in all probability, misbehaving scientists were less likely to respond and those responding were more likely to underreport their deviance. The problems such unprofessional practices create would not be solved, however, even if all fraudulent, biased, or otherwise tainted articles were eventually retracted or tagged. Tagging the retracted articles online can do nothing to purge the literature of the many citations to flawed articles, citations that permanently infect the literature.[40] Indeed, flawed articles are sometimes cited, even after correction or retraction, partly because they are sometimes cited though not consulted.

A recent case of fraud suggests that times may have changed thanks to watchdog blogs. The case bears some resemblances to that of the Bulfone-Paus group. On January 30, 2014, *Nature* published two articles by Haruko Obokata and coworkers claiming to have discovered a simple method for converting the blood cells of newborn mice to stem cells. It too involved papers with many authors. It too appeared in a high-impact journal. It too involved repeated denials of wrongdoing by the principal investigator. However, the time between publication and revelation of probable fraud and retraction was far shorter. Starting on the day of official publication, a blog by researcher Paul Knoepfler reported the articles as "really important" but perhaps "too good and too simple of a method to be true."[41] Almost immediately, someone posted his concerns on the watchdog blog called "PubPeer."[42] That opened the floodgates. Bloggers almost immediately raised serious doubts about the articles' contents: in particular, doctored images, plagiarized texts, and, most damning of all, questions about data reproducibility. On April 1, within only two months, an investigating committee formed by the affiliated research institute found Obokata guilty of scientific misconduct.[43] Having allowed time to confirm the irreproducibility of the reported method by others, *Nature* retracted both articles in July 2014, five months after publication. At that time, the electronic versions of both articles were prominently time stamped in the front matter as "Retracted." In September of the same year, "Retraction Watch" published the negative peer review comments of a 2012 manuscript submitted to *Science* by Obokata and coworkers on the same subject.[44] It had been rejected. The case is encouraging. But one swallow does not make a summer.

HOW WATCHDOG BLOGS WORK

The websites of Marcus, Oransky, and Zwirner are engaged in a heroic quest, designed to rescue not just bioscience, but all science from the throes of error and self-deception. To do so, they turn the recent past into a story with a moral, a Pilgrim's Progress of scientists caught in the snares of institutional constraints, tempted by sin into deviance. But can such moral journeys rest, as those of Marcus, Oransky, and Zwirner largely rest, on the accusations of anonymous whistleblowers? Should not accusations of plagiarism, error, and fraud be pursued only through proper institutional channels, behind closed doors, rather than aired in public? And if pursued beyond proper channels, should whistleblowers be permitted to remain anonymous?

Those in favor of proper channels ignore the evidence that these fail to work properly more often than not, a fact that "Retraction Watch" and "Abnormal Science" regularly document and as the Bulfone-Paus and other similar cases amply support. Speaking of the German Ombudsman in charge of investigating fraud, Zwirner vents his understandable frustration at the approach through proper channels:

> Fig. 3C is obviously and unequivocally manipulated. The correct control stain (double color stain) could prove it beyond doubt . . . Instead you accept the wrong control stain (single color). An analogy to your approach would be that a court accepted a kitchen knife as weapon in a homicide case although the victim had a gunshot wound in the forehead and the suspect offender was in possession of the gun in question.[45]

Those against the option of anonymity seem unaware that the public forum afforded by a blog is well suited for exposing the evidence for plagiarism, error, and fraud. What counts in the cases reported in "Retraction Watch" and "Abnormal Science" is, after all, not the motive of the whistleblower but the evidence produced in defense of claims. Moreover, those against anonymity seem also unaware that whistleblowing legislation has repeatedly failed to protect whistleblowers from retaliation.[46] Those against anonymity also ignore the fact that blogs allow anyone to respond almost immediately to an accusation, including those most knowledgeable about what really happened, the alleged perpetrator. Finally, those in favor of anonymity ignore the existence of libel law as a protection for those falsely accused of plagiarism or fraud.

Stories with a moral like those in "Retraction Watch" and "Abnormal Science" are the routine products of investigative journalism. In such journalism, "narrative is an instrument of both cognitive and moral understanding. More than that, narrative is the instrument by which these two intellectual impulses are united."[47] It is a union abetted by irony, a tool designed to persuade readers to share the authors' indignation at the violation of Merton's norms and to spur the demand for a return to their adherence.[48] In telling Bulfone-Paus's story, for example, "Retraction Watch" combined cognitive and moral understanding in a single narrative, one honed throughout by structural and verbal irony. Structural irony contrasted Bulfone-Paus's respected position with her alleged misconduct, apparently trying to quash a whistleblower in her lab and threatening to sue another. This ironic stance was seconded by its verbal counterpart:

> Some of the notices have gone into great detail about what was wrong with the original papers, and journals have even allowed the team to declare that some of the results had been replicated. One simply said there had been misconduct.
> Then there's this [retraction notice]:
> This article has been withdrawn by the authors.
> That certainly clears things right up.[49]

This verbal irony was also seconded by readers who commented on the case, one of whom was none other than Joerg Zwirner:

> EMBO Journal editor Bernd Pulverer has done science a disservice. Without good cause he provided platform to people (shall we still call them scientists?) who gambled away their credibility. Key experiments reproduced and confirmed? No proof? No evidence? Come on! Bulfone-Paus is not worthy of our trust anymore.[50]

In other "Retraction Watch" cases, where the violation seems particularly outrageous, irony's siblings, sarcasm and ridicule, play a significant role:

> A team of Australian medical writers who analyzed four decades worth of retractions has reached the conclusion—we trust you're sitting—that people in their profession are more honest than, well, the rest of us.[51]

This freedom to belittle does not extend to the web equivalent of face-to-face interaction, an indication that Marcus and Oransky's moral compass is in order.

Responding to a comment, Marcus's tone is as always sober, indicating by a modulation that ridicule extends only to the article, not to its authors:

> Our skepticism stems largely from the significant limitation of the study—the inability to analyze papers in which the work of medical writers has not been disclosed—and the implicit claim that medical writers add a veneer of ethical purity. In our view, transparency and the willingness to disclose (authorship, pharma involvement, etc.) probably are the best insurance against misconduct.[52]

While "Abnormal Science" was Zwirner's personal blog, "Retraction Watch" is also a forum open to a public discussion aimed at reaching a rational consensus on the subject of scientific misconduct. A commitment to Habermasian ideals is embodied in Marcus and Oransky's policy statement: "It may not be clear to those who feel the need to resort to . . . personal attacks that they destroy the discourse that we and others have worked so hard to build on Retraction Watch, but it is abundantly clear to us and many others. The same goes for unfounded allegations and unverified facts."[53]

Marcus and Oransky and Zwirner also extend the permissible scope of investigative reporting by their willingness to editorialize, to make their moral mission explicit. It is this willingness that is behind a "Retraction Watch" entry that attempts to give journals retraction grades. Of 12 retraction notices, the most impressive acknowledge misconduct and do not permit the authors to make unsubstantiated claims concerning the remaining worth of their retracted papers. Less worthy notices mention that there are irregularities but do not tell us what they are. Even less worthy notices say nothing whatever about the cause of the retraction. The four worst notices specify exactly what was wrong but then allow "the authors to claim—without the journal editors having reviewed any findings, one of them told us—that the data and conclusions had been confirmed." For example, "The authors declare that key experiments presented in the majority of these figures were recently reproduced and that the results confirmed the experimental data and the conclusions drawn from them."[54]

Zwirner goes even further out on a moral limb in his attack on a melanoma study that, he alleges, continues to recruit patients in defiance of medical plausibility. His less-than-perfect English does not interfere with his message:

> The official Website of the Department of Dermatology, the first and foremost purpose of which is to inform patients, their physicians as well as scientists and students delivers false, misleading informations on a large scale dendritic

cell-based tumor vaccination trial. The Website is an important tool for the recruitment of melanoma patients in future trials with dendritic cell-based immune therapy. From the perspective of patients and their physicians it is totally inacceptable that the true fate of this multicenter study and the inefficacy of the dendritic cell therapy as found in that trial is not revealed.[55]

Reader commentary extends investigative reporting's scope even further. In "Retraction Watch," dozens comment, some only once, some seldom, some frequently. Some prefer pseudonyms; some reveal their identity either directly or indirectly. The case of ktwop, alias Krishna Pillai, a research engineer with a doctorate, reveals what a frequent commentator can contribute to reinforce the goals of investigative journalism by employing its methods: straight reporting informed by structural irony, criticism edged with sarcasm, editorializing. Concerning the precarious state of academic integrity in Chinese science, ktwop employs structural irony:

After a quick trial, a local court in Beijing convicted urologist Xiao Chuang-Guo on 10 October of assaulting two well-known advocates of academic integrity in China. One victim of the attacks was Fang Shimin, freelance writer and self-appointed watchdog of research misconduct. Fang had questioned Xiao's academic achievements, but this was not what prompted the attack, Xiao claimed. Xiao told the court that he had a decade-long personal conflict with Fang, mainly because Fang had insulted Xiao's wife and teacher.[56]

A comment on an English case of scientific fraud is edged with sarcasm:

Perhaps friend Jatinder can follow the example of "zu Googleberg" [a reference to a German Defense Minister, Karl Theodor zu Guttenberg, dismissed over a plagiarism scandal]. As the plagiarist he has retracted his own PhD and Angela Merkel has let him continue in his job. But he has a personal fortune of € 300 million to fall back on![57]

Of a journal editor who was not forthcoming about the reasons for retraction, ktwop editorializes:

It is increasingly obvious that it is not just the ethics of researchers which can be involved in retractions. The ethics of the journal editors and the journals themselves (including their peer-review process) are obviously very relevant. He may be a wonderful surgeon and husband for all I know but as an editor-in-chief he is no role-model and he does not impress.[58]

For Marcus and Oransky, for Zwirner, and for their reader-commentators, narrative tinged with irony is the tool with which to judge and to transform the moral order so that it conforms more closely to the acknowledged norms of science.

There are limits to this approach. "Retraction Watch" never probes beneath the surface to the source behind misconduct, to science as a social institution, to an enterprise that has silently incorporated into itself incentives at odds with its norms. To its credit, "Abnormal Science" does raise this issue, though Zwirner, a scientist but not a social scientist, lacks the tools to address it fully:

> There has been a neglect of the sociological aspects of scientific misbehavior to this day. One might argue that misconduct in science is as much a sociological phenomenon as a scientific or legal issue. Such reasoning has already been voiced in regard to doping in sports. . . . However, to keep sports as well as science clean, it might prove to be insufficient to focus exclusively on the scientist who personally fabricated, falsified or plagiarized, or the athlete who used performance enhancers. Such a personalization of misconduct might distract from other, equally important causes of failures of compliance with accepted standards in science and sports.[59]

Still, it would be unfair to judge these blogs against a standard they were not designed to meet. In Ivan Oransky and Adam Marcus's "Retraction Watch," and Joerg Zwirner's "Abnormal Science," everyday professional life is encountered, reflected on, and infused with moral purpose. Marcus, Oransky, and Zwirner see themselves as successful only to the extent that scientific journals openly retract erroneous, plagiarized, or fraudulent articles and at the same time tell the scientific public exactly why they are doing so. They are conservative, motivated by the pressing need to keep science true to an established principle: self-correction. In our view, "Retraction Watch" and "Abnormal Science" succeed in the task they undertake: setting the scientific record straight by turning their personal blogs into a form of investigative journalism, reborn on the web. The error, plagiarism, and fraud that Marcus, Oransky, and Zwirner expose and publicize cannot be easily dismissed; nor can their insistence on open acknowledgment be readily gainsaid.

HUMANITIES POST-PEER REVIEW

In the seven decades since they were first articulated, Merton's norms have been subject to a small library of commentary and controversy. However, in all that time, so far as we can tell, no one has noticed what seems to us obvious: Communalism, universalism, disinterestedness, organized skepticism, and originality are norms central to *any* enterprise devoted to the creation of knowledge.[60] In saying this, we are not trying to turn the humanities into sciences. We are saying only what we take to be commonplace: Scholars in the humanities are expected to share their results freely with others, to apply common disciplinary standards in their work, to be motivated only by a search for truth, to be skeptical of the truth of their own statements as well as those of others, and to generate new knowledge from their efforts. Setting the record straight, in the humanities as well as in the sciences, means heeding the norms of disinterestedness and organized skepticism; it means acknowledging one's own errors of fact and interpretation when they inadvertently occur, and pointing out those of others, whether inadvertent or not.

To do so, however, requires appropriate channels of communication. In the sciences, concerning the genre of preference, the article, several mechanisms are already in place to supplement peer review. In the sciences, it is possible to write letters to the editor for publication; in a great many cases, it is possible to comment on articles online without any barrier due to editorial filtering and without the delays inherent on a world of print (see Chapter 2). In all cases, it is possible independently to intervene on the web, as did Martin Frost and Karen Wiebauer. In addition, watchdog blogs like "Retraction Watch" and "Abnormal Science" supplement these traditional routes to correction, making up for some of their deficiencies. An ambitious Internet project, The Faculty of 1000, offers for a modest fee a large online archive of postpublication peer reviews of articles from 3,500 biological and medical journals. Its more than a hundred thousand recommendations give each reviewed article a star rating and a ranking. Of this venture, Martin Raff, a Fellow of the Royal Society, writes: "I find Faculty of 1000 useful for three reasons: identifying key papers in areas outside my own; highlighting papers in journals I don't normally read; and providing confirmation by an expert of a paper I have read (i.e. a second opinion)."[61]

In the humanities, few such resources along the lines of "Retraction Watch" or "Abnormal Science" or Faculty of 1000 exist. Serious conceptual clarification and the correction of error after publication, of course, is just as important to the humanities as to the sciences. Plato's early dialogue on friendship, his *Lysis*, exemplifies at its birth the dialectical process by which such clarification may be achieved. It exemplifies Socrates's perception that new insights can be achieved only through rigorous interrogation among peers, a process that must be never-ending because we experience the truth not as a goal, but as a horizon. In this dialog, Socrates, Lysis, and Menexenus are participants in a mutual effort as, step by inferential step, they attempt to define friendship, a concept that consistently eludes their grasp. In providing the face-to-face interchange that makes serious conceptual clarification possible, blog commentary and discussion forums can duplicate, even enhance, this process, albeit virtually. They are Habermasian exchanges dedicated to rational consensus through mutual understanding.

Witness this Internet exchange with Richard Stallman (RS) incorporated into the "Digital Humanities Blog" run by Dan Cohen (DC). It concerns a blog post of Cohen's, "Open Access Publishing and Scholarly Values":

> RS: ["Green OA" and "Gold OA"] are new to me—can you tell me what they mean? [In addition, you say:] "So my colleagues worry more about truly open publications 'counting' vs. publications that are simply open to reading on a commercial publisher's Website." I don't understand that sentence.
>
> DC: Green O[pen] A[ccess] = when a professor deposits her finished article in a university repository after it is published. Theoretically that article will then be available (if people can find the Website for the institution's repository) even if the journal keeps it gated. Gold OA = ~~when an author pays a journal (often around $1-3K) to make their submissions open access.~~ when a journal itself (rather than a repository) is open access; may involve the author paying a submission fee. Still probably doesn't have a redistribution license, but it's not behind a publisher's digital gates. Counting = counting in the academic promotion and tenure process. Much of the problem here is (I believe misplaced) concern about the effect of open access on one's career.
>
> RS: Are you saying that the social realm contains the obstacle to the adoption of ethical publication methods?
>
> DC: Correct. And much of it has to do with the meekness of academics (especially in the humanities, bastion of liberalism in most other ways) to challenge the system to create a more ethical publication system, one controlled by the community of scholars rather than commercial publishers who profit from our work.[62]

This exchange was just a segment of blog commentary open to the public. Comments on this post soon arrived from interlocutors as far apart geographically as California, Montreal, Edinburgh, Ithaca, Madison, and Washington, D.C. Professional librarians—the majority of respondents—were joined by Stevan Harnad, a professor in the School of Electronics and Computer Science at the University of Southampton, and Jean-Claude Guédon, a professor of comparative literature at the Université de Montréal. Participants reacted first of all to the blog post. The crossed-out sentence, for example, corrects an error pointed out by Dorothea Salo, a librarian based in Madison, Wisconsin. Respondents also interacted with each other: Librarian Kevin Ashley questioned librarian Peter Hirtle's definition of Green Open Access, and Hirtle responded. The range of expertise so quickly and effectively deployed, the partial erasure of time, and the total erasure of distance—these are truly astonishing improvements in the same intellectual task that Plato set: conceptual clarification.

Not unexpectedly, interest in Cohen's post waned quickly. Six of the 13 comments were made on the first day; except for one, they were all completed within five days. It is this traffic—so rapid, so spontaneous, and so transient—with which the blogosphere is most comfortable. These characteristics might seem anathema to genuine intellectual advance. Our blog example shows that this is not always the case. But it is also true that the Internet can facilitate serious conceptual clarification in the case of the two central genres of scholarly communication—the article and the book. In both cases we next examine, we will find that this potential falls somewhat short of being realized. Although all the ingredients for intellectual advance are present, they have not yet coalesced. Nevertheless, since such coalescence is only a small step away—only an editorial decision away—we see no reason to despair.

POSTPUBLICATION PEER REVIEW: THE ARTICLE

Behavioral and Brain Sciences is an outstanding example of a print-era vehicle designed to generate and disseminate a version of the ideal speech situation, to offer to its readers extended evaluations after peer review has taken place. An article by Hugo Mercier and Dan Sperber, the same article we analyzed in the last chapter, will be our example.[63] Having passed editorial and peer review, their contribution was circulated electronically to two dozen scholars for comment concerning the cogency of their central thesis. The article was then published in April 2011 along with these commentaries and an author response. While this article appears in a journal devoted to the social sciences, it would, if properly disseminated, have an impact across the board—from the "hardest" of the sciences to the "softest" of the humanities.[64]

According to Mercier and Sperber, many have asserted that "the role of reasoning is to critically evaluate our beliefs so as to discard wrong-headed ones and thus create more reliable beliefs—knowledge."[65] If so, why are humans so poor at reasoning in general? Mercier and Sperber's explanation is that reasoning is an evolutionary adaptation designed to win arguments, to persuade others of their validity. It is primarily a survival strategy, and only secondarily a vehicle for discovering the truth. Of course, arguing would not help us survive if it did not have on average some correspondence with truth.

Mercier and Sperber draw upon hundreds of psychological studies to justify the claims their theory incorporates. In constructing arguments, they contend, arguers exhibit "confirmation bias"—that is, they tend to find evidence in their favor and to bypass evidence against their claims. Arguers are also proactive—that is, they try to anticipate the arguments they expect their opponents to make, an activity that makes it easier for them to favor claims in which they already believe. The deleterious effects of this confirmation bias, Mercier and Sperber feel, are best held in check in groups focused on the same issue, where the group members can exercise "epistemic vigilance," calibrating the arguer's credibility and checking the argument's coherence with their own beliefs. It is in these group settings in which arguers and evaluators participate that performance improves. Even in such contexts, however, participants tend to exhibit motivated reasoning—that is, they seek out flaws in arguments with which they disagree rather than evaluating them objectively. Moreover, they persist in holding beliefs that, on the evidence, are clearly false.

In *Behavioral and Brain Sciences*, Mercier and Sperber's article was thrown open to the epistemic vigilance of expert commentators. Unlike peer reviewers, these were not assigned the task of evaluating whether the essay was worthy of publication; that had already been decided by the editor and four anonymous readers. The emphasis of the commentaries was not on clarity or originality or disciplinary significance—characteristics handled largely by peer review—but on argumentative competence.

Not all commentaries were critical. Some confirmed Mercier and Sperber's claim.[66] Some extended it to other areas.[67] Others found the theory persuasive but sought to limit its scope or object to its single-minded emphasis on the persuasive role of argumentation. According to Evans, the article left out higher reasoning: "In particular, theorists have emphasized the ability of some individuals . . . to engage in hypothetical thinking and mental stimulation, decoupling their actual beliefs in order to support suppositional reasoning."[68] To Frankish, the theory slighted individual cognition.[69] According to Connolly and Reb, it omitted the role of the emotions in reasoning.[70] According to Uleman, Kressel, and Rim, it paid too little attention to intuitive processes.[71]

Some detected not limitations, but serious flaws. According to Narvaez, the theory was "deeply flawed" because it was largely founded on psychological studies of college students from Western countries, whom she characterized as "immature reasoners from an abnormal culture."[72] Harrell was sweeping in her condemnation, saying that "In fact, the experimental evidence from a variety of studies, including surprisingly many that are cited favorably by M&S, suggests that people do not have these particular [argumentative] skills."[73] According to De Neys, the theory slighted the evidence that people reason well in decontextualized tasks, those typical of laboratory experiments.[74] According to Stemberg, the empirical evidence does not support the increased efficacy of group reasoning, and the theory itself was a manifestation of a major societal ill: "Society has come to care more about reasoning in the service of persuasion than reasoning in the service of truth or even some kind of ethical good. This trend risks leading not to better adaptation of humans but, rather, to their ultimate destruction."[75] According to Stupple and Ball, Mercier and Sperber greatly underestimated people's ability to engage in formal reasoning and to hold their current beliefs in abeyance.[76] Finally, Opfer and Sloutsky dismissed Mercier and Sperber's evolutionary explanation in toto: "Put simply, reasoned argumentation is no more likely to have evolved for social communication than is the posture of the foot to have evolved for disco."[77]

In their response published in the same issue of *Behavioral and Brain Sciences*, Mercier and Sperber stood firm and argued against the accusations of errors in interpretation, pointing out that their critics misinterpreted either them or the evidence they adduced in favor of their counterclaims.[78] They argued that some commentators unfairly broadened their own very specific definition of reasoning—"the mental act of constructing or evaluating an argument"—into intuitive inference—"a process that yields a conclusion without articulating the reasons to accept it."[79] They also countered that others had not fully understood their claim about evolution and the function of reasoning and confirmation bias. As they stated in the abstract to their response: "we stress that reasoning is not only for convincing but also for evaluating arguments, and that as such it has an epistemic function."[80] As they wrote in the target article: "people are quite capable of reasoning in an unbiased manner, at least when they are evaluating arguments rather than producing them, and when they are after the truth rather than trying to win a debate."[81] Moreover, "reasoning evolved in part to make people change their minds by giving them *good* reasons to do so."[82] Hence, Stemberg need not fear for human survival, at least not on account of Mercier and Sperber's theory.

To argue against accusations of errors in fact, Mercier and Sperber revisited their sources. For example, when Harrell said of Sà et al.'s 2005 study that "participants have difficulty producing evidence for a claim,"[83] Mercier and Sperber countered that Harrell misrepresented Sà et al.'s results. In fact, participants generated an average of "nearly six arguments to defend their opinion."[84] To Narvaez's charge of Western bias in the psychological studies that formed their evidential basis, Mercier and Sperber countered that "while there certainly are differences in reasoning and argumentative style . . . there is no report of a culture that would be deprived of these skills."[85] To Stupple and Ball's charge that the literature clearly shows that some people attempt to argue logically when faced with problems, Mercier and Sperber "agree that in reasoning tasks people try to provide the correct, logically valid answer. What is more interesting is that most of them fail. Given that the tasks are not computationally hard, this indicates that reasoning is not geared towards pure logical validity, but that it takes into account other factors, such as believability."[86]

In this *Behavioral and Brain Sciences* issue, Mercier and Sperber participated in a process that made their claims clearer and the originality and importance of their argument more defensible, a process that minimized their confirmation bias and motivated reasoning by maximizing epistemic vigilance. The authors also acknowledged they gained insights from several commentators who pointed out promising lines of research to better understand the algorithmic implementation of reasoning. This is an example of the value added by group participation in argument evaluation. All participants gained from the knowledge that they were joining in a task designed to enhance the coherence, and therefore the value, of the discipline to which they belong. Finally, all readers of the debate gained a much fuller appreciation of the strengths and possible weaknesses of Mercier and Sperber's argument.

In the print era, official publication would have normally brought debate to a close. But this is the Internet era: Robust debate and further promulgation of the essay's claims also took place in the public arena of blogs and discussion groups, as well as online newspapers and magazines. Actually, that discussion started in March 2010, more than a year before official publication of the target article. At that time, blogger Morendil had posted a preprint of the article and a summary of its contents on the blog "Less Wrong."[87] The blog received 28 responses, all but four on the same day. In July 2010, the "online salon" *Edge* hosted a conference in Connecticut called the "The New Science of Morality."[88] The Mercier and Sperber article was a central point of discussion in the first presentation, in which psychologist Jonathan Haidt applied the theory to moral reasoning. *Edge* posted video, audio, and text versions of Haidt's talk. In the same month as publication of the *Behavioral and Brain Sciences* issue, *Edge* also posted a video in which Mercier explained the theory for a general audience.

On June 15, 2011, the *New York Times* featured "Why Do Humans Reason?" as a possible breakthrough in understanding human behavior.[89] The day after the *Times* article was posted—on a blog called "New APPS: Art, Politics, Philosophy, Science"—Catarina Dutilh Novaes, a research fellow at the City University of New York, summarized the article's arguments, praised it, and expressed several points of disagreement.[90] At the end of the same month, on another blog, "Rationally Speaking," professor Massimo Pigliucci, also from the City University of New York, denounced the whole theory as "bad reasoning about reasoning," mainly taking issue with Mercier and Sperber's claim that reasoning evolved in a Darwinian sense.[91] On July 19, in a blog of the *Chronicle of Higher Education*, Laurie Fendrich editorialized about its implications for higher education ("It'll take down the whole edifice of Western thought").[92] On August 15, a podcast appeared on the website

Point of Inquiry in which Chris Mooney engaged in a debate with Mercier about the theory.[93] The website also posted numerous comments by listeners of the podcast, to many of which the remarkably patient and always civil Hugo Mercier wrote a reply. A podcast on the discussion forum *Philosophy Bites* appeared in which philosophers David Edmonds and Nigel Warburton interviewed Dan Sperber.[94]

To illustrate more deeply the value of public commentary, we focus on the *New York Times* discussion forum appended to Cohen's article. This article received 345 online comments from all over the world: 225 on the day it was posted, another 104 over the next three days, and the remaining 16 over the next month or so, after which commentary was closed. While for many commentators "Actually, this research makes sense,"[95] a sizable fraction wrote in to criticize and question. Commentary fell into three broad categories: originality with regard to past major thinkers in Western civilization, significance of the knowledge claims to the real world, and argumentative competence. Many thought the claims were obvious. "This is thought to be news?"[96] "Duh!"[97] "Quelle surprise!"[98] "In summary: Competitive debate is competitive,"[99] and "I've known this since I was six years old."[100] Many others noted that much earlier thinkers had made similar claims, including Aristotle, Plato, the Sophists, Epictetus, Thomas Aquinas, David Hume, Friedrich Nietzsche, William James, and Michel Foucault. One respondent quoted a wonderfully apt line from an old Paul Simon song, "The Boxer": "A man hears what he wants to hear and disregards the rest."

Many *Times* commentators found the theory explained the "irrational" discourse of those with whom they disagreed. Not surprising, given the liberal bent of the *Times*, especially prominent among those allegedly prone to confirmation bias were members of the Republican Party. A typical derogatory comment was "Republicans don't care about winning arguments; they don't even READ the evidence; they just go by belief and try impose their will by fiat."[101] Also mentioned in the same company are Fox News, Tea Party members, AM talk radio, climate change deniers, and all politicians. One commentator even aimed a barb at those who comment on discussion forums in general: "The theory explains the blowhard amateur punditry found in Internet comments."[102] For about a half-dozen commentators, the theory did not earn their trust. They could not believe *French* theorists could have anything significant to say about anything or have any hard evidence for their claims: "it figures French philosophers would come up with that."[103] At least some of these commentators would seem to be displaying the confirmation bias that is a keystone in Mercier and Sperber's theory.

Quite a few respondents noted the apparently paradoxical nature of Mercier and Sperber's argument. Was their own motivation winning an argument as opposed to finding the truth? If so, wouldn't that be an argument against their argument?

As one respondent noted, "How are they exempt from their own conclusions?"[104] (A subsequent *Times* blog post by philosopher Gary Gutting addressed that question.[105]) Several respondents asked whether widely known instances of the failure of "groupthink" contradicted a central premise in the argument. Another respondent wondered "what about the fact that we reason with ourselves too? What's that all about then, to win an argument with ourselves?"[106] And in line with several of the *Behavioral and Brain Sciences* peer commentators, four questioned the theory's universality, since it is based on psychological studies of Westerners. Many also questioned whether the authors had any evidence for the evolution of flaws in reasoning as adaptive behavior. In particular, they wondered exactly how reason and argument emerged in prehistory, a topic about which Mercier and Sperber are understandably silent since "linguistic behavior does not fossilize,"[107] nor does it lend itself to DNA analysis, nor are they evolutionary biologists. One commentator did note an apparent paradox in the evolutionary explanation: "Their argument is itself irrational. If reason evolved then we have to assume at some point a human ancestor who did not reason. Creatures who do not reason do not argue, and thus reason could not have evolved as a means of winning arguments."[108]

Quite a few others asserted that the theory apparently violates a central tenet of evolutionary theory: "Ugh. Traits don't appear for a reason. They appear, most often by chance."[109]

On the basis of the first 200 or so comments, co-author Mercier wrote a reply in the *Times*. In it, he restated the main claim: Reasoning evolved "to improve communication by allowing people to debate with each other: to produce and evaluate arguments during a discussion."[110] He further assured the skeptical commentators that he and Sperber had amassed "a lot of evidence in support of our theory." He then addressed the criticisms related to the relativism charge: "We do not claim that reasoning has nothing to do with the truth. We claim that reasoning did not evolve to allow the lone reasoner to find the truth. We think it evolved to argue." Moreover, Mercier denied that reasoning evolved mainly to trick others, as many commentators had inferred, asserting that it is only one of many cognitive mechanisms humans employ to fulfill social functions.

There is no reason to believe that more than a few of the *Times* respondents read the original scholarly article, the peer commentary, or Mercier and Sperber's response. The *Times* article had a link to only an abstract for the Mercier and Sperber article; all the rest was behind a paywall in the journal. Nor do we expect they read Sperber's and his colleagues' earlier scholarly article on "Epistemic Vigilance,"[111] where they explained at great length how this "suite of cognitive mechanisms" keeps humans from being "accidentally or intentionally misinformed," the important counterweight to "confirmation bias," the main focus of the *Times* article.

"Epistemic Vigilance" was also behind a paywall. As a consequence of total reliance on the *Times* article, some comments reflected unwarranted extrapolation, attributing positions about reasoning and argument that Mercier and Sperber do not hold. Indeed, the *Times* article itself claimed that, for Mercier and Sperber, truth and accuracy are "beside the point." This misleading statement led many commentators to infer the authors were advocating a philosophically relativistic position with regard to the "truth." One commentator unfairly characterized Mercier and Sperber's theory as "an amorphous blob of relativism."[112]

Given the restricted access to Mercier and Sperber's complete arguments and the limited response space, as well as the short attention span in newspaper journalism, the *Times* comments did not accomplish what the early Platonic dialogues so clearly exemplify. There was no sense in which commentators engaged in the debate at the intellectual level the editors of *Behavioral and Brain Sciences* took for granted. Still, the degree to which these online forums approach the criteria of the ideal speech situation cannot fail to impress.

A solution to the problem of response quality is readily available. To invite intelligent commentary, scholarly journals could find a way to eliminate paywalls (see Chapter 7) and to permit and even encourage commentary on every article. To foster intelligent debate and commentary, journals themselves could start a discussion forum by following the outstanding example set by *Behavioral and Brain Sciences*, posting solicited peer commentary to target articles selected by the editors, or even by readers. Only by such means can Habermasian ideals be more fully approximated.

POSTPUBLICATION PEER REVIEW: THE BOOK

In the humanities, the genre of preference for communicating new knowledge is the book-length scholarly monograph, and the primary mechanism for postpublication evaluation is the book review. Unlike the scientific journal, humanities journals often include a fairly substantial section devoted to such reviews: They can occupy a third or more of a given issue. In this section, we will explore the Internet potential for the postpublication peer review of books. We will compare the book reviews of two history-of-science monographs: Daniel J. Cohen's *Equations from God: Pure Mathematics and Victorian Faith*[113] and Peter Galison's *Image and Logic: A Material Culture of Microphysics*.[114] Cohen's is a first monograph, based on his dissertation, a *rite de passage* absolutely necessary to achieve tenure at a research university. We compare the reception of this useful first effort with that of Galison's *magnum opus*.

We show that in both cases the current system of evaluation erects unreasonable barriers against reaching disciplinary consensus over the truth of the claims these authors make. Cohen asserts that religion was an important factor in the philosophy of pure mathematics in England and America during the 19th century, a motivation that vanished at the century's end. Galison asserts that the 20th century saw two cultures in microphysics, one based on the centrality of images, the other on the centrality of statistical proofs. But, Galison claims, this *dis*unity was overcome by the creation of "trading zones" that permitted the two cultures to communicate and, eventually, to merge. Galison feels that his focus on material culture, on machines, is the best way of avoiding the sterile debate between positivists who insist that facts drive theory or postpositivists who insist that theory, in the form of paradigms, drives facts. Cohen hopes to change the way historians and philosophers of mathematics view the Victorian period; Galison hopes to change the way historians of science conceive of and practice their profession. We review the reviews of each book in turn, then propose how the Internet might be used to make better use of them.

We found 14 reviews of *Equations from God*. In these, Cohen was charged with errors of fact, of omission, and of methodology. As reviewer Judith Grabiner pointed out, Cohen was simply mistaken when he defined the parallel postulate as "that time-honored law [that] held that given a line and a point not on that line, one could draw only one parallel line through the point."[115] Reviewer Ivor Grattan-Guinness,[116] writing in the *American Historical Review*, took Cohen to task for placing Bertrand Russell in Germany, hobnobbing with mathematicians rather with Social Democrats, as was actually the case.[117,118] These errors are, to be sure, only marginally relevant to Cohen's interpretation of the past. Errors of omission and methodology are more serious. Grabiner was concerned that Cohen omitted important precursors to ideas crucial to his central thesis:

> Unfortunately, the author often does not consider alternative sources for the views he attributes to nineteenth-century theology. For instance, Leibniz took the first steps in constructing a symbolic logic, a "universal characteristic," which he said would end disputes by reducing them to calculation; Cohen does not even mention this. Condorcet, whose name does not appear in Cohen's index, described symbolic algebra as potentially applicable to all combinations of ideas. Although Cohen alludes to the Cambridge Analytical Society, he does not discuss the influence of their formalism on Boole.[119]

These omissions weaken Cohen's central thesis that the philosophy of British and American pure mathematics altered in motivation from the religious to the secular as the 19th century progressed; methodological deficiencies, however, undermine the thesis. Grattan-Guinness pointed out that Cohen's choice of the discovery of Neptune was distinctly odd, given that this discovery was a triumph of *applied* mathematics, followed by observational confirmation. Worse, apparently, was Cohen's choice of cases, as reviewers Fernando Gouvêa, writing in *First Things: A Monthly Journal of Religion and Public Life*,[120] and Karen Parshall, writing in *Isis*,[121] pointed out. The case study method depends on judicious selection, but Cohen's choice of Benjamin Peirce, George Boole, and Augustus De Morgan was far from judicious. According to Parshall, Cohen

> assumes that there was one, monolithic "philosophy of mathematics," somehow shared by nineteenth-century mathematicians in the United States and Great Britain, to be abandoned. Had different case studies been taken, however—say, those of James Joseph Sylvester and Arthur Cayley instead of Boole and De Morgan—a very different picture would have emerged.[122]

On this point, Gouvêa concurred. Moreover, Parshall argued that it is a serious error to conflate the social and political influences on American and English mathematics, to place Benjamin Peirce in the same category as George Boole and Augustus De Morgan. Reviewer Jeremy Gray, writing in the *Newsletter* of the London Mathematics Society, summed up: "Cohen's narrative begins to fall apart in the final chapter of the book. The later Victorian period was dominated by Cayley, who said little about his faith, Sylvester, who as a Jew kept away from specifically Christian debates, and Clifford, a polemicist who died young. None of these figures help the author to spell out his thesis about the growing secularization of mathematics, correct though it is, and important theologians are missing."[123]

These reviewers were not trashing Cohen's book; they were simply weighing it against communal standards. If the book's reviewers found it wanting, they hardly found it valueless. Grabiner summed up the consensus: "Cohen has successfully situated the work of Peirce, Boole and De Morgan in social and religious context, making this book a valuable contribution to the literature on the mathematics of the English-speaking world in the nineteenth century."[124] Hannibuss, writing in the *English Historical Review,* concurred: "Cohen's study makes the case for some interesting parallels between the interaction of mathematical and religious ideas in the work of Peirce, Boole, and de Morgan, and can certainly be recommended for that, despite its somewhat unfocused final chapter."[125]

This synthesis of expert judgments ought to be available to all those who are interested in Cohen's book and in the history and philosophy of Victorian mathematics. But the reviews on which our synthesis is based are for the most part available only to scholars at major research universities and to subscribers of the individual journals in which the reviews appear. With the exception of Gray, all serious criticism is behind a paywall and, in any case, can be discovered only with persistence.

Those who considered purchasing the book from the blurbs provided by either the publisher or Amazon.com[126] would be greeted with a set of opinions that, to say the least, misrepresent what their authors said. Gouvêa and Grattan-Guinness are both severely critical of the book; indeed, Grattan-Guinness is dismissive. But the excerpt from Gouvêa is "One can only welcome *Equations from God*," while the excerpt from Grattan-Guinness is "The main strength of the book comes from Cohen's archival research."

From Cohen's reviews we might legitimately infer that his audience was relatively narrow: historians of mathematics and some Victorian scholars. From Galison's reviews, we might legitimately infer that audience was relatively wide: not only historians of science who read the *British Journal for the History of Science*, *Metascience*, and *Isis*; historians of technology who read *History and Technology*, *Technology and Culture*, and *Science, Technology, and Human Values*; general historians who read *Journal of Modern History* and *Minerva*; and scientists who read *Science, Nature, Physics Today, New Scientist*, and *American Scientist*, but also the general reading public interested in science, readers of *TLS, The New York Times, The Chronicle of Higher Education*, and *The New Republic*. Moreover, in many cases, reviewers of high status have been put to work, always a mark of significant publication. They include such distinguished students of science as John Ziman and Daniel Kevles and such distinguished scientists as W. K. H. Panofsky[127] and the Nobelist Martin L. Perl.[128] It is also comforting to know that these physicists-reviewers can vouch for the accuracy of Galison's science—for example, physicist Ed Hinds in *New Scientist* says that "the physics is remarkably accurate, except for the occasional minor slip."[129] We are probably not alone in our inability to read Galison's discussion of these technical matters with an appropriately critical eye.

Given its potentially wide audience, we might expect the book would avoid entangling readers in technical details of microphysics. If so, we would be disappointed. Nine of Galison's reviewers emphasized how difficult it is to read a work Kevles called "huge, sprawling, and inadequately disciplined."[130] Ed Hinds called reading *Image and Logic* "very heavy work."[131] Joseph Pitt described the book as follows: "written over a period of ten years, it looks as if it has seven case studies, each with its own theme, but with new beginning and ending paragraphs that nod in the directions laid out in the introductory and concluding chapter."[132] To Florian Hars, "the first impression of *Image and Logic* is intimidating: almost one thousand pages, and, to make things worse, typeset in Times New Roman at an unreadable eighty characters per line."[133]

Reviewers were not simply complaining that the book was difficult—no one expects such books to be beach reading; they were complaining that it was unnecessarily so, that in his zeal to write a book absolutely faithful to the history of

20th-century microphysics, Galison lost touch with the many readers whose knowledge of this science, and whose interest in its details, is far less than his. For these reviewers, this loss was a pity, since the two concepts at the center of the book—the image–logic distinction and the trading zone—have implications that go far beyond its confines. The first is designed to revolutionize the history of particle physics; the second, borrowed from anthropology and linguistics, to revolutionize the way we think about interactions within and among scientific disciplines.

Writing in *American Scientist*, Richard Cook said of the trading zone that it "is a powerful idea when applied to high-energy physics, but it will have great impact elsewhere. Such zones exist in the intensive care units of research hospitals and elsewhere."[134] In *Minerva*, John Ziman reiterated the point about the idea's power and added that the concept has an important philosophical implication: "This novel concept of a 'trading zone' between contacting research cultures applies in every field of science. To my mind, it effectively settles the debate that has long raged about the supposed 'incommensurability' of competing or successive paradigms."[135]

Although the idea of trading zones received high praise not only from several reviewers but also in back-of-the-book blurbs from Ian Hacking and Clifford Geertz, C. W. F. Everitt and Anna Muza[136] in an *Isis* review expressed their concern that "trading" might not be the right word for the concept, since the traffic in ideas may be more a matter of simplification than of intellectual interchange between equals. Andrew Pickering had another criticism, a dissent from Ziman's entirely positive assessment of the book's philosophical implications. He complained that Galison had gone too far in dismissing a modified Kuhnian view that research traditions in particle physics are not so easily reconciled or bridged: "as it happens," he said, "there is a big quasi-Kuhnian break in the history of particle physics."[137]

Galison's second central concept—the distinction in 20th-century microphysics between an image and a logic tradition—also did not escape criticism. Ziman,[138] Jeff Hughes,[139] and Hars[140] felt it was overdrawn. Ziman was most forceful on this point:

> these two traditions are not so distinct epistemologically as Galison seems to think. A logic experiment is performed against a background of visual representations, such as diagrams of the arrangements of the counters in space. Conversely, an image of a "track" implies numerous logical propositions concerning inclusion, exclusion, continuity, etc., which we automatically impute to it. That is to say, these experiments—as physicists would themselves rightly insist—are both producing essentially the same type of knowledge, abstracted in different modes.[141]

In his article on *Image and Logic*, Staley made the even more damaging claim that the arguments both traditions make are fundamentally the same. From this Staley concluded that "the epistemic divide between these two traditions was not so great as to make an interlanguage necessary for them to communicate, cooperate and, eventually to unite in a single experimental pursuit."[142] Galison may even agree with this view, at least in part, since in Staley's acknowledgments Galison was thanked for helpful comments and criticisms. If Staley is right, Galison's radical difference is, at bottom, not really radical, but only a difference in emphasis.

Reviewers also alleged that Galison's problem is not as new as he seems to claim, nor is his solution as original as he implies. David Gooding[143] pointed out that problems of cross-cultural coordination within the sciences did not begin with 20th-century particle physics; William McKinney[144] and Robert Crease[145] asserted that were Galison more familiar with the phenomenological-hermeneutical tradition, he would be aware that his reorientation of science, a refiguring that takes the history of instrumentation seriously into consideration, had long ago been anticipated by that tradition. McKinney even quoted Martin Heidegger on instrumentation's centrality:

Modem physics is not experimental physics because it applies apparatus to the questioning of nature. Rather, the reverse is true. Because physics, indeed already as pure theory, sets nature up to exhibit itself as a coherence of forces calculable in advance, it therefore orders its experiments precisely for the purpose of asking whether and how nature reports itself when set up in this way.[146]

Because aggregate reviews such as ours of Cohen and Galison are not readily available, scholarly communities are unnecessarily deprived of information that would continually refresh their knowledge and form the basis for intellectual advance. Book reviews should not be entombed in print or hidden behind online paywalls, like Fortunato in the *Cask of Amontillado*; instead, they should be placed on aggregate websites freely accessible to all Internet users. Should journals balk at making these reviews freely available, citing copyright, summaries would be a good substitute for the real thing, as they are in this chapter. In fact, such review summaries could be relatively short if an extended summary of the book headed the website, a real advantage in saving reader time, as most of most reviews are in large part summaries of the book in question. A provision for reader commentary could easily be added to keep such aggregate sites, and thus the knowledge base, current. Book reviews so treated can contribute mightily to rational consensus concerning the worth of serious scholarship in the humanities, the Habermasian ideal.

There are four ways of achieving this goal. The first already exists in the print and online literature, *Metascience*'s "Review Symposium," the source for four of the reviews of *Image and Logic* we have consulted. The print Symposium consists of the author's extended summary of the book, the reviews, and, finally, the author's reaction. Online, H-France Review follows a similar format. Bryn Mawr Classical Review illustrates a second possibility, a site that hosts lengthy single reviews by appointed peers. There is also an opportunity for readers to comment. Naturally, this feature is used only on occasion, when strong views are held and contested; the issue of plagiarism in translations of the *Iliad* is an example.[147] There is also a lengthy response to a negative review, a defense of the book in question by a scholar other than the author.[148] A third possibility is the electronic book review of the Open Humanities Press, "a peer-reviewed journal of critical writing published by the emergent digital literary network."

A final possibility is far less conventional: Rotten Tomatoes, a movie review aggregation website. In addition to movie summaries, links to reviews, and reader comments, the site employs algorithms that generate numerical ratings of movie quality. An analogous rating algorithm might be considered for scholarly monographs, such as the five-star system used in the open-access Public Library of Science journals. In such a system, we would give Cohen four stars for readability and two for significance, Galison two and a half stars for readability and four and a half for significance. Other readers might disagree; that is exactly the point of an aggregation site. We present a model for such a site in the next page.

A natural host for such sites would be the web pages of a professional society; in the case of such monographs as *Equations from God* and *Image and Logic*, the History of Science Society would seem the obvious choice. In *Digital History* Cohen and Roy Rosenzweig make clear that only a website with institutional sponsorship can survive in the long term, given that individuals may lose interest, retire, or die.[149]

We can see two objections to the feasibility of such a site. The first concerns copyright: Will journals agree to open their gated reviews so they can be linked to an aggregate site? We find it difficult to believe that there are sound arguments in favor of the continued gating of reviews, a practice that is in the interests neither of authors, the profession, nor the publishers themselves who, like the University of Chicago Press or Oxford University Press, publish books as well as journals. Even were such refusals to occur, two options would still be open. Authors of reviews can agree to share with the site their manuscripts or proofs, arguably theirs to share. In the worst case, judicious excerpts can be employed without links to the full review.

A second argument concerns the lack of professional reward for such labor on the part of scholars. But what, pray tell, is the professional reward for the lengthy reviews in H-France Forum? Or for book reviews in general? Bryn Mawr Classical

Image and Logic: A Material Culture of Microphysics
University of Chicago Press, 1997. Peter Galison

Readibility: 2.5/5
Significance 4.5/5

Summary

Galison asserts that the 20th century saw two cultures in microphysics, one based on the centrality of images, the other, on the centrality of statistical proofs. But, Galison claims, this *dis*unity was overcome by the creation of "trading zones" that permitted the two cultures to communicate and, eventually, to merge. Galison feels that his focus on material culture, on machines, is the best way of avoiding the sterile debate between positivists who insist that facts drive theory or post-positivists who insist that theory, in the form of paradigms, drives facts.

Synthesis

Galison's book is a difficult read because of its level of technical detail and because it consists of case studies that insufficiently cohere. Nevertheless, there is little doubt that it is exemplary historical scholarship. Galison promotes three central ideas—the existence of independent image and logic traditions in experimental micro-physics, the creation of "trading zones" that facilitate communication and cooperation between them, and the importance of focusing on material culture in the study of science. The first idea is sound and insightful; the second, a possible solution to the problem of incommensurablity; the third, a way of avoiding sterile philosophical debates. Given their provocative nature, it is unsurprising that these ideas do not escape criticism.

Reviews

- Joseph Pitt in *Science Technology and Human Values:* "Peter Galison's *Image and Logic* is a big book. It is also a good book. Rich in details, *Image and Logic* gives us a microhistory of the material culture of twentieth-century microphysics." <u>Read more</u>.
- Martin Perl in *Science:* "Practicing scientists—particle physicists or gene sequencers—can get a broader view of their own experimental technology. Students of the history or philosophy of science who have overdosed on paradigms and the nature of scientific truth will find detailed material for more realistic thoughts about the practice of science." <u>Read more</u>.
- Daniel Kevles in *New Republic:* "Peter Galison drives an original cut through the great trunk of twentieth-century physics, exposing how its practitioners have gone about finding, identifying, and comprehending the elementary particles that comprise the building blocks of matter and energy." <u>Read more</u>.
- Richard Cook in *American Scientist:* "Galison shows how [trading zones allow] people with disparate roles to create modern physics by delimiting meanings in ways that allow productive work to go forward. This is a powerful idea when applied to high-energy physics, but it will have great impact elsewhere. Such zones exist in the intensive care units of research hospitals and elsewhere." <u>Read more</u>.
- And so on.

Author Response...

Review provides a model for the enterprise. Books are sent to the Review and are subsequently doled out to qualified reviewers. Provided their supervisor agrees to monitor the procedure, graduate students writing their dissertations can also review. We see no problem in routinely extending such invitations to graduate students for the purpose of contributing to an aggregate review on an appropriately chosen research monograph. The assignment seems like a learning experience at least equal to many others they might encounter.

CONCLUSION

Without the Internet, enterprises like "Retraction Watch" and "Abnormal Science" are inconceivable. Neither newspapers nor television nor radio could focus so relentlessly on a single topic of no interest to a general audience but of considerable importance to every citizen. No other medium could maintain an instantly available archive of cases, a history of scientific misconduct and retraction as it unfolds. No other medium could make reader comments an integral part of its developing stories. No other medium could provide Twitter feeds that keep the blog up to date, minute by minute. No other medium could provide such ready access to other relevant Internet sources, including other blogs or related articles. The story of "Retraction Watch" and "Abnormal Science" is the tale of nodes in a network of expanding knowledge and epistemic, social, and moral critique. Such blogs can seriously influence how we know. By correcting error, "Abnormal Science" did so directly; by publicizing error and opening a window to the efforts of others in so doing, "Retraction Watch" has done so indirectly. Bulfone-Paus's exposure is a prime example of private endeavors working in the public interest, an enterprise made possible and made public by the Internet. As mentioned earlier, another watchdog blog, "PubPeer," was instrumental in the retraction of two high-profile *Nature* articles on stem cells. These and other cases demonstrate that science is far from self-correcting, but that it can no longer insulate its lapses from wider public opinion operating in virtual space. As a result of the efforts of these bloggers, we—all of us—have a firmer sense of the state of knowledge at the research front in particular fields of scientific endeavor.

The Internet revolution can also have a serious impact on the postpublication evaluation of the two central genres of the humanities—articles and books. We suggest in this chapter that the Internet is especially well suited to the more widespread adaptation of sites that allow online peer and community commentary, and that the format developed for the print version of *Behavioral and Brain Sciences* can serve as a model for imitation and adaptation in open-access scholarly journals, a form of publication that is becoming increasingly widespread. We also suggest an overhaul in an established enterprise, scholarly book reviewing. If this practice remains unchanged, we contend, it will not succeed in its larger purpose: keeping the record straight in the humanities. Book reviews, often delayed many months or years, will continue to be scattered over various periodicals, hidden, for the most part, behind paywalls. Even for those with access, these reviews will remain difficult to find and time consuming to synthesize. The discussion forum and aggregation site we suggest will go a long way to solving this problem.

The Internet revolution can do more than help keep the humanities record straight; it can promote intellectual advance. Mercier and Sperber's target article and its wealth of responses reveal a new and important research question: Why has argument evolved? Aggregated and analyzed, the reviews of *Equations from God* reveal a coherent research question that can now be addressed: What exactly is the role of religion in 19th-century English and American mathematics? Aggregated and analyzed, the reviews of *Image and Logic* ask importantly: What exactly are the mechanisms of cooperation in disciplinary collaborations? In all cases, commentators and reviewers give scholars a sense of the possible directions of future research into these questions. In Mercier and Sperber's case, ways are needed to strengthen the bridge between argument studies, cognitive psychology, and evolutionary biology. In Cohen's case, we need a better choice of exemplars and a firmer sense of the differences between intellectual climates in British and American mathematics. In Galison's case, we require a subtler definition of the trading zone, as well as a better sense of where in 20th-century microphysics the differences between the image and logic traditions reside.

To continue in the present well-worn path of print journals is to squander commentators' and reviewers' efforts, and to nullify the effect of their combined critique. Opening the door to author and reader responses turns such sites into forums for scholarly debate about the issues aggregation and analysis raise, the cutting edge of research they reveal, a process whose goal is always rational consensus, the best approximation possible to the ideal speech situation.

7

OVERCOMING THE OBSTACLES TO INTERNET EXPLOITATION

THE OPPORTUNITIES

The Internet presents an opportunity for the sciences and humanities to transform the generation, communication, and evaluation of new knowledge. Indeed, the elite scientific journals are already reinventing the traditional research article via the Internet. Its methods are being communicated by a combination of video demonstration and verbal description, its gist, not only by verbal, but by visual abstracts, video abstracts, summaries for the general reader, and podcasts. Its contents take advantage of the computer screen; its results are communicated by multicomponent computer-generated images in color, videos of events in the laboratory or simulations of the natural world, graphs that automatically turn into tables and vice versa, maps displayed so that the viewer can zoom in and out, and 3D interactive images. Links are sending readers to a wealth of supplementary material: data, images, related readings. Community response to articles is being captured in new ways. Innovative processes for the evaluation of proposed new knowledge, before and after publication, are being developed and adopted. Upon publication and even before, articles and the data in them are becoming part of virtual archives that give new meaning to "body of knowledge." See Video 7.1 [▶]. Researchers are inviting commentary from the professional community as their data are generated; they are posting data and images online that others are free to use—with appropriate attribution, of course. Enthusiastic amateurs or the simply curious in large numbers are once again able to actively participate in scientific research projects.

For the humanities, the Internet is no less promising. Film scholars are interposing film clips in their critique of classic films. Historians are including videos of historical events or computerized recreations, as well as reproductions of key documents of historical interest such as court testimony and reproductions of handwritten letters. Art and architectural historians are displaying interactive 3D reconstructions of sculptures and buildings and historical sites. See Video 7.2 [▶]. Musical scholars are incorporating not only musical scores but also recorded performances (audio and video). But it is in archival websites that we see an extraordinary outburst of creativity and innovation. In them you can access a vast library of works by well-known writers and artists, as well as scholarly annotations for those works and links to biographies; scholarly articles and critical reviews, videos, or podcasts about the authors and artists; photographs of them and interviews with them. And like the sciences, the humanities are experimenting with new ways to capture community response and solicit research assistance. Although these are not yet everyday practices, many will likely become so.

Although these achievements are true to the Internet's potential, we have deliberately slighted the obstacles that might interfere with, even undermine its realization. Our first four obstacles affect both the sciences and the humanities. The first consists of the limitations in the circulation of knowledge that gated access imposes; the second, tenure and promotion codes better suited to an era of print; the third, digital preservation over the long term. The fourth obstacle affects the sciences and the humanities differently. In the sciences, patent legislation inhibits innovation, while copyright legislation and institutional barriers make difficult or impossible the mining of gated journals and vast private datasets for the valuable data they contain, data that can facilitate scientific progress.[1] In the humanities, copyright legislation places barriers in the way of those who would employ music or still and moving images in their work. A fifth obstacle faces only scholars in the humanities whose research focuses on government documents. Historians and political scientists have been impeded in their archival work by the overclassification of such documents and by unreasonable prohibitions on their release. At the same time, the quantity of material and the demand for its use are increasing exponentially as a consequence of Freedom of Information legislation, forcing a competition between scholars and the general public that Internet access can alleviate. Only by overcoming these obstacles can we release the full creative energy that C. P. Snow saw in the "clash" between the sciences and the humanities; only then can both fully exploit the Internet in the interest of the generation, communication, and evaluation of knowledge.

GATED ACCESS: THE FIRST OBSTACLE

With few exceptions, scholarly and scientific books and articles generate not income, but reputation, the universal currency of academe. Because of this "economic" system, most scholars and scientists prefer that their ideas have the widest circulation. They give their work away to publishers. Because they do so, some authors might feel that their work ought to be free to their readership. But, of course, it is not: Publishers control access to most knowledge by placing a paywall between that knowledge and its potential consumers. In exchange for publication, authors must generally transfer their rights to their own work to publishers, who then place their wares on the open market. In this system of monetizing new knowledge, scholars and universities buy back intellectual content from publishers what publishers obtain for nothing. The dilemma is, How is it possible to satisfy publishers entitled to a reasonable profit for their services and scholars and scientists who require full access in the pursuit of new knowledge?

While the price of access to any journal or book may be affordable for individual scholars and scientists, the price of access to all journals and books is not. No scholar or scientist can afford to purchase all she needs; for this, she must rely on university libraries and institutional subscriptions. And no library, not Harvard itself,[2] can keep up with the rapid increase in the number and cost of academic books and journals. Open-access peer-reviewed publication offers a way out of this dilemma. Other advantages are the ability to include hyperlinks to full documents and "the time that researchers would save when trying to access or read papers that were no longer lodged behind paywalls."[3] The advantage of open access is social as well. Professors at universities and colleges not ordinarily involved in original research can now become more readily involved, either on their own or as part of teams.

How may reasonable access to the scholarly and scientific literature be achieved? At first, a cost-effective solution seemed to be self-archiving, where authors post their own papers and book chapters online before publication. This "preprint" solution bypasses traditional academic publishing dominated by commercial presses like Reed Elsevier, university presses like Harvard and Chicago, and learned societies who act as publishers like the Modern Language Association and the American Chemical Society. Self-archiving comes in two varieties, institutional and disciplinary. Typical institutional repositories are at Harvard and Minnesota; typical disciplinary repositories are arXiv for physics and mathematics, the Social Science Research Network for the social sciences, Research Papers in Economics (RePEc) for economics, and PubMed for biomedicine. At first glance, it would seem that both sorts of repository would be supremely efficient: Any scholar or scientist could accomplish her literature search simply by using an engine such as Google Scholar.

But there are problems with this apparently elegant solution. In the first place, it is not cost free: The site must be hosted and curated. These are costs *additional* to journal subscriptions that must be maintained. Second, many submissions to self-archiving sites have been simply citations, or abstracts, not whole articles. In the case of the University of Strathclyde, for example, only 9% of submissions were found to be full text.[4] In addition, many links are dead links: In the University of Southampton's repository more than half the links to full texts were dead on arrival.[5] Third, many publishers do not allow final PDFs to be posted, only submitted drafts before any peer review. When Alan Gross tried to download his published articles to the University of Minnesota's Digital Conservancy he was told that only eight of a total of 59 could be freely accessed, despite the fact that some were 20 years old. Finally, literature searches in the humanities can span decades, even centuries; no subject-matter repository can accommodate such searches.

Some of these problems relate only to institutional repositories. By far, these do not work as well as their disciplinary counterparts. Academics or scientists lack a strong motive to post their documents, as submission does little to enhance their reputations or their chances for tenure and promotion.[6] Even a mandate endorsed by a faculty vote, as at Harvard, does not necessarily help: After institutional mandates were in place, only 69% of repositories experienced an increase in content; 15% actually experienced a decrease.[7] We may wish to conclude that universities have become involved in an area where disciplines function more effectively. Still, disciplinary repositories lack universal acceptance; the majority of disciplines have none (arXiv, the Social Science Research Network, RePEc, and PubMedCentral are notable exceptions).

The principal alternative to self-archiving is open-access publishing. While there is faculty consensus that open access to academic journals and books is a good idea,[8] opinion is divided as to whether it is economically feasible. Someone must bear the brunt of costs associated with article or book publication. Concerning those costs, there is, apparently, no consensus. In the United Kingdom, there have been two extensive reports, those of the Joint Information Systems Committee[9] and the Research Information Network.[10] While the two differ in their modeling assumptions—the Joint Information Systems Committee includes editorial costs, and the Research Information Network does not—both argue convincingly that a move to online open-access article publishing would effect a cost saving, a modest $42 million in the latter case, a more robust $162 million in the former.[11] According to the Joint Information Systems Committee report, moreover, the shift to e-only academic monographs would reduce those costs per item from $24,000 to $11,440, a substantial savings.

These conclusions, however, must be balanced against an American report by Mary Waltham of eight humanities and social science journals, an examination that shows open-access publishing in those disciplines might not be a "sustainable business model."[12] Waltham's analysis found that costs for an article in the humanities or social sciences (average of $7,000) are about twice those in the sciences.[13] Reasons given for the discrepancy include longer average article length, higher costs for peer review due to a much higher rejection rate (only about 10% accepted), and in any given journal issue, higher content of material that is not original research (mainly book reviews). Even if average article charges were the same, a fact of life is that the humanities and social sciences are much less well funded than the sciences, making the financing of journal publication through author or affiliated organization payment problematic. These problems notwithstanding, Waltham acknowledges that various forms of open access are on the rise in the humanities and social sciences.[14] Indeed, arguments that open access is not economically feasible fail to account for the existence of such robust freestanding open-access journals as the *International Journal of Communication, Music Theory Online,* and the *European Journal of Comparative Economics,* as well as the family of journals sponsored by the European Geosciences Union. At the very least, one might conclude from Waltham's and other similar studies that open access need be no more costly than its gated counterpart.

To supplement the results from open-access modeling and economic analyses, we offer two existence proofs. The first is a consortium formed to buy back open access from publishers. The Sponsoring Consortium for Open Access Publishing in Particle Physics (SCOAP3), an arm of CERN, the European high-energy physics consortium, was formed to buy open-access rights from publishers of journals in high-energy physics. This initiative is funded by proportional contributions from university libraries to be paid in lieu of subscription fees. Although CERN does not envision any cost savings, the worldwide scientific community will gain free access to the journals in question. Despite the existence of the very successful subject-matter website, arXiv, CERN is willing to pay for the benefits of peer review and for professional editing.[15] Moreover, hard bargaining may well lead to cost savings:

> Libraries typically must pay 4 to 6 times as much per page for journals owned by commercial publishers as for journals owned by non-profit societies. These differences in price do not reflect differences in the quality of the journals. In fact the commercial journals are on average less cited than the non-profits and the average cost per citation of commercial journals ranges from 5 to 15 times as high as that of their non-profit counterparts.[16]

The second existence proof consists of two instances of open rebellion. The *ACM Transactions on Algorithms* was created out of frustration with the high cost of Elsevier's *Journal of Algorithms*[17]; while not free access, the new journal can be purchased by members for $40 per annum after payment of a yearly membership fee of $99. Another journal, *Economics Bulletin*, was founded for two reasons: frustration with cost and with the slow pace with which articles were published in the existing journal, *Economic Letters*. Library subscriptions to *Economic Letters* ran around $1,500 per annum, personal subscription was not an option, and there was an eight-month delay in publishing. In 2012, the turnaround time of the open access *Economics Bulletin* had been reduced from eight to two months.

It is worth noting that a sizable fraction of the journal literature is already freely available on the web. In a 2006 survey of 1,350,000 journal articles, Bo-Christer Björk estimated about 20%; a more recent study shows that the tipping point has been reached, and that more than 50% of papers are now available.[18,19] Moreover, in the scientific literature, researchers have free access to abstracts for nearly all journal articles in English from the 20th and 21st centuries.

The current situation is not quite as bright for scholarly books. We suspect the majority of current readers intending to carefully read a scholarly book front to back still prefer the print version. Still, most university presses are now selling both electronic and print versions of their recent books at a similar cost, while Amazon offers electronic versions at about three-quarters the price of their print counterparts. The recently launched Amherst College Press has entered the fray of open-access scholarly publishing with a bold business plan involving no author charges. Its open-access books will be funded out of the library budget and the endowment fund. Founded by a group of distinguished scholars in 2007, Open Humanities Press also offers open access, with no author charges, to a relatively small list of monographs. And several commercial presses such as Springer and Brill now offer open access to monographs by authors willing to pay in the neighborhood of $10,000 to $20,000 per title.[20] On the negative side, we know of no major university press that has adopted open access for its books. Unless the Amherst or similar business model catches on with other universities, that might never prove economically viable. On the positive side, many websites provide open access to scholarly and scientific books that are in the public domain, and Google Books and Amazon upload major portions of many new scholarly titles along with abstracts, reader commentary and ratings, and more.

CURRENT TENURE RULES: THE SECOND OBSTACLE

If Internet science and humanities scholarship are to flourish, tenure must be transformed from what it is now, a hindrance to the full exploitation of the web's potential, to what it could be, a component of a comprehensive plan to exploit that potential. One possibility for such reform has already been broached. Ernest Boyer's

Scholarship Reconsidered[21] suggested a radical broadening of tenure requirements, one that would include, in addition to the traditional scholarship of discovery, three new forms: scholarships of integration, application, and teaching. Boyer assumed that sweeping change was needed. We do not think so. To spearhead the integration of the Internet into the work of science and scholarship, we need only ask that provosts and deans employ the powers they already have, that faculty employ skills and prerogatives already inherent in their positions, that all heed norms already in place.

As a first step, we suggest that provosts and deans appoint faculty committees charged with rethinking the probationary period for tenure, a choice of seven years that was, as Walter Metzger makes clear, perfectly arbitrary: It "had the desirable property of falling between the very few years of probationary service advocated by the teachers' union and rejected by the AAUP [American Association of University Professors] as amounting to instant tenure and the founders' double-digit standard, which would have alienated from the AAUP most academics under thirty or thirty-five."[22]

Seven years to demonstrate appropriate academic standing may well have been too short in 1938 when the compromise was achieved; it was clearly too short in 1993 when Metzger's words were written, a time before the Internet loomed; it is clearly too short now, in the wake of the Internet revolution, at least if that revolution is to be properly harnessed by young scientists and scholars who need to learn unaccustomed skills. Moreover, as anyone who has served on college or university tenure committees can attest, this period is too short for all but a few scholars and scientists to achieve a national or international reputation, an appropriate goal at a research institution; too short to achieve a reputation for research productivity, an appropriate goal at a comprehensive university; too short to achieve a reputation for research integrated into classroom instruction, an appropriate goal at a liberal arts college. Ten years would seem to be a reasonable period in which to accomplish these tasks. So as not to challenge AAUP guidelines, any extension should be only by mutual consent.

Accompanying this lengthened probationary period should be a revised set of policies for tenure and promotion, ones that take the Internet, and the collaborative efforts it encourages, seriously into consideration. The Modern Language Association has an exemplary set. These insist that born-digital projects be taken seriously, that their collaborative nature in no way undermine a candidate's case, that such projects be viewed in the media for which they were produced, and, finally, that reviewers be engaged who are competent to judge, scholars who may well be found only outside the candidate's home department.[23] Tenure and promotion policies need to be explicit concerning the value of such activities as founding and editing an Internet journal or creating and curating a database designed to advance knowledge.

In turn, candidates for tenure or promotion intent on exploiting the Internet need to have clarified in writing just how their online achievements will be credited. For their part, they need to document these achievements for those who may not be well acquainted with the challenges and possibilities of the Internet, or who may be skeptical of its achievements. For instance, candidates need to provide evidence that the online journals they found and edit have had an impact or that the databases they curate are regularly used.

While the existence of new guidelines is no guarantee that tenure and promotion committees will heed them, provosts and deans are not lacking in persuasive power to guide and administrative power to correct. Of course, no such decisions can be made if no new faculty members are hired with the skills and motivation to pursue Internet science and scholarship. In this matter, provosts and deans can usefully intervene; they can aim their department negotiations in the direction of new hires eager to explore the Internet's potential. They can encourage the selection of candidates who intend to use the Internet as a vehicle for the generation, communication, and evaluation of knowledge as well as those whose interest is the subjection of such Internet use to analysis, to exploring its social, political, economic, or philosophical implications. Provosts and deans can also influence hiring and work assignments in technology support so that Internet projects are efficiently brought to fruition. Finally, they can redirect programs of internal grants so as to encourage Internet projects.

DIGITAL PRESERVATION: THE THIRD OBSTACLE

In general, digitization is not an obstacle; it is a boon. Digitization preserves 19th-century books and articles, for example, printed on acid-based paper that crumbles when touched; the digitization of Blake's corpus gives you ready access to a trove of widely scattered products of a literary and artistic genius (see Chapter 4). Although the effect of digitization has been largely salutary, it has left two problems in its wake. The first is the aptly named "link rot," the tendency of connections between web documents and their Uniform Resource Locators or URLs to vanish over time. In a study of link rot in legal resources, the Chesapeake Digital Preservation Group found a precipitous decline in live links from 2008 to 2013.[24] Although link rot cannot be repaired after the fact, it can be prevented by archiving documents in the Wayback Machine or WebCite, two very useful apps. Moreover, many books and journal articles now have Digital Object Identifiers or DOIs, a unique and permanent code. If they are not gated, these can be accessed using CrossRef, another app.

The second problem created in the wake of digitization concerns the preservation of complex digital objects, such as *Valley of the Shadow*, which went digital in 1993. Edward Ayers, one of the project's creators, estimates that $1 million went into the effort of producing it. When the project was chosen for technical updating by the University of Virginia Library, however, the cost increased by another $100,000. This is an update so good that visitors to the site would not perceive that it had occurred:

> "What we essentially had to do was standardize it all," Bradley J. Daigle [director of digital curation services at the University of Virginia Library] says. He compares the process to what auto mechanics used to do in the 1950s. "We basically swapped out all the parts and rebuilt the engine," he says. "We took the entire site and atomized it into several hundred thousand individual files," then analyzed them to see if they were damaged or in still-usable formats. Monitoring software now keeps tabs on the site to make sure it continues to function well. Users can email the library to report problems they encounter.[25]

Anyone who doubts the complexity of the task ought to consult the reports on the project, a truly astonishing list of fix after fix.[26,27] Obviously, not every web project can get the royal treatment *Valley of the Shadow* received. But even long-term preservation may not be out of reach for ordinary mortals. Faculty can certainly increase their chances if they consult professionals at the planning stages. An article published in 2002 outlines the task still with us:

> Data grows, lives, and dies, as do delivery systems. As never before, the task of keeping data alive requires frequent adaptations to and perpetual evolution of the archival system. To keep pace with technological flux, an ongoing process of selection—of media platforms, of preservation structures, of migratory patterns—is necessary to avoid data extinction.[28]

The rapidity of change in hardware and software is staggering, as a timeline produced by the Cornell University Library clearly reveals.[29] Remember Word Star? Remember Apple II? If you do, you see the problem. You also see the problem if you do not. In the long term, stability of valuable web projects will obviously depend upon institutions, not individuals. At present, for example, Cornell University Library maintains arXiv; the Research Collaboratory for Structural Bioinformatics, the Protein Data Bank in the United States; and the University of North Carolina and Library of Congress, the William Blake Archive.

PATENTS AND COPYRIGHT: THE FOURTH OBSTACLE

In the sciences, the Internet is an ideal medium for sharing and mining the large databases the sciences accumulate, and for maximizing access to such resources as genes, biobank samples, stem cells, and the building blocks of synthetic biology—but not if copyrights inhibit access to the first, and patents to the rest. On this turf, universities and industry are at war, a contest in which universities are also arrayed against each other.[30] By inhibiting sharing, present arrangements retard the generation and communication of new knowledge that would otherwise result.

The relationship between universities and industry is particularly fraught. Academic researchers' requests for drugs, whether from industry or from fellow researchers, were only one-twelfth as likely to be filled as those for other materials. Moreover, while academic researchers refused requests for materials from other academic researchers only 6% of the time, they refused requests from industry in 31% of cases.[31] Worse, in the last decades, the lure of profit has created in universities themselves an atmosphere detrimental to the advance of knowledge:

> A survey of more than 2,000 biomedical faculty conducted in 1993 . . . found that 20 percent of respondents had delayed publication of research results for at least six months. Nearly half of these faculty reported that they had delayed publication of research results in order to protect the patentability of these findings. This survey also found that 9 percent of respondents had denied other scientists' requests for access to their research results. In a follow-up survey . . . conducted in 2000, 73 percent of respondents working in genetics indicated that difficulties in obtaining access to data or materials had slowed scientific progress in this field.[32] [See also McLennon[33] and Agovic.[34]]

Even in publication there has been a reluctance to share the data that ground conclusions. The *Journal of Pharmacology and Experimental Therapeutics* withdrew a paper when its authors refused fully to characterize the chemical structure at issue.[35] It is not surprising that, more and more, journals in science and medicine are making full data disclosure mandatory.[36] The reluctance to share may persist even after publication.[37]

Patents inhibit the sharing and collaboration that the Internet makes possible. In both industry and the academy, patents on life forms have been routinely granted far enough upstream—far enough from actual application—to impede research further downstream, work that would focus on application.[38–41] This trend is especially deleterious when we consider how valuable upstream openness is to innovation in such areas as drug synthesis.[42] A reform would not be to forgo patents altogether, but to apply for them further downstream, where profits and the public good coincide. Deleterious practices are not only a matter of industrial practice; the patents held by the Wisconsin Alumni Research Foundation have apparently created a formidable barrier to innovation.[43] Moreover, even when licenses are obtained from patent holders, patents create a roadblock of formidable transaction costs and considerable delays.[44,45] This is particularly significant since most research involves the use of not one or two but of numerous biological products.

There is another problem. In America, at least, copyright extends only to that portion of an endeavor that is creative. This principle is embodied in *Feist v. Rural*, a case in which the Supreme Court determined that a telephone directory could not be copyrighted. Its content—the facts of subscriber names, addresses, and telephone numbers—certainly could not; and its form, alphabetical order, was transparently routine. In Europe, matters markedly differ, one reason why harmonization with European law is avidly sought by American copyright holders. In Europe, even data can be copyrighted, provided it is contained in a database whose construction required a substantial investment. This investment, not inherent creativity, confers ownership, even government ownership of data generated under its sponsorship. Such data can be withheld or sold, a situation impossible in the United States.[46,47]

Even after Bayh-Dole, an American law that permits universities to patent inventions based on government-generated data, researchers are not permitted to place that data itself beyond common use. Still, after Bayh-Dole the situation has seriously worsened for the advocates of open data sharing online. Since 1980 there has been an explosion of university interest in the revenue stream license revenues create. This stream can be robust indeed. In 1980 the University of California took in just over $1 million in patents; in 1995 the figure was over $39 million. Of course, such impressive gains must not allow us to overstate the *general* impact of patents on the academic research community: At the University of California, the five top earners—all biomedical patents—earned 85% of the whole.[48]

While such numbers are impressive, the present system is far from maximizing reputational and financial gains for universities or industry. The increase available from successful wide-scale collaboration would be greater still. Stubborn diseases like Alzheimer's, Parkinson's, and the various cancers have by and large not given up their secrets to isolated efforts. Big Pharma, especially, is in crisis. Patents on lucrative drugs are expiring; moreover, new drugs that may have looked promising "upstream," before rigorous testing, have more and more proved to be failures "downstream," at the level of the clinic.

While Big Pharma has in its possession banks of testable material now under lock and key, academic researchers have the skills—currently underutilized—with which to test new drugs.[49,50] A partnership between universities and industry would reduce wasteful targeting and would create an innovative community comprising

> individuals or firms interconnected by information transfer links which may involve face-to-face, electronic, or other communication. These can, but need not, exist within the boundaries of a membership group. They often do, but need not, incorporate the qualities of communities for participants, where "communities" is defined as meaning "networks of interpersonal ties that provide sociability, support, information, a sense of belonging, and social identity."[51]

Successful communities of this sort abound. Within academia we have the International Cancer Genome Consortium[52]; within industry we have the Biomarkers Consortium and the Predictive Safety Testing Consortium.[53] Examples that combine industry and academia are the 1000 Genomes Project[54] and the Alzheimer's Disease Neuroimaging Initiative.[55] Projects of this sort are increasing as international collaborative networks increase, a gain that can be readily tracked by patterns of co-authorship.[56,57] Numerous models for scaling such systems up also exist.[58–62] Almost invariably, these recommend restricted access to at least some of this data and material. One important reason is patient confidentiality.[63,64] Marc Rodwin cites the Veterans Administration and Kaiser Permanente as successful public and private ventures in the management of patient data,[65] models to be imitated so that patient data vital to medical research can be extracted and transferred to an Internet database without violating confidentiality.

All of these communities are designed to overcome the inhibiting effect of over-zealous patent and copyright enforcement:

> In retrospect, it seems ironic that just as new technologies were producing significant breakthroughs in scientific research, and as digitally networked sites and other information technologies began empowering new models of collaborative investigation, innovation policies that should embrace these developments were instead using intellectual property rights to control or, in many cases, impede them. The successive use of public and private law to preclude access to basic knowledge resources, as well as knowledge-based goods, has increased the political and social burden of an intellectual property regime that, in theory, remains dedicated to the public interest of society at large.[66]

Universities ought to lead in establishing "digitally networked sites" and "new models of collaborative investigation" by data sharing; they ought to cease to be at war, either with themselves or with industry. Indeed, as we have just seen, in more and more cases peace treaties have been signed that facilitate mutually beneficial trade.[67]

Subject to contractual, administrative, and ethical constraints, scientists control the data they generate; in contrast, the humanities more often have as their subject a product owned by others, at least for a time. In the United States, for works published after 1978 that time is now the life of the author plus 70 years, a recent extension that has been challenged before the Supreme Court on the grounds of the Constitution's stipulation of copyright's purpose: to encourage learning for the public good by providing authors with a *temporary* monopoly. Mickey Mouse, who celebrated his 80th birthday in 2008, is still under copyright, and "orphan works" whose copyright holder cannot be found are still presumed to be under copyright and not in the public domain.

Nevertheless, the latest extension of copyright has been judged constitutional. In *Eldred v. Ashcroft*, the Supreme Court denied the plaintiff's allegations that the Copyright Term Extension Act (CTEA) was unconstitutional.[68] The Court found that the Act

> is a rational enactment; we are not at liberty to second-guess congressional determinations and policy judgments of this order, however debatable or arguably unwise they may be. Accordingly, we cannot conclude that the CTEA which continues the unbroken congressional practice of treating future and existing copyrights in parity for term extension purposes is an impermissible exercise of Congress' power under the Copyright Clause.[69]

In our view, this opinion represents a peak of injudicious adjudication. The Act is clearly contrary to the Founders' intent. It has initiated a process in which what had been intended as a temporary monopoly over publication rights is transformed into a right of ownership in perpetuity. In so doing, the Act has conflated the idea of a physical book, which can be so owned, with the right to access and use the contents of the book, which the Constitution never intended to be so owned beyond a severely limited period.[70,71]

One might think this decision is irrelevant to scholarship in the humanities. Scholars have a right to fair use that permits comment and critique of all copyrighted culture, not excluding that of the 20th and 21st centuries. While it is true that no permission is generally needed in order to reproduce short prose excerpts from extended works, much of 20th- and 21st-century culture consists not of printed words, but of music and moving and still images. Concerning these, fair use does not readily apply.

Or so it proved in our case. We reproduced over 130 images from scientific books and articles in *Science from Sight to Insight: How Scientists Illustrate Meaning*.[72] To do so, in 2012 we paid over $2,500 in permissions. In addition, we invested a week of work, struggling, often unsuccessfully, to discover who actually owned what, trying not without anxiety to convince our publisher that our powers of persuasion did not extend to publishers who had vanished and authors two decades dead. The barrier of copyright is also pertinent to communications on the web. In his dissent in *Eldred* Justice Breyer details typical problems:

> the American Association of Law Libraries points out that the clearance process associated with creating an electronic archive, *Documenting the American South*, "consumed approximately a dozen man-hours" per work ... The College Art Association says that the costs of obtaining permission for use of single images, short excerpts, and other short works can become prohibitively high; it describes the abandonment of efforts to include, e.g., campaign songs, film excerpts, and documents exposing "horrors of the chain gang" in historical works or archives; and it points to examples in which copyright holders in effect have used their control of copyright to try to control the content of historical or cultural works.[73]

Nor is the problem confined to reproduction of 20th- and 21st-century cultural products. One need only read Katherine Rudy's account of her difficulties in obtaining access to brick-and-mortar archives and permission to reproduce images therein in her pursuit of medieval scholarship.[74]

Right now, fair use does not behave like a right. I have a right not to incriminate myself. It is absolute; I can assert it without penalty. I have a right to free speech. True, I cannot yell "fire" in a crowded theater. But within these well-known limitations, I need not ask permission to air my views in public. If, however, I assert my right to reproduce any portion of *Rhapsody in Blue*, *Friendly Persuasion*, or *Guernica* for the purpose of scholarly comment and critique, my reward might well be a letter threatening to sue. Susan Scafidi comments:

> It is frightening to get a cease-and-desist letter. I am certainly not a digital native. I speak with an accent. I am terrified when I get them. I usually bare my teeth and send back a nasty letter. I have always, in the few cases it has been, gotten an "Oh sorry, professor"—in one case, exactly those two words. But it is still nerve-wracking to get that.[75]

Most of us are not law professors like Susan Scafidi. Most of us would cease and desist. We would be wise to do so. Even a summary judgment—one that avoids a trial—can run in the "tens of thousands of dollars."[76] Moreover, a decision against a defendant—you—can be very costly:

> The range for statutory damages is between $750 and $30,000 per infringed work, and this amount can be increased to $150,000 per work if willful infringement is proven. In many cases, the real threat is the fee-shifting provision by which defendants can be made to pay the copyright owner's attorney's fees, which can exceed the amount of damages.[77]

Fair use in contested areas—those beyond simple prose quotation—is not so much a right as a suggestion to hire an attorney. Suppose we do. Our advocate will build an affirmative defense according to the following criteria:

(1) the purpose and character of the use, including whether such use is of a commercial nature or is for nonprofit educational purposes;
(2) the nature of the copyrighted work;
(3) the amount and substantiality of the portion used in relation to the copyrighted work as a whole; and
(4) the effect of the use upon the potential market for or value of the copyrighted work.[78]

There is a difference of opinion concerning the degree to which these factors constrain decisions judges and juries make, the extent to which they permit plaintiffs and defendants to predict outcomes. Some believe that the degree is close to zero.[79] Others are more optimistic; they believe that a firm distinction is emerging between mere reproduction and a use that is "transformative."[80–82] Transformative uses include the rap parody of *Pretty Woman*, as well as a case in which Grateful Dead posters owned by the Bill Graham Archive were reproduced in a biography of the music group. In *New Era Publishing International v. Carol Publishing*, a case involving a biography of Scientology founder L. Ron Hubbard, an important point was made concerning the strength of a defendant's claim of fair use: Defendants were more likely to prevail if they gave reasons for their reuse of copyrighted material. It would be especially pertinent if these reasons coincided with their professional organization's code of fair use. Some believe a trend is emerging in which transformative uses never violate copyright law. Of course, no one can predict what a plaintiff will do or what a judge will determine.

Still, the more optimistic point of view might prevail. It is incorporated in Madison's pattern-oriented approach to fair use.[83] It is a strategy recommended in Aufderheide and Jaszi's *Reclaiming Fair Use.*[84] It is embodied in such scholarly codes of fair use as that of the International Communication Association.[85] Nevertheless, we would be unwise to count on scholarly opinion or on codes. Despite all optimistic assessments, the scope of fair use remains unclear because, as Samuelson points out, "the relevant case law is quite thin."[86] Nevertheless, it is getting thicker every day.

Moreover, trepidation may be unwarranted, at least for state universities, all of which have sovereign immunity. In *Cambridge University Press v. Becker et al.*, a suit filed against Georgia State University over the propriety of its making copies for electronic reserves, had the plaintiff won, injunctive relief is all Cambridge would have achieved: Georgia State University would have had to stop producing and sharing these reserves. A state university whose press asserted fair use would thus risk only legal fees, as in a civil suit each side usually pays its own. Even in this case a judge might decide that the plaintiff must pay all fees on the grounds that its suit was frivolous. Furthermore, if the publications that aggressively asserted fair use were entirely electronic, entirely online, potential plaintiffs would have been offered the smallest possible target. In case of loss, no books or journals would need to be pulped; only an offending movie clip or two would have to be excised.

FREEDOM OF INFORMATION: THE FIFTH OBSTACLE

A fifth obstacle faces scholars of contemporary history, indeed any scholar whose research relies on access to recent national and local government documents, as well as related images, video, and audio recording: Many legal, ethical, and financial impediments stand in the way of making such materials open to all through digital archives, a situation that Internet access is in the process of transforming.

In the past, scholars have relied on regular deposits into brick-and-mortar archives after a number of years, usually 20 or 30. In addition, it had been possible—in fact, it still is possible—to request documents still shielded under these timelines. These will be released when, in the judgment of agency officials, they do not compromise current government operations or reveal protected personal data, such as health records. Such documents might still be released with their sensitive information redacted. This situation has been made more complex, however, especially in the last two or three decades, by the passage of various national and state Freedom of Information acts designed to give not only scholars, but also the general public access to a behind-the-scenes look at the workings of government. By 2010, 90 countries had such acts.[87] By 2012, while many Asian and African nations lagged behind, 90% of the nations in Europe and the Americas had one.[88]

Freedom of Information acts are beset with problems. Because requests for government documents have dramatically increased, scholars now compete with the general public on an equal basis, leading to delays of months and sometimes years. Although senior scholars may be able to accommodate to such delays, for graduate students writing theses and dissertations, they are clearly unworkable. These management problems are exacerbated by overclassification, creating unnecessary refusals and lengthy procedural delays.[89],[90] Added to management problems are those of convenient access. In the United States, although presidential papers are covered by the Freedom of Information Act as are other state papers, they are scattered in presidential libraries throughout the country.[91] In formerly totalitarian regimes, moreover, Freedom of Information acts must struggle against an ingrained habit of secrecy.[92]

There is another difficulty with Freedom of Information acts, the worry that open access will lead to empty archives, that as a consequence of their enactment wary politicians will entrust fewer of their views to writing or other means of recording. An informed observer from Sweden gives this worry anecdotal substance:

I have amused myself by asking a number of [Swedish] senior corporate managers whether they have ever written to the government on a matter that was important to them. The answer was no—important issues are discussed orally, by telephone or in some other way.[93]

While it is too early to tell whether such reluctance is so general as to constitute a worry for scholars, Gill Bennett's view seems only common sense: "in practice … it is impossible for public servants to do their jobs without writing things down."[94] Perhaps also they need not worry. The evidence is hardly robust, but it does point to the possibility that open access might not interfere with legitimate government operations. In Scotland, for instance, open access "has not caused 'a chilling effect' or altered government effectiveness and decision-making."[95]

There is another source of government documents: whistleblowers. Although in countries such as the United States and Sweden these men and women are protected by legislation, it is not clear whether that protection applies in a particular case. It is clear, however, that scholars using such leaked material are under no legal obligation to refrain from doing so.[96] Anyone can use the video of an Apache gunship attack on civilians in Baghdad, released by WikiLeaks.[97] This video is an excellent candidate for analysis within the context of the war in Iraq as a whole and concerning the rules of engagement in particular, an analysis that can be best carried out frame by frame. Of course, while scholars can use such leaked material with impunity, governments and commercial entities can try to deny organizations such as WikiLeaks access and support; indeed, they have done so. But their measures were punitive in vain. Anonymous, a group of hackers, have attacked those who choose to limit access and have created "mirror" sites to sidestep any attack on WikiLeaks itself.[98]

While legal issues concerning scholarly use are reasonably clear, ethical issues are less so. It is one thing for the *New York Times* to balance the public's right to know against the harm that release will cause; the Pentagon Papers is a case in point. It is quite another for this balance test to be in the hands not only of the *Times* but also of *The Guardian* and *Der Spiegel*, organizations that have, as the WikiLeaks case proved, very different scales for measuring harm. The ethical dilemma is further complicated when, acting as a newspaper, WikiLeaks releases documents on its own, following its own dramatically different sense of balance.[99],[100] These problems mount because WikiLeaks is not an isolated phenomenon; it is part of a general trend, the deinstitutionalization of the news business. Leaking sensitive or false information through the web creates a situation in which legal and ethical responsibility may be difficult or impossible to fix.

Still, there is little doubt that most unauthorized releases enrich scholarly resources with material that is of historical, political, or social significance, material that may cause embarrassment but no real harm and that, consequently, raises no ethical problems. The Apache gunship incident is an example. It is also an example of the power of Internet access. You can see unfold before your eyes what looks every bit like an American war crime. Despite any legal or ethical difficulties, there is little doubt that enhanced access to government materials offers scholars an historic opportunity to understand the recent past and to document their conclusions more completely. Given that these digital troves now include still images and audio and video records, scholars of the recent past also have the opportunity to put the affordances of the Internet to good use.

Universities ought to recognize the difficulties such scholars face; they ought to encourage and acknowledge their pursuits in their reward systems. They also ought to mobilize their lobbyists and their academic and professional organizations to increase openness. Citizens need access, to be sure; scholars need privileged access. Of course, as more and more of these documents and related materials from government agencies find their way to open-access sites on the Internet, less and less privilege will be required.

A PATH FORWARD

The primary institution with the means to substantially reduce all five obstacles to Internet exploitation is the research university. It is in the best position to lead in removing the obstacles to the gated circulation of new knowledge, updating of tenure and promotion codes, implementing long-term preservation of complex digital projects, encouraging open data sharing and more reasonable policies for fair use, and promoting timely access to government or other restricted documents. In organizations as large and diverse as research universities, however, collective action is difficult to achieve so long as employees behave like rational actors concerned only with their self-interest, economic machines who maximize their gains and minimize their expenditures of effort. Such model men and women have little incentive to participate in actions costly to them, actions that, because these organizations are so large, promise only meager benefits to most. In any case, any change for the better will benefit all whether or not they participate in effecting it; they will get a "free ride."

Perhaps, however, rational actor theory is an unreasonable oversimplification of the way human beings actually behave. Perhaps they do not have one order of preference they unvaryingly apply, regardless of the situation. Indeed, anyone who acted that way, Nobelist Amartya Sen believes, would be a "bit of a fool" and "close to being a social moron."[101] Nobelist Douglass C. North is critical of rational actor theory for the same reason: He feels that its chief proponent, Mancur Olson,[102] misses "evolving ideological perspectives that have led individuals to have contrasting views of the fairness of their situation and to act upon those views."[103]

It is such criticisms that motivated work on a theory that could explain why some collective action succeeds. This has been the task of Nobel laureate Elinor Ostrom, her students, and her collaborators. Her landmark book *Governing the Commons* appeared in 1990.[104] Since then, she has advanced her theory through numerous articles and edited collections. In the first two decades, her focus was on the management of such natural resources as fisheries. In 2011, however, with the publication of *Understanding Knowledge as a Commons*, she broadened the scope of her theory.[105] In 2011, in a parallel effort, in *The Penguin and the Leviathan*, Yochai Benkler[106] provided a cascade of evidence that this theory makes sense in a broad range of applications—real-life examples supported by a host of experimental studies showing that human beings are actually prone to cooperative behavior.

Our task parallels that of Ostrom and Benkler. We are concerned with the possibility of change through collective action in institutions whose chief business is the generation, communication, and evaluation of knowledge. We acknowledge that there is good reason to question the ability of universities to employ rapid technological change in the interest of advancing these goals. Existing rules can be out of step with technological potentials, impeding positive change. In addition, new rules generated by newly adopted technologies, such as computer programs, can apply constraints that interfere with rather than support institutional priorities. Indeed, technological inversion is possible, a state of affairs in which "the capabilities of technology contradict traditional missions, values, or even constitutional rights."[107]

While it would be foolish to make light of the difficulties posed by complex and changing university environments, we think that we can afford to be optimistic that barriers to advance can be overcome. Our first cause for optimism concerns the nature of the resource in question. Data, information, and knowledge they generate have a peculiar character: To give them away is not to lose them, unlike a commodity such as a car or a computer. Moreover, unimpeded access to knowledge has a value far higher than the cost of providing it.[108] Because this is so, faculty and administration are well motivated to address any imbalance. Moreover, altruism—giving away knowledge to all institutions of higher learning, especially to those in developing countries—costs no more than creating and maintaining a system that makes access possible.[109] These resources are already available to scholars and scientists in research positions in the West: There is only relative scarcity, a condition in which no scarcity at all can easily seem within reach.[110]

We are also struck by how closely the organization of universities conforms to potentially progressive design principles. First, they have clearly defined and well-policed boundaries, honed by centuries of practice. Second, not only are the rules they follow well matched to local needs and conditions but their faculties participate in governance—that is, in enforcing and modifying these rules. Third, systems are in place that monitor the behavior of faculty and administrators, seeing to it that they conform to accepted norms. When those norms are violated, moreover, a graduated system of sanctions exists; low-cost conflict-resolution procedures are also available. Fourth, the right of institutions to behave independently in this way is well accepted by the larger society. Finally, institutional activities are nested: There is an intricate, interlocking, and well-integrated hierarchy to manage both daily operations and long-term planning.[111] No one who has lived in a university setting for any length of time would argue these sub-systems work efficiently. Such a person might argue, however, that they do not have to work efficiently to work, equally, to the benefit of the professoriate and the advance of knowledge.

This is especially true because this structure leads to two other features conducive to positive institutional change. First, outcomes are highly predictable—an internal grant program designed to foster Internet innovation in science and scholarship will tend to do so. Second, given that universities prefer incremental changes that entail low transaction costs, those that require relatively little time and effort, a change in tenure and promotion guidelines so as not to discriminate against Internet publication easily falls in this category. Of course, positive change will not likely occur in the absence of leadership, always a rare commodity. Its most probable occurrence will be among top-tier research universities, a guarantee that the changes instituted have met the highest academic standards and can be widely and safely adopted.

Most of what we suggest need not involve substantive additional cost, and nothing need involve university administrations and their faculties in large-scale procedural or institutional innovation. Ours is a conservative program designed to accommodate radical epistemic and communicative change, to contain this change well within the boundaries of established policies, procedures, priorities, and budgets, and well within the realm of scholars and scientists who make claims and back up those claims with evidence and arguments.

Nevertheless, we have no illusions that the program we suggest will be easy to implement. Our claim is only that it is better than two far-less-desirable alternatives: to insist on radical institutional change or to do nothing whatever. As Yochai Benkler makes clear, change will occur regardless. File sharing is a dramatic instance:

> Alongside these institutionally instantiated moves to create a self-reinforcing set of common resources, there is a widespread, global culture of ignoring exclusive rights. It is manifest in the widespread use of file-sharing software to share copyrighted materials. It is manifest in the widespread acclaim that those who crack copy-protection mechanisms receive. This culture has developed a rhetoric of justification that focuses on the overreaching of the copyright industries and on the ways in which the artists themselves are being exploited by rights holders. While clearly illegal in the United States, there are places where courts have sporadically treated participation in these practices as copying for private use, which is exempted in some countries, including a number of European countries. In any event the sheer size of this movement and its apparent refusal to disappear in the face of lawsuits and public debate present a genuine countervailing pressure against the legal tightening of exclusivity.[112]

Change will occur; it just will not occur according to plan unless there is a plan. Although Internet science and scholarship will advance regardless, colleges and universities will have lost a leadership role of the process. They will not govern events; events will govern them.

Notes

CHAPTER I

1. C. P. Snow, *Two Cultures and a Second Look* (Cambridge: Cambridge University Press, 1964), 14 and 15.

2. Ibid., 16.

3. "The One Hundred Most Influential Books Since the War," *Times Literary Supplement*, October 6, 1995, p. 39.

4. Snow, 12–13.

5. Ibid., 14–15.

6. Sharon Traweek, *Beamtimes and Lifetimes: The World of High Energy Physicists* (Cambridge, MA: Harvard University Press, 1988), 79.

7. Ibid., 273.

8. Max Weber, *The Protestant Ethic and the Spirit of Capitalism*, translated by Stephen Kalberg, 3rd ed. (Los Angeles: Roxbury Publishing Company, 2002), 101.

9. Jerome Kagan, *Three Cultures: Natural Sciences, Social Sciences, and Humanities in the 21st Century* (Cambridge: Cambridge University Press, 2009).

10. Paul Arthur Schilpp, ed., *Albert Einstein, Philosopher-Scientist*, 2 vols. (New York: Harper and Row, 1959).

11. René Descartes, *Discourse on Method, Optics, Geometry, and Meteorology*, translated by Paul J. Olscamp, revised ed. (Indianapolis: Hackett Publishing, 2001).

12. Edward L. Ayers, *In the Presence of Mine Enemies: War in the Heart of America, 1859–63* (New York: W. W. Norton, 2003).

13. William G. Thomas, *The Iron Way: Railroads, the Civil War, and the Making of America* (New Haven: Yale University Press, 2011).

14. Alan G. Gross, Joseph Harmon, and Michael Reidy, *Communicating Science: From the 17th Century to the Present* (New York: Oxford University Press, 2002).

15. James E. McClellan III, *Science Reorganized: Scientific Societies in the Eighteenth Century* (New York: Columbia University Press, 1985).

16. Timothy Lenoir, *Instituting Science: The Cultural Production of Scientific Disciplines* (Stanford: Stanford University Press, 1987), 53.

17. Robert K. Merton, *The Sociology of Science: Theoretical and Empirical Investigations*, ed. Norman W. Storer (Chicago: University of Chicago Press, 1973), 380.

18. J. A. Fernández, "The Transition from an Individual Science to a Collective One: The Case of Astronomy," *Scientometrics* 42, no. 1 (1998): 61–74.

19. Yves Gingras, "The Transformation of Physics from 1900 to 1945," *Physics in Perspective* 12 (2010): 248–265.

20. Timothy L. O'Brien, "Change in Academic Coauthorship: 1953–2003," *Science, Technology, & Human Values* 37, no. 3 (2012): 210–234.

21. Elena Arnova, Karen S. Baker, and Naomi Oreskes, "Big Science and Big Data in Biology: From the International Geophysical Year through the International Biological Program to the Long Term Ecological Research (LTER) Network, 1957–Present," *Historical Studies in the Natural Sciences* 40, no. 2 (2010): 183–224.

22. Hugo Horta and T. Austin Lacy, "How Does Size Matter for Science? Exploring the Effects of Research Unit Size on Academics' Scientific Productivity and Information Exchange Behaviors," *Science and Public Policy* 38, no. 6 (2011): 449–460.

23. Stefan Wuchy, Benjamin F. Jones, and Brian Uzzi, "The Increasing Dominance of Teams in Production of Knowledge," *Science* 316 (2006): 1036–1039.

24. Clifford Geertz, *The Interpretation of Cultures* (New York: Basic Books, 1973), 25.

25. Aristotle, *The Nicomachean Ethics*, translated by David Ross (New York: Oxford University Press, 1998).

26. John Austin, *How to Do Things with Words*, 2nd ed. (Cambridge, MA: Harvard University Press, 1975).

27. Northrup Frye, *Anatomy of Criticism: Four Essays* (Toronto: Toronto University Press, 2007).

28. Thomas S. Kuhn, *The Structure of Scientific Revolutions*, 50th anniversary ed. (Chicago: University of Chicago Press, 2012).

29. Walter Benjamin, "The Work of Art in the Age of Mechanical Reproduction," in *Illuminations*, translated by Hannah Arendt (London: Fontana, 1968).

30. H. Paul Grice, "Logic and Conversation," in P. Cole and J. Morgan, eds., *Syntax and Semantics*, vol. 3 (New York: Academic Press, 1975).

31. John Locke, *An Essay Concerning Human Understanding* (Oxford: Oxford University Press, 1979).

32. Martin Heidegger, *Being and Time*, translated by J. Macquarrie and E. Robinson (New York: Harper and Row, 1962).

33. Plato, *Lysis* (Cambridge: Cambridge University Press, 2005).

34. Ludwig Wittgenstein, *Philosophical Investigations* (New York: Macmillan, 1953).

35. Friedrich Schleiermacher, *Lectures on Philosophical Ethics*, ed. Robert B. Louden, translated by Louise Adey Huish (Cambridge: Cambridge University Press, 2002).

36. Ferdinand de Saussure, *Writings in General Linguistics*, eds. Simon Bouquet and Rudolf Engler (New York: Oxford University Press, 2006).

37. John T. E. McTaggart, "The Unreality of Time," *Mind* 17 (1908): 457–474.

38. Denis Corish, "McTaggart's Argument," *Philosophy* 80 (2005): 77–99.

39. Isaac Newton, "New Theory About Light and Colors," *Philosophical Transactions* 6 (1671): 3075–3087.

40. Wilhelm Konrad Röntgen, "On a New Kind of Rays," translated by Arthur Stanton, *Nature* 53 (1896): 274–276.

41. Ptolemy, *Almagest*, translated by G. J. Toomer (Princeton: Princeton University Press, 1998).

42. Ibn al-Haytham, *On the Configuration of the World*, translated by Y. Tzvi Langermann (New York: Garland, 1990).

43. Nicholas Copernicus, *On the Revolutions of the Heavenly Bodies*, translated by Edward Rosen, (London: Macmillan, 1972).

44. Charles Darwin, *On the Origin of Species*, 1st ed. (Cambridge, MA: Harvard University Press, 1859, 1964).

45. E. O. Wilson, *Sociobiology: The New Synthesis* (Cambridge, MA: Harvard University Press, 1975).

46. Yochai Benkler, *The Wealth of Networks: How Social Production Transforms Markets and Freedom* (New Haven: Yale University Press, 2006), 1 and 5.

47. Elizabeth Eisenstein, *The Printing Press as an Agent of Change: Communications and Cultural Transformations in Early Modern Europe* (Cambridge: Cambridge University Press, 1979).

48. H. Mercier and D. Sperber, "Why Do Humans Reason? Arguments for an Argumentative Theory," *Behavioral and Brain Sciences* 34 (2011): 57–74.

CHAPTER 2

1. John Stewart Owen, *The Scientific Article in the Age of Digitization* (Ph.D. thesis, University of Amsterdam, 2005), 5 and 11. Also published by Springer, Netherlands (2006).

2. Ibid., 55.

3. Stevan Harnad, "Post-Gutenberg Galaxy: The Fourth Revolution in the Means of Production of Knowledge," *Public-Access Computer Systems Review* 2 no. 1 (1991): 39–53.

4. A. G. Gross, J. E. Harmon, and M. Reidy, *Communicating Science: The Scientific Article from the 17th Century to the Present* (Oxford: Oxford University Press, 2002), 213.

5. H. M. Goodman and A. Rich, "Formation of a DNA-Soluble RNA Hybrid and Its Relation to the Origin, Evolution, and Degeneracy of Soluble RNA," *Proceedings of the National Academy of Sciences* 48 (1962): 2101–2109.

6. L. Aron, P. Klein, T.-T. Pham, E. R. Kramer, W. Wurst, and R. Klein, "Pro-survival Role for Parkinson's Associated Gene DJ-1 Revealed in Trophically Impaired Dopaminergic Neurons," *PLOS Biology* 8, no. 4 (2010), e1000349.

7. Gross et al., 185.

8. D. Harley, S. K. Acord, and C. Judson King, *Assessing the Future Landscape of Scholarly Communication: An Exploration of Faculty Values and Needs in Seven Disciplines* (Berkeley: Center for Studies in Higher Education, 2010), 12.

9. Charmaine Y. Pietersen, Maribel P. Lim, Tsung-Ung W. Woo, "Obtaining High Quality RNA from Single Cell Populations in Human Postmortem Brain Tissue," *Journal of Visualized Experiments* 30 (2009): doi: 10.3791/1444.

10. Michael Nielsen, "Is Scientific Publishing about to be Disrupted?" June 29, 2009, http://michaelnielsen.org/blog/is-scientific-publishing-about-to-be-disrupted.

11. L. Bintu, T. Ishibashi, M. Dangkulwanich, Y.-Y. Wu, L. Lubkowska, M. Kashlev, and C. Bustamante, "Nucleosomal Elements that Control the Topography of the Barrier to Transcription," *Cell* 151 (2012): 738–49.

12. Kent Anderson, "The Article of the Future—Just Lipstick Again?" July 21, 2009, http://scholarlykitchen.sspnet.org/2009/07/21/the-article-of-the-future-lipstick-on-a-pig.

13. Online Journalism Blog, "Elsevier's Article of the Future Resembles Websites of the Past," July 27, 2009, http://onlinejournalismblog.com/2009/07/27/elseviers-article-of-the-future-resembles-websites-of-the-past.

14. Thomson Reuters, "Science Watch, Top Ten Most-Cited Journals, 1999–2009," 2009, http://sciencewatch.com/dr/sci/09/aug2-09_2.

15. Jeffrey Beall, *Scholarly Open Access: Critical Analysis of Scholarly Open Access Publishing*, June 2014, http://scholarlyoa.com/publishers.

16. Jeffrey Beall, "Predatory Publishers Are Corrupting Open Access," *Nature* 489 (2012): 179.

17. Declan Butler, "Investigating Journals: The Dark Side of Publishing," *Nature* 495 (2013): 433–435.

18. Peter Woit, *Not Even Wrong: American Journal of Modern Physics*, June 2014, http://www.math.columbia.edu/~woit/wordpress/?p=5607.

19. Gross et al.

20. Aron et al.

21. Goodman and Rich, 2101.

22. Gross et al., 231.

23. Cameron Neylon, "More Than Just Access: Delivering on a Network-Enabled Literature," *PLOS Biology* 10 (2012): e1001417.

24. Gary Ward, "PLOS Expands Mission," September 28, 2012, http://archive-org.com/page/389908/2012-10-08/http://www.plos.org/plos-expands-mission.

25. Gross et al., 175.

26. S. Wuchty, B. F. Jones, and B. Uzzi, "The Increasing Dominance of Teams in Production of Knowledge," *Science* 316 (2007): 1036–1039.

27. B. F. Jones, S. Wuchty, and B. Uzzi, "Multi-university Research Teams: Shifting Impact, Geography, and Stratification in Science," *Science* 322 (2008): 1259–1262.

28. International Multiple Sclerosis Genetics Consortium and Wellcome Trust Case Control Consortium, "Genetic Risk and a Primary Role for Cell-Mediated Immune Mechanisms in Multiple Sclerosis," *Nature* 476 (2011): 214–219.

29. Aron et al., 1.

30. Ibid., 14.

31. P. B. Nina, J. M. Morrisey, S. M. Ganesan, H. Ke, A. M. Pershing, M. W. Mather, and A. B. Vaidya, "ATP Synthase Complex of Plasmodium Falciparum: Dimeric Assembly in Mitochondrial Membranes and Resistance to Genetic Disruption," *Journal of Biological Chemistry* 286 (2011): 41312–41322.

32. J. Harder, J. V. Moloney, and S. W. Koch, "Temperature-Dependence of the Internal Efficiency Droop in GaN-Based Diodes," *Applied Physics Letters* 99 (2011): 181127.

33. Charles Bazerman, "Intertextuality: How Texts Rely on Other Texts," in Charles Bazerman and Paul A. Prior, eds., *What Writing Does and How It Does It* (Mahwah, NJ: Lawrence Erlbaum Associates, 2003), 83–84.

34. George P. Landow, *Hypertext 3.0: Critical Theory and New Media in an Era of Globalization* (Baltimore: Johns Hopkins Press, 2006), 4.

35. Gross et al., 85 and 131.

36. Ibid., 169 and 180.

37. Eugene Garfield, "When to Cite," *The Library Quarterly* 66 (1996): 449–458.

38. Gross et al., 181–186.

39. Michael Nielsen, "The Future of Science," July 17, 2008, http://michaelnielsen.org/blog/the-future-of-science-2.

40. Goodman and Rich, 2106.

41. Edward R. Tufte, *Envisioning Information* (Cheshire, CT: Graphics Press, 1990), 81–82.

42. J. Ma and W. Yang, "Three-Dimensional Distribution of Transient Interactions in the Nuclear Pore Complex Obtained from Single-Molecule Snapshots," *Proceedings of National Academy of Sciences* 107 (2010): 7305–7310.

43. O. Yizhar, L. E. Fenno, M. Prigge, F. Schneider, T. J. Davidson, D. J. O'Shea, V. S. Sohal, I. Goshen, J. Finkelstein, J. T. Paz, K. Stehfest, R. Fudim, C. Ramakrishnan, J. R. Huguenard, P. Hegemann, and K. Deisseroth, "Neocortical Excitation/Inhibition Balance in Information Processing and Social Dysfunction," *Nature* 477 (2011): 171–178.

44. I. Konvalinka, Dimitris Xygalatas, Joseph Bulbulia, Uffe Schjødt, Else-Marie Jegindø, Sebastian Wallot, Guy Van Orden, and Andreas Roepstorff, "Synchronized Arousal Between Performers and Related Spectators in a Fire-Walking Ritual," *Proceedings of National Academy of Sciences* 108 (2011): 8514–8519.

45. C. Sayrin, I. Dotsenko, X. Zhou, B. Peaudecerf, T. Rybarczyk, S. Gleyzes, P. Rouchon, M. Mirrahimi, H. Amini, M. Brune, J.-M. Raimond, and S. Haroche, "Real-Time Quantum Feedback Prepares and Stabilizes Photon Number States," *Nature* 477 (2011): 73–77.

46. K. Bodin, S. Ellmerich, M. C. Kahan, G. A. Tennent, A. Loesch, J. A. Gilbertson, W. L. Hutchinson, P. P. Mangione, J. Ruth Gallimore, D. J. Millar, S. Minogue, A. P. Dhillon, G. W. Taylor, A. R. Bradwell, A. Petrie, J. D. Gillmore, V. Bellotti, M. Botto, P. N. Hawkins, and M. B. Pepys, "Antibodies to Human Serum Amyloid P Component Eliminate Visceral Amyloid Deposits," *Nature* 468 (2010): 93–97.

47. B. Boehm, H. Westerberg, G. Lesnicar-Pucko, S. Raja, M. Rautschk, J. Cotterell, J. Swoger, and J. Sharpe, "The Role of Spatially Controlled Cell Proliferation in Limb Bud Morphogenesis," *PLOS Biology* 8, no. 7 (2010): e1000420.

48. D'Arcy Thompson, *On Growth and Form* (London: Cambridge University Press, 1917). Reprinted in abridged form in 1945.

49. Julian Huxley, *Problems of Relative Growth* (New York: Dial Press, 1932), 105.

50. Fred L. Bookstein, "The Measurement of Biological Shape and Shape Change," in S. Levin, ed., *Lecture Notes in Biomathematics* (Berlin: Springer-Verlag, 1978), 69.

51. Thompson, 751.

52. Ibid., 736.

53. Huxley, 106.

54. Ibid., 292.

55. Thompson, 106.

56. Huxley, 17.

57. Ibid., 31.

58. Ibid., 270.

59. Ibid., 275.

60. Ibid., 299.

61. Ibid., 81; see also 116.

62. Ibid., 96, 98, 103.

63. Karl Pearson and G. M. Morant, "The Wilkinson Head of Oliver Cromwell and its Relationship to Busts, Masks and Painted Portraits," *Biometrika* 26 (1934): 1–116.

64. Fred L. Bookstein, "A Hundred Years of Morphometrics," *Acta Zoologica Academiae Scientiarum Hungaricae* 44 (1998): 7–59, 16.

65. Pearson and Morant, between 104 and 105.

66. Ibid., 85.

67. Ibid., 100.

68. Ibid., 104 and 105.

69. Ibid., 101.

70. Ibid., 103.

71. Ibid., 105.

72. Ibid., 106.

73. Ibid., 105.

74. David Kendall, "The Diffusion of Shape," *Advances in Applied Probability* 9 (1977): 428–430, 428.

75. Dean C. Adams, F. James Rohlf, and Dennis E. Slice, "Geometric Morphometrics: Ten Years of Progress Following the Revolution," *Italian Journal of Zoology* 7 (2004): 5–16, 5.

76. Ibid., 13.

77. F. James Rohlf and Leslie F. Marcus, "A Revolution in Morphometrics," *Tree* 8 (1993): 129–132, 132.

78. Adams et al., 13.

79. Michael Coquerelle, Fred L. Bookstein, José Braga, and Demetrios J. Halazonetis, "Fetal and Infant Growth Patterns of the Mandibular Symphysis in Modern Humans and Chimpanzees (*Pan troglodytes*)," *Journal of Anatomy* 217 (2010): 507–520, 509.

80. Ibid., 511.

81. Adams et al., 11.

82. Miriam Leah Zelditch, Donald Swiderski, H. David Sheets, and William L. Fink, *Geometric Morphometrics for Biologists: A Primer* (Amsterdam: Elsevier, 2004), 393.

83. Adams et al., 13.

84. Coquerelle et al., 512.

85. Marcia Ponce de León and Christoph P. E. Zollikofer, "Neanderthal Cranial Ontogeny and its Implications for Late Hominid Diversity." *Nature* 412 (2001): 534–538.

86. Ibid., 536.

87. Fred Bookstein, e-mail communication with Alan Gross (June 16, 2011).

88. Paul Ginsparg, "ArXiv at 20," *Nature* 476 (2011): 145–147.

CHAPTER 3

1. Eugene Garfield, "Arts and Humanities Journals Differ from Natural and Social Sciences Journals—but Their Similarities Are Surprising," in *Essays of an Information Scientist*, Vol. 5 (Philadelphia: ISI Press, 1982), 761–767.

2. David Kolb, "Socrates in the Labyrinth," in G. P. Landow, ed., *Hyper/Text/Theory* (Baltimore: Johns Hopkins University Press, 1994), 323–342.

3. David Kolb, "The Revenge of the Page," in *Proceedings of 19th ACM Conference on Hypertext and Hypermedia* (Pittsburgh, PA: ACM Digital Library, 2008).

4. Anne Friedberg, "Virtual Window Interactive," *Vectors: Journal of Culture and Technology in a Dynamic Vernacular*, 3, no. 1 (2007), http://vectors.usc.edu/projects/index.php?project=79 &thread=ProjectCredits.

5. Anne Friedberg, *The Virtual Window: From Alberti to Microsoft* (Cambridge, MA: MIT Press, 2009).

6. Robert Darnton, *The Case for Books: Past, Present, and Future* (New York: Public Affairs, 2010), 79.

7. Deirdre Murphy, "On the Tenure Track with an e-Book," *Perspectives: Newsletter of the American Historical Association* 41 (May 2003): 34–36, https://www.historians.org/publications-and-directories/perspectives-on-history/may-2003/on-the-tenure-track-with-an-e-book.

8. Donald J. Waters and Joseph S. Meisel, *Scholarly Publishing Initiatives: 2007 Annual Report* (New York: Andrew W. Mellon Foundation, 2008), http://www.mellon.org/news_publications/annual-reports-essays/annual-reports/content2007.pdf.

9. Helena Pohlandt-McCormick, *"I Saw a Nightmare . . . Doing Violence to Memory: The Soweto Uprising, June 16, 1976* (New York: Columbia University Press, 2002), http://www.gutenberg-e.org/pohlandt-mccormick/index.html.

10. Ibid., "Introduction."

11. Ibid., "Introduction," fn. 1.

12. Ibid., Chapter 1, sec. 1, para. 15.

13. Ibid., *Asingeni*, para. 11.

14. Ibid., Chapter 4, The Participants, Zakes Molotsi, para. 16.

15. Ibid., Chapter 2, sect. 1, fn. 29.

16. Ibid., Chapter 4, sec. 2, para. 11.

17. Edward L. Ayers, "Narrating the New South," *Journal of Southern History* 61 (1995): 555–566.

18. Jack Censer and Lynn Hunt, eds., "Imaging the French Revolution," *American Historical Review* 110 (Feb. 2005), http://chnm.gmu.edu/revolution/imaging/home.html.

19. Jack Censer and Lynn Hunt, "Imaging the French Revolution: Depictions of the French Revolutionary Crowd," *American Historical Review* 110, no. 1 (2005): 38–45.

20. Jack Censer and Lynn Hunt, "Introduction," in "Imaging the French Revolution," *American Historical Review* 110 (Feb. 2005), http://chnm.gmu.edu/revolution/imaging/essays/introessay.html.

21. George Rudé, *The Crowd in the French Revolution* (London: Oxford University Press, 1959).

22. Warren Roberts, "Images of Popular Violence in the French Revolution: Evidence for the Historian?" in "Imaging the French Revolution," *American Historical Review* 110 (Feb. 2005), http://chnm.gmu.edu/revolution/imaging/essays/roberts1.html.

23. Richard Mowery Andrews, "Social Structures, Political Elites and Ideology in Revolutionary Paris, 1792–94: A Critical Evaluation of Albert Soboul's *Les Sans-Culottes Parisiens en l'an II*," *Journal of Social History* 19 (1985): 71–112, 78.

24. Joan Landes, "Discussion: On Material Objects and Digital Technology," in "Imaging the French Revolution," *American Historical Review* 110 (February 2005), http://chnm.gmu.edu/revolution/imaging/discussion/gh5.html.

25. Wayne Hanley, "Discussion: On-line Collaboration," in "Imaging the French Revolution," *American Historical Review* 110 (Feb. 2005), http://chnm.gmu.edu/revolution/imaging/discussion/gh5.html.

26. William G. Thomas III and Edward L. Ayers, *The Differences Slavery Made: A Close Analysis of Two American Communities* (Charlottesville, VA: Virginia Center for Digital History at the University of Virginia, 2003), http://www2.vcdh.virginia.edu/AHR.

27. Robert Fogel and Stanley Engerman, *Time on the Cross: The Economics of American Negro Slavery* (Boston: Little Brown, 1974).

28. Lennart Jörberg, "Robert Fogel and Douglass C. North: Award Ceremony Speech," in Torsten Persson, ed., *Nobel Lectures, Economics 1991–1995* (Singapore: World Scientific Publishing Co., 1997), http://www.nobelprize.org/nobel_prizes/economics/laureates/1993/presentation-speech.html.

29. Thomas Weiss, "Review of *Time on the Cross: The Economics of American Negro Slavery* by Robert Fogel and Stanley Engerman," EH.net, Economic History Association, 2001, http://eh.net/book_reviews/time-on-the-cross-the-economics-of-american-negro-slavery.

30. Ayers, "Narrating the New South."

31. Thomas and Ayers, "Introduction: Presentation."

32. Ibid., "Introduction: Overview."

33. Ibid., "Points of Analysis: Campaign of 1860."

34. Ibid., "Summary of Argument: Conclusion."

35. Ibid., "Evidence: Cash value of farms per capita comparison, 1850 and 1860."

36. Ibid., "Evidence: Acres of Farm Land, 1860."

37. Ibid., "Evidence: Augusta County, Va., Agricultural Production."

38. Ibid., "Crops."

39. Christine L. Borgman, "The Digital Future is Now: A Call to Action for the Humanities," *DHQ: Digital Humanities Quarterly* 3 (2009), http://www.digitalhumanities.org/dhq/vol/3/4/000077/000077.html.

40. William G. Thomas III, "Writing a Digital History Journal Article from Scratch: An Account," *Digital History Project: Essays*, December 2007, http://digitalhistory.unl.edu/essays/thomasessay.php.

41. Philip J. Ethington. "Los Angeles and the Problem of Urban Historical Knowledge," *American Historical Review* 112 (December 2007), http://www.usc.edu/dept/LAS/history/historylab/LAPUHK.

42. Ibid., "The Complexity of Political Space: Los Angeles County, 1849–1994."

43. Friedberg, *The Virtual Window*, 121.

44. Ethington, "Along Central."

45. Ibid., "Hispanic Population: 1970 and 1990."

46. Ibid., "2150 South Central Avenue."

47. Ibid., "Essay."

48. Ibid., "1905 and 2000 Panorama."

49. Diane Favro and Christopher Johanson, "Death in Motion: Funeral Processions in the Roman Forum," *Journal of the Society of Architectural Historians* 69 (2010): 12–37.

50. Ibid., 12.

51. Ibid., 15.

52. Ibid., 12.

53. Diane Favro, "In the Eyes of the Beholder: Virtual Reality Re-creations and Academia," *Journal of the Roman Archaeology Supplementary Series* 61, no. 1 (2006): 321–334, 321–322.

54. Diane Favro and Christopher Johanson, "Google Earth Model: An Image of the Roman Forum and Environs via Google Earth," accessed June 2014, http://www.jstor.org/action/showP opup?citid=citart1&id=figure0&doi=10.1525%2Fjsah.2010.69.1.12.

55. Christopher Johanson, *Spectacle in the Forum: Visualizing the Roman Aristocratic Funeral of the Middle Republic* (Ph.D. Thesis: University of California, Los Angeles, 1999), 22.

56. Roger Scruton, *Understanding Music: Philosophy and Interpretation* (London: Continuum, 2009), 11.

57. Ibid., 38.

58. Daniel Barenboim, "Beethoven and the Quality of Courage," *New York Review of Books*, April 4, 2013, http://www.nybooks.com/articles/archives/2013/apr/04/beethoven-and-quality-courage.

59. William E. Caplin, "Beethoven's 'Tempest' Exposition: A Response to Janet Schmalfeldt," *Music Theory Online* 16, no. 2 (2010), http://www.mtosmt.org/issues/mto.10.16.2/mto.10.16.2.caplin.html.

60. James Hepokoski, "Formal Process, Sonata Theory, and the First Movement of Beethoven's 'Tempest' Sonata," *Music Theory Online* 16, no. 2 (2010), http://www.mtosmt.org/issues/mto.10.16.2/mto.10.16.2.hepokoski.html.

61. Janet Schmalfeldt, "One More Time on Beethoven's 'Tempest,' from Analytic and Performance Perspectives: A Response to William E. Caplin and James Hepokoski," *Music Theory Online* 16, no. 2 (2010), http://www.mtosmt.org/issues/mto.10.16.2/mto.10.16.2.schmalfeldt3.html.

62. Dorottya Fabian and Emery Schubert, "Baroque Expressiveness and Stylishness in Three Recordings of the D Minor Sarabanda for Solo Violin (BWV 1004) by J. S. Bach," *Music Performance Research* 3 (2009): 36–55.

63. Robert Kolker, "The Moving Image Reclaimed," *Postmodern Culture* 5, no. 1 (1994), https://muse.jhu.edu/journals/postmodern_culture/summary/v005/5.1kolker.html.

64. Adrian Miles, "*Singin' in the Rain*: A Hypertextual Reading," *Postmodern Culture* 8, no. 2 (1998), http://muse.jhu.edu/login?auth=0&type=summary&url=/journals/postmodern_culture/v008/8.2miles.html.

65. Ibid., "*Singin' in the Rain:* Inside."

66. Stephen Mamber, "Who Shot Liberty Valance?" (Los Angeles: UCLA Department of Film, Television, and Digital Media), accessed June 2014, http://mamber.filmtv.ucla.edu/LibertyValance.

67. Ibid., "The Direction of the Bullets."

68. Ibid., "Scholarship."

69. Stephen Mamber, "The Mediascape Q&A: Stephen Mamber, Professor, Cinema and Media Studies," *Mediascape: UCLA's Journal of Cinema and Media Studies*, February 11, 2013, http://www.tft.ucla.edu/mediascape/blog/?p=1366.

70. Stephen Mamber, "Simultaneity and Overlap in Stanley Kubrick's *The Killing*," *Postmodern Culture*, 8, no. 2 (1998), http://muse.jhu.edu/login?auth=0&type=summary&url=/journals/postmodern_culture/v008/8.2mamber.html.

71. Stephen Mamber, "Narrative Mapping," in *New Media: Theories and Practices of Intertextuality*, ed. Anna Everett and John Caldwell (London: Routledge, 2003), 149.

72. Mamber, "Stanley Kubrick's *The Killing*."

73. Clifford James Galiher, *Mediascape: UCLA's Journal of Cinema and Media Studies,* January 27, 2013, http://www.tft.ucla.edu/mediascape/Winter2013_ThreeFates.html.

74. Bruno Latour, *An Enquiry into Modes of Existence: An Anthropology of the Moderns* (Cambridge, MA: Harvard University Press, 2013). See also http://www.modesofexistence.org.

CHAPTER 4

1. Helena Pohlandt-McCormick, *"I Saw a Nightmare ... Doing Violence to Memory: The Soweto Uprising, June 16, 1976* (New York: Columbia University Press, 2002), Chapter 1, sec. 2, para. 47, http://www.gutenberg-e.org/pohlandt-mccormick/PM.c1p2.html.

2. A. S. G. Edwards, "Back to the Real?" *Times Literary Supplement,* June 7, 2013, http://www.the-tls.co.uk/tls/public/article1269403.ece.

3. Ed Folsom, "Database as Genre: The Epic Transformation of Archives," *PMLA* 122 (2007): 1571–1579, 1576.

4. Alan G. Gross, Joseph Harmon, and Michael Reidy, *Communicating Science: From the 17th Century to the Present* (New York: Oxford University Press, 2002).

5. Jerome McGann, "The Rationale of Hypertext," *Radiant Textuality: Literature After the World Wide Web* (New York: Palgrave, 2001), 71.

6. Brigham Young University, "Overview: Corpus of Historical American English," accessed July 1, 2013, http://corpus.byu.edu/coha.

7. Harvey L. Molloy, "Before and After the Web: [An Interview with] George P. Landow," *electronic book review*, September 13, 2003, http://www.electronicbookreview.com/thread/technocapitalism/uncenterable.

8. Gregory R. Crane, "The Mission of Perseus," *Perseus Digital Library*, accessed July 1, 2013, http://www.perseus.tufts.edu/hopper/research.

9. Walt Whitman, *Leaves of Grass*, ed. Gay Wilson Allen (New York: New American Library, 1980), 82.

10. Ibid., 250.

11. Ibid., 389.

12. Geoffrey Keynes, ed., *The Complete Writings of William Blake* (New York: Random House, 1957), 887.

13. Ibid., 894.

14. Joseph S. Viscomi, e-mail communication with Alan Gross, August 2, 2013.

15. William J. Mitchell, *Blake's Composite Art: A Study of the Illuminated Poetry* (Princeton: Princeton University Press, 1978), 76.

16. Helen S. Ettlinger, "The Iconography of the Columns in Titian's Pesaro Altarpiece," *The Art Bulletin* 6 (1979): 59–67.

17. Mitchell, 6–9, 11–13, 210–211, 26–28.

18. Geoffrey Keynes, ed., *The Complete Writings of William Blake* (New York: Nonesuch Press, 1957), 778.

19. Anthony Blunt, "Blake's 'Ancient of Days': The Symbolism of the Compasses," *Journal of the Warburg Institute* 2 (1938): 54, 56.

20. Madeline Doran, *The Text of King Lear* (Palo Alto: Stanford University Publications, 1931), Vol. 4, No. 2.

21. Gary Taylor and Michael Warren, eds., *The Division of the Kingdoms: Shakespeare's Two Versions of King Lear* (Oxford: The Clarendon Press, 1983).

22. E. A. J. Honigmann, "The New Lear," *New York Review of Books*, February 2, 1984, http://www.nybooks.com/articles/archives/1984/feb/02/the-new-lear.

23. "The *Science* Contributors FAQ: What's the Policy on Publication of Data Sets?" *Science*, accessed December 2012, http://www.sciencemag.org/site/feature/contribinfo/prep/gen_info.xhtml#datadep.

24. "Understanding PDB Data: Looking at Structures," *Protein Data Bank*, accessed December 2012, http://www.rcsb.org/pdb/101/static101.do?p=education_discussion/Looking-at-Structures/intro.html.

25. H. M. Berman, B. C. Narayanan, L. D. Costanzo, S. Dutta, S. Ghosh, B. P. Hudson, C. L. Lawson, E. P. Andreas Prlić, P. W. Rose, C. Shao, H. Yang, J. Young, and C. Zardecki, "Trendspotting in the Protein Data Bank," *FEBS Letters* 587 (2013): 1036–1045.

26. L. Pauling, H. A. Itano, S. J. Singer, and I. C. Wells, "Sickle Cell Anemia, a Molecular Disease," *Science* 110 (1949): 543–548.

27. D. J. Harrington, K. Adachi, and W. E. Royer, Jr., "The High Resolution Crystal Structure of Deoxyhemoglobin S," *Journal of Molecular Biology* 272 (1997): 398–407.

28. H. M. Berman, J. Westbrook, Z. Feng, G. Gilliland, T. N. Bhat, H. Weissig, I. N. Shindyalov, and P. E. Bourne, "The Protein Data Bank," *Nucleic Acids Research* 28 (2000): 235–242.

29. T. J. W. Clark, S. A. Houck, and J. I. Clark, "Hemoglobin Interactions with αB Crystallin: A Direct Test of Sensitivity to Protein Instability," *PLOS ONE* 7 (2012): e40486.

30. E. Hodis, E. Martz, M. M. Walls, and J. Prilusky, "The High Resolution Crystal Structure of Deoxyhemoglobin S," *Proteopedia*, accessed June 2014, http://proteopedia.org/wiki/index.php/2hbs.

31. Paul Ginsparg, "It Was 20 Years Ago Today . . .," *ArXiv*, August 14, 2011, http://arxiv.org/abs/1108.2700.

32. "ArXiv Stats," *ArXiv*, April 2015, http://arxiv.org/stats/monthly_submissions.

33. "First Clay Mathematics Institute Millennium Prize Announced Today Prize for Resolution of the Poincaré Conjecture Awarded to Dr. Grigoriy Perelman," Clay Mathematics Institute, March 18, 2010, http://www.claymath.org/sites/default/files/millenniumprizefull.pdf.

34. Nadejda Lobastova and Michael Hirst, "Maths Genius Living in Poverty," *The Sydney Morning Herald*, August 21, 2006, http://www.smh.com.au/news/world/maths-genius-living-in-poverty/2006/08/20/1156012411120.html.

35. Tracy Vence, "Q&A: One Million Preprints and Counting: Conversation with ArXiv founder Paul Ginsparg," *The Scientist*, December 23, 2004, http://www.the-scientist.com/?articles.view/articleNo/41677/title/Q-A--One-Million-Preprints-and-Counting.

36. Ginsparg.

37. "Figshare Partners with Open Access Mega Journal Publisher PLOS," *Figshare Blog*, January 2013, http://figshare.com/blog/figshare_partners_with_Open_Access_mega_journal_publisher_PLOS/68.

38. Yochai Benkler, *The Wealth of Networks: How Social Production Transforms Markets and Freedom* (New Haven: Yale University, 2006), 81.

39. Tim Adams, "Galaxy Zoo and the New Dawn of Citizen Science," *The Guardian*, March 18, 2012, http://www.guardian.co.uk/science/2012/mar/18/galaxy-zoo-crowdsourcing-citizen-scientists.

40. "An Introduction to Foldit," *YouTube*, accessed May 2015, https://www.youtube.com/watch?v=DvYFjo3vC-k&list=UUGjfDFjL-7rvhRRl2keqhcA&index=2.

41. S. Cooper, F. Khatib, A. Treuille, J. Barbero, J. Lee, M. Beenen, A. Leaver-Fay, D. Baker, Z. Popović, and Foldit players, "Predicting Protein Structures with a Multiplayer Online Game," *Nature* 466 (2010): 756–760.

42. "The Story So Far," *Galaxy Zoo*, accessed December 2012, http://www.galaxyzoo.org/#/story.

43. Graham Silsby, "Objects at or Beyond the Limits of Resolution," *Galaxy Zoo Forum*, September 27, 2012, http://www.galaxyzooforum.org/index.php?topic=280427.0.

44. Tom Zolotor, "Objects at or Beyond the Limits of Resolution," *Galaxy Zoo Forum*, October 11, 2012, http://www.galaxyzooforum.org/index.php?topic=280427.0.

45. Hanny Van Arkel, "The Hanny's Voorwerp," *Galaxy Zoo Forum*, August 13, 2007, http://www.galaxyzooforum.org/index.php?topic=3802.0.

46. Chris Lintott, Kevin Schawinski, William Keel, Hanny van Arkel, Nicola Bennert, Edward Edmondson, Daniel Thomas, Daniel Smith, Peter Herbert, Matt Jarvis, Shanil Virani, Dan Andreescu, Steven Bamford, Kate Land, Phil Murray, Robert Nichol, Jordan Raddick, Anze Slosar, Alex Szalay, and Jan Vandenberg, "Galaxy Zoo : 'Hanny's Voorwerp', a Quasar Light Echo?" *ArXiv*, June 29, 2009, http://arxiv.org/abs/0906.5304.

47. Michael Nielsen, *Reinventing Discovery: The New Era of Networked Science* (Princeton: Princeton University Press, 2012), 170.

48. Sally McGrane, "Crowdsourcing Tolstoy," *New Yorker*, October 14, 2013 http://www.newyorker.com/online/blogs/books/2013/10/crowdsourcing-tolstoy.html.

49. Edward O. Wilson, "The Encyclopedia of Life," *TRENDS in Ecology and Evolution* 18 (2003): 77–80, 77.

50. "What Is the Encyclopedia of Life?" *Encyclopedia of Life*, accessed July 2013, http://eol.org/about.

51. "Who Uses EOL?" *Encyclopedia of Life*, accessed July 2013, http://eol.org/info/disc_scientists.

52. C. Michael Hogan, "My Info," *Encyclopedia of Life*, accessed July 2013, http://eol.org/users/40106.

53. J. Rosindell and L. I. Harmon, "OneZoom: A Fractal Explorer for the Tree of Life," *PLOS Biology* 10, No. 10 (2012): e1001406.

54. Ed Folsom, "Reply," *PMLA* 122 (2007): 1608–1612, 1611.

55. E. Curry, A. Freitas, and S. O'Riain, "The Role of Community-Driven Data Curation for Enterprises," in David Wood, ed., *Linking Enterprise Data*, David Wood (Springer, 2010), 25–47.

CHAPTER 5

1. David M. Raup, *The Nemesis Affair: A Story of the Death of Dinosaurs and the Ways of Science* (New York: W. W. Norton, 1999), 175.

2. H. Zuckerman and R. K. Merton, "Institutionalized Patterns of Evaluation in Science," in Robert K. Merton and Norman W. Storer, eds. *The Sociology of Science: Theoretical and Empirical Investigations* (Chicago: University of Chicago Press, 1973), 460.

3. D. Harley and S. K. Acord, *Peer Review in Academic Promotion and Publishing: Its Meaning, Locus, and Future* (Berkeley: University of California, Berkeley, Center for Studies in Higher Education, 2011), 1.

4. Reinhardt Schuhmann, "Editorial: Peer Review per Physical Review," *Physical Review Letters* 100 (2008): 050001.

5. "Open Journal Systems," Public Knowledge Project, accessed June 22, 2014, http://pkp.sfu.ca/ojs.

6. Sheryl P. Denker, "2014: By the Numbers," *PLOS: BLOG*, February 17, 2015, http://blogs.plos.org/plos/2015/02/2014-numbers.

7. L. Bornmann, "Scientific Peer Review," *Annual Review of Information Science and Technology* 45 (2011): 199–245.

8. L. Bornmann, C. Weymuth, and H-D. Daniel, "A Content Analysis of Referees' Comments: How Do Comments on Manuscripts Rejected by a High-Impact Journal and Later Published in either a Low- or High-Impact Journal Differ?" *Scientometrics* 83, no. 2 (2010): 493–506.

9. J. S. Gans, S. Joshua, and George B. Shepherd, "How Are the Mighty Fallen: Rejected Classic Articles by Leading Economists," *Journal of Economic Perspectives* 8, no. 1 (1994): 165–179.

10. D. P. Peters and S. L. Ceci, "Peer-Review Practices of Psychological Journals: The Fate of Published Articles, Submitted Again," *Behavioral and Brain Sciences* 5 (1982): 187–195.

11. Steven Cole, "Review of *Peerless Science: Peer Review and U.S. Science Policy* by Daryl E. Chubin," *Contemporary Sociology* 20 no. 4 (1991): 603–605.

12. D. E. Chubin and E. J. Hackett, *Peerless Science: Peer Review and U.S. Science Policy* (Albany: SUNY Press, 1990).

13. Ibid., 65–57.

14. Ibid., 72.

15. Ibid., 73.

16. Michèle Lamont, *How Professors Think: Inside the Curious World of Academic Judgment* (Cambridge, MA: Harvard University Press, 2009).

17. Ibid., 235.

18. Ibid., 153.

19. R. H. Fletcher and S. W. Fletcher, "The Effectiveness of Journal Peer Review," in Fiona Godlee and Tom Jefferson, eds., *Peer Review in the Health Sciences*, 2nd ed. (London: BMJ Publishing Group, 2003), 72.

20. D. Mohr and A. R. Jadad, "How to Peer Review a Manuscript," in Fiona Godlee and Tom Jefferson, eds., *Peer Review in the Health Sciences*, 2nd Ed. (London: BMJ Publishing Group, 2003), 184–185.

21. British Academy, *Peer Review: The Challenges for the Humanities and Social Sciences* (London: British Academy, 2007), 28.

22. Bernard Donovan, "The Truth about Peer Review," *Learned Publishing* 11 (1998): 179–184.

23. David M. Schultz, "Rejection Rates for Journals Publishing in the Atmospheric Sciences," *Bulletin of the American Meteorological Society* 91 (2010): 231–243.

24. S. Turner and R. Hanel, "Peer-Review in a World with Rational Scientists: Toward Selection of the Average," *European Physical Journal B* 84 (2011): 707–711.

25. H. Mercier and D. Sperber, "Why Do Humans Reason? Arguments for an Argumentative Theory," *Behavioral and Brain Sciences* 34 (2011): 57–74.

26. John Brockman, "The Argumentative Theory: A Conversation with Hugo Mercier," April 27, 2011, *Edge*, http://www.edge.org/conversation/the-argumentative-theory.

27. Mercier and Sperber, 57.

28. Ibid., 72.

29. D. Sperber, F. Clément, C. Heintz, O. Mascaro, H. Mercier, G. Origgi, and D. Wilson, "Epistemic Vigilance," *Mind & Language* 25, no. 4 (2010): 359–393, 382–383.

30. Amartya K. Sen, "Rational Fools: A Critique of the Behavioral Foundations of Economic Theory," *Philosophy & Public Affairs* 6, no. 4 (1997): 317–344, 335–336.

31. Mercier and Sperber, 60–72.

32. Jürgen Habermas, *Communication and the Evolution of Society*, translated by Thomas McCarthy (Boston: Beacon Press, 1979).

33. Jürgen Habermas, "A Reply to My Critics," in John B. Thompson and David Held, eds., *Habermas: The Critical Debates* (Cambridge, MA: MIT Press, 1982), 219–283.

34. The first author has previously written about the connection between peer review and the ISS in Alan G. Gross, *Starring the Text: The Place of Rhetoric in Science Studies* (Carbondale: Southern Illinois University Press, 2006), 99–101.

35. Margaret Canovan, "A Case of Distorted Communication: A Note on Habermas and Arendt," *Political Theory* 11, no. 1 (1983): 105–116.

36. Thomas McCarthy, *The Critical Theory of Jürgen Habermas* (Cambridge, MA: MIT Press, 1982), 258–259.

37. Chubin and Hackett, 109.

38. Lamont, 199.

39. Ibid., 86–87.

40. Michael Polanyi, *Science, Faith, and Society* (Chicago: University of Chicago Press, 1964), 51.

41. Isaiah Berlin, *Concepts and Categories: Philosophical Essays* (New York: Viking Press, 1978), 95, 102.

42. Editorial, "Overview: *Nature*'s Peer Review Trial," *Nature*, December 2006, doi: 10.1038/nature05535.

43. Editorial, "Peer Review and Fraud," *Nature* 444 (2006): 971–972.

44. D. Dingwell, P. Crutzen, A. Richter, U. Pöschl, and M. Masmussen, *A Short History of Interactive Open Access Publishing* (Göttingen, Germany: Copernicus Publications, 2011).

45. L. Bornmann, C. Neuhaus, and H. D. Hans-Dieter Daniel, "The Effect of a Two-Stage Publication Process on the Journal Impact Factor: A Case Study on the Interactive Open Access Journal *Atmospheric Chemistry and Physics*," *Scientometrics* 86 (2011): 93–97.

46. Ulrich Pöschl, "Interactive Open Access Publishing and Public Peer Review: The Effectiveness of Transparency and Self-Regulation in Scientific Quality Assurance," *International Federation of Library Associations and Institutions* 36, no. 1 (2010): 40–46.

47. L. Bornmann, H. Schier, W. Marx, and H. D. Daniel, "Is Interactive Open Access Publishing Able to Identify High-Impact Submissions? A Study on the Predictive Validity of *Atmospheric Chemistry and Physics* by Using Percentile Rank Classes," *Journal of the American Society for Information Science and Technology* 62, no. 1 (2011): 61–71.

48. L. Bornmann, M. Wolf, and H. D. Daniel, "Closed Versus Open Reviewing of Journal Manuscripts: How Far Do Comments Differ in Language Use?" *Scientometrics* 91 (2012): 843–856.

49. A. G. Gross and J. E. Harmon, *Science from Sight to Insight: How Scientists Illustrate Meaning* (Chicago: University of Chicago Press, 2013), 178–188.

50. M. N. Juckes, M. R. Allen, K. R. Briffa, J. Esper, G. C. Hegerl, A. Moberg, T. J. Osborn, and S. L. Weber, "Millennial Temperature Reconstruction Intercomparison and Evaluation," *Climate of the Past* 3 (2007): 591–609.

51. Bornmann et al., "Interactive Open Access Publishing."

52. W. Eschenbach, Interactive Comment, *Climate of the Past Discussion* 2 (2006): S715–S719, http://www.clim-past-discuss.net/2/S715/2006/cpd-2-S715-2006.pdf.

53. S. McIntyre, Interactive Comment, *Climate of the Past Discussion* 2 (2006): S697–S702, http://www.clim-past-discuss.net/2/S697/2006/cpd-2-S697-2006.pdf.

54. Ibid., S701–S702.

55. Ibid., S702.

56. M. N. Juckes, Interactive Comment, *Climate of the Past Discussion* 2 (2007): S918–S921, http://www.clim-past-discuss.net/2/S918/2007/cpd-2-S918-2007.pdf.

57. Anonymous referee #1, Interactive Comment, *Climate of the Past Discussion* 2 (2006): S689–S691, http://www.clim-past-discuss.net/2/S689/2006/cpd-2-S689-2006.pdf.

58. H. Goosse, Interactive Comment, *Climate of the Past Discussion* 2 (2007): S964–S966, http://www.clim-past-discuss.net/2/S964/2007/cpd-2-S964-2007.pdf.

59. W. Eschenbach, Interactive Comment, *Climate of the Past Discussion* 2 (2006): S587, http://www.clim-past-discuss.net/2/S587/2006/cpd-2-S587-2006.pdf.

60. S. McIntyre, "Hugues Goosse and the Unresponsiveness of Juckes," *Climate Audit*, September 24, 2007, http://climateaudit.org/2007/09/24/hugo-goosse-and-the-unresponsiveness-of-juckes.

61. Martin Claussen, *Climate Audit*, September 24, 2007, http://climateaudit.org/2007/09/24/hugo-goosse-and-the-unresponsiveness-of-juckes.

62. Andrew Murphy, "Comment on Paragraph 5," in "Networks of Deep Impression: Shakespeare and the History of Information," *Shakespeare Quarterly: Shakespeare and New Media: Open Review*, March 13, 2010, http://mcpress.media-commons.org/ShakespeareQuarterly_NewMedia/networks-of-deep-impression/1-shakespearean-computing.

63. Alan Galey, "Comment on Paragraph 5," in "Networks of Deep Impression: Shakespeare and the History of Information," *Shakespeare Quarterly: Shakespeare and New Media: Open Review*, May 4, 2010, http://mcpress.media-commons.org/ShakespeareQuarterly_NewMedia/networks-of-deep-impression/1-shakespearean-computing.

64. "How to Comment on these Essays," in *Shakespeare Quarterly: Shakespeare and Performance: Open Review*, 2011, http://mcpress.media-commons.org/shakespearequarterlyperformance/how-to-comment-on-these-essays.

65. Joshua Gutzkow, Michèle Lamont, and Grégoire Mallard, "What is Originality in the Humanities and Social Sciences?" *American Sociological Review* 69 (2004): 190–212.

66. Jonathan Hope and Michael Witmore, "The Hundredth Psalm to the Tune of 'Green Sleeves': Digital Approaches Shakespeare's Language of Genre," in *Shakespeare Quarterly: Shakespeare and New Media: Open Review*, 2010, http://mcpress.media-commons.org/ShakespeareQuarterly_NewMedia/hope-witmore-the-hundredth-psalm.

67. Zeno Ackermann, "'Playing Away' and 'Working Through': The *Merchant of Venice* in West Germany, 1945 to 1960," in *Shakespeare Quarterly: Shakespeare and Performance: Open Review*, 2011, http://mcpress.media-commons.org/shakespearequarterlyperformance/ackermann.

68. Kate Rumbold, "From 'Access' to 'Creativity': Shakespeare Institutions, New Media and the Language of Cultural Value," in *Shakespeare Quarterly: Shakespeare and New Media: Open Review*, 2010, http://mcpress.media-commons.org/ShakespeareQuarterly_NewMedia/rumbold-from-access-to-creativity.

69. Todd A. Borlik, "General Comment," in "Othello in Tokyo: Performing Patriarchy, Race, and Empire in 1903 Japan," in *Shakespeare Quarterly: Shakespeare and Performance: Open Review*, March 8, 2011, http://mcpress.media-commons.org/shakespearequarterlyperformance/tierney.

70. Robert Tierney, "*Othello* in Tokyo: Performing Patriarchy, Race, and Empire in 1903 Japan," in *Shakespeare Quarterly: Shakespeare and Performance: Open Review*, 2011, http://mcpress.media-commons.org/shakespearequarterlyperformance/tierney.

71. Claude E. Shannon, "A Mathematical Theory of Communication," *The Bell System Technical Journal* 27, no. 3 (1948): 379–423, 379.

72. Alan Galey, "Networks of Deep Impression: Shakespeare and the History of Information," in *Shakespeare Quarterly: Shakespeare and New Media: Open Review*, 2011, http://mcpress.media-commons.org/ShakespeareQuarterly_NewMedia/networks-of-deep-impression/5-conclusion.

73. Alan Galey, "Comments on Paragraph 12," in *Shakespeare Quarterly: Shakespeare and New Media: Open Review*, May 4, 2010, http://mcpress.media-commons.org/ShakespeareQuarterly_NewMedia/networks-of-deep-impression/5-conclusion.

74. Alan Galey, "Comments on Paragraph 11," in *Shakespeare Quarterly: Shakespeare and New Media: Open Review*, April 7, 2010, http://mcpress.media-commons.org/ShakespeareQuarterly_NewMedia/shakespeare-remediated/murphy-shakespeare-goes-digital.

75. Andrew Murphy, "Shakespeare Goes Digital: Three Open Internet Editions," 2010, in *Shakespeare Quarterly: Shakespeare and New Media: Open Review*, http://mcpress.media-commons.org/ShakespeareQuarterly_NewMedia/shakespeare-remediated/murphy-shakespeare-goes-digital.

76. Kathleen Fitzpatrick, *Planned Obsolescence: Publishing, Technology, and the Future of the Academy* (New York: New York University Press, 2011).

77. Kathleen Fitzpatrick, "Community-Based Filtering," in *Planned Obsolescence: Publishing, Technology, and the Future of the Academy*, 2009, http://mediacommons.futureofthebook.org/mcpress/plannedobsolescence/one/community-based-filtering.

78. Ibid.

79. Kathleen Fitzpatrick, "Mediacommons and Peer-to-Peer Review," in *Planned Obsolescence*, 2009, http://mediacommons.futureofthebook.org/mcpress/plannedobsolescence/one/mediacommons-and-peer-to-peer-review.

80. Kathleen Fitzpatrick, "Notes, Chapter 1," in *Planned Obsolescence*, 2009, http://mediacommons.futureofthebook.org/mcpress/plannedobsolescence/notes/notes-chapter.

81. Fitzpatrick, *Planned Obsolescence*, 189.

CHAPTER 6

1. Geoffrey Chaucer, *The Poetical Works*, edited by F. N. Robinson (Boston: Houghton Mifflin, 1933), 314 [our translation].

2. A. Marcus and I. Oransky, "Why Was That Paper Retracted?" *Retraction Watch*, January 5, 2011, http://retractionwatch.wordpress.com/2011/01/05/why-was-that-paper-retracted-editor-to-retraction-watch-its-none-of-your-damn-business/#more-1261.

3. P.-S. Tsou, N. N. Talia, A. J. Pinney, A. Kendzicky, S. Piera-Velazquez, S. A. Jimenez, J. R. Seibold, K. Phillips, and A. E. Koch, "Effect of Oxidative Stress on Protein Tyrosine Phosphatase 1B in Scleroderma Dermal Fibroblasts," *Arthritis and Rheumatism* 64, no. 6 (2012): 1978–1989, 1987.

4. A. Marcus and I. Oransky, "Freedom from Information Act? Another *JBC* Retraction Untarnished by the Facts," *Retraction Watch*, March 21, 2011, http://retractionwatch.wordpress.com/?s=matsuda.

5. A. Marcus and I. Oransky, "What People Are Saying about Retraction Watch," August 10, 2011, *Retraction Watch*, http://retractionwatch.wordpress.com/?s=craig+silverman.

6. Craig Silverman, "Retraction Action," *Columbia Journalism Review*, August 9, 2010, http://www.cjr.org/the_observatory/retraction_action.php?page=all.

7. Ben Goldacre, "Now You See It, Now You Don't: Why Journals Need to Rethink Retractions," *The Guardian*, January 14, 2011, http://www.theguardian.com/commentisfree/2011/jan/15/bad-science-academic-journal-retraction.

8. Editorial, "Making Science Transparent," *Vancouver Sun*, August 17, 2011, http://www.canada.com/story_print.html?id=42256b12-90f0-4a77-8376-4da98aa81e64&sponsor.

9. A. Marcus and I. Oransky, "MD Anderson's Bharat Aggarwal Threatens to Sue Retraction Watch," *Retraction Watch*, April 10, 2013, http://retractionwatch.wordpress.com/2013/04/10/md-andersons-bharat-aggarwal-threatens-to-sue-retraction-watch.

10. Joerg Zwirner, "German Ombudsman et al., Systematic Suppression of Evidence," *Abnormal Science*, September 27, 2011, http://abnormalscienceblog.wordpress.com/2011/09/27/german-ombudsman-et-al-systematic-suppression-of-evidence/#more-790. [Site defunct]

11. A. Marcus and I. Oransky, "Authors of *Journal of Immunology* Paper Retract It after Realizing They Have Ordered the Wrong Mice," *Retraction Watch*, January 7, 2011, http://retractionwatch.wordpress.com/2011/01/07/authors-of-journal-of-immunology-paper-retract-it-after-realizing-they-had-ordered-the-wrong-mice/#more-1274.

12. A. Marcus and I. Oransky, "A Lightning-Fast JNCI Retraction Shows How Science Should Work," *Retraction Watch*, http://retractionwatch.wordpress.com/2011/01/19/a-lightning-fast-jnci-retraction-shows-how-science-should-work/#more-1416, January 19, 2011.

13. A. Marcus and I. Oransky, "Nearly Identical Twins: *European Respiratory Journal* Retracts Another Asthma in Pregnancy Paper Similar to Another by the Same Group," *Retraction Watch*, December 28, 2010, http://retractionwatch.wordpress.com/2010/12/28/nearly-identical-twins-european-respiratory-journal-retracts-asthma-in-pregnancy-paper-similar-to-another-by-same-group/#more-1199.

14. Grant Steen, "Retractions in the Scientific Literature: Do Authors Deliberately Commit Research Fraud?" *Journal of Medical Ethics* 37 (2011): 113–117.

15. Martin Frost, "Frost's Meditations," December 2010, http://www.martinfrost.ws/htmlfiles/dec2010/blame-elena-vadim.html. [Site defunct.]

16. A. Marcus and I. Oransky, "Three More Bulfone-Paus Retraction Notices, in *Journal of Immunology*," *Retraction Watch*, February 3, 2011, http://retractionwatch.wordpress.com/2011/02/03/three-more-bulfone-paus-retraction-notices-out-in-journal-of-immunology/#more-1656.

17. A. Marcus and I. Oransky, "Bulfone-Paus Retraction Notice Appears in the *Journal of Biological Chemistry*," *Retraction Watch*, February 15, 2011, http://retractionwatch.wordpress.com/2011/02/15/bulfone-paus-retraction-notice-appears-in-the-journal-of-biological-chemistry/#more-1747.

18. A. Marcus and I. Oransky, "As Last of 12 Bulfone-Paus Retractions Appears, a (Disappointing) Report Card on Journal Transparency," *Retraction Watch*, March 14, 2011, http://retractionwatch.wordpress.com/2011/03/14/as-last-of-12-promised-bulfone-paus-retractions-appears-a-disappointing-report-card-on-journal-transparency/#more-2048.

19. Editorial, "A Destabilizing Force," *Nature* 467 (2010): 133.

20. Frost.

21. Board of Directors of the Research Center Borstel, "Response—To Whom It May Concern," April 6, 2011, http://www.fzborstel.de/cms/fileadmin/content_fz/downloads/Pressemitteilungen/2011/Responsetoopenletter.pdf

22. Robert Merton, *Social Theory and Social Structure* (New York: The Free Press, 1968), 270–278.

23. I. Boutron, S. Dutton, P. Ravaud, and D. G. Altman, "Reporting and Interpretation of Randomized Controlled Trials with Statistically Nonsignificant Results for Primary Outcomes," *JAMA* 303, no. 20 (2010): 2058–2064.

24. C. Hewitt, N. Mitchell, and D. Torgerson, "Listen to the Data When Results Are Not Significant," *BMJ* 336 (2008): 23–25.

25. Peter C. Gøtzsche, "Believability of Relative Risks and Odds Ratios in Abstracts: Cross Sectional Study," *BMJ* 333 (2006): 231–234.

26. B. C. Martinson, M. S. Anderson, and R. de Vries, "Scientists Behaving Badly," *Nature* 435 (2005): 737–738.

27. Charles L. Bennett, "Association Between Pharmaceutical Support and Basic Science Research on Erythropoiesis-Stimulating Agents," *Archives of Internal Medicine* 170, no. 16 (2010): 1490–1498.

28. V. Yank, D. Rennie, and L. A. Bero, "Financial Ties and Concordance Between Results and Conclusions in Meta-analyses: Retrospective Cohort Study," *BMJ* 335 (2007), doi: 10.1136/bmj.39376.447211.BE.

29. P. Norris, A. Herxheimer, J. Lexchin, and P. Mansfield, *Drug Promotion: What We Know, What We Have Yet to Learn: Reviews of Materials in the WHO/HAI Database on Drug Promotion*, World Health Organization, WHO/EDM/PAR/2004.3 (2005), 48–55.

30. G. ter Riet, P. Chesley, A. G. Gross, L. Siebeling, P. Muggensturm, N. Heller, M. Umbehr, D. Vollenweider, T. Yu, E. A. Akl, L. Brewster, O. M. Dekkers, I. Mühlhauser, B. Richter, S. Singh, S. Goodman, and M. A. Puhan, "All That Glitters Isn't Gold: A Survey on Acknowledgment of Limitations in Biomedical Studies," *PLOS One* 8, no. 1 (2013): e73623.

31. S. Hopewell, S. Dutton, L.-M. Yu, A.-W. Chan, and D. G. Altman, "The Quality of Reports of Randomized Trials in 2000 and 2006: Comparative Study of Articles Indexed in PubMed," *BMJ* 340 (2010). doi: 10.1136/bmj.c723.

32. Martinson et al.

33. T. Jefferson, C. Di Pietrantonj, M. G. Debalini, A. Rivetti, and V. Demicheli, "Relation of Study Quality, Concordance, Take Home Message, Funding, and Impact in Studies of Influenza Vaccine: Systematic Review," *BMJ* 338 (2009): doi: 10.1136/bmj.b354.

34. Yank et al.

35. A. W. Jørgensen, J. Hilden, and P. C. Gøtzsche, "Cochrane Reviews Compared with Industry Supported Meta-analyses and Other Meta-analyses of the Same Drugs: Systematic Review," *BMJ* (2006): doi: 10.1136/bmj.38973.444699.OB.

36. ter Riet et al.

37. Norris, 54.

38. B. K. Redman, H. N. Yarandi, and J. F. Mertz, "Empirical Developments in Retraction," *Journal of Medical Ethics* 34 (2008): 807–809.

39. Martinson et al.

40. Jennifer Howard, "Despite Warnings, Biomedical Scholars Cite Hundreds of Retracted Papers," *Chronicle of Higher Education*, April 10, 2011, http://chronicle.com/article/Hot-Type-Despite-Warnings/127050.

41. Paul Knoepfler, "Review of Obokata Stress Reprogramming *Nature* Paper," January 29, 2014, http://www.ipscell.com/2014/01/review-of-obokata-stress-reprogramming-nature-papers.

42. *PubPeer*, January 29, 2014, https://pubpeer.com/publications/8B755710BADFE6FB0A8 48A44B70F7D#fb6381.

43. David Cyranoski, "Stem-Cell Scientist Found Guilty of Misconduct," *Nature*, April 1, 2014, http://www.nature.com/news/stem-cell-scientist-found-guilty-of-misconduct-1.14974.

44. Retraction Watch, "'Truly Extraordinary,' 'Simply not Credible,' 'Suspiciously Sharp': A STAP Stem Cell Peer Review Report Revealed," September 10, 2014, http://retractionwatch.com/2014/09/10/truly-extraordinary-simply-not-credible-suspiciously-sharp-a-stap-stem-cell-peer-review-report-revealed

45. Zwirner.

46. Terence Morehead Dworkin, "Sox and Whistleblowing," *Michigan Law Review* 105 (2007): 1757–1780.

47. T. S. Ettems and T. S. Glasser, *Custodians of Conscience: Investigative Journalism and Public Virtue* (New York: Columbia University Press, 1998), 128.

48. Ibid., 87.

49. A. Marcus and I. Oransky, "Bulfone-Paus Retraction Notice Appears in the *Journal of Biological Chemistry*," *Retraction Watch*, February 15, 2011, http://retractionwatch.wordpress.com/2011/02/15/bulfone-paus-retraction-notice-appears-in-the-journal-of-biological-chemistry/#more-1747.

50. A. Marcus and I. Oransky, "Three More Bulfone-Paus Rejection Notices, in *Journal of Immunology*," *Retraction Watch*, February 3, 2011, http://retractionwatch.wordpress.com/2011/02/03/three-more-bulfone-paus-retraction-notices-out-in-journal-of-immunology/#more-1656.

51. A. Marcus and I. Oransky, "Want to Avoid a Retraction? Hire a Medical Writer, Say Medical Writers," *Retraction Watch*, April 15, 2011, http://retractionwatch.wordpress.com/2011/04/15/want-to-avoid-a-retraction-hire-a-medical-writer-say-medical-writers/#more-2315.

52. Marcus and Oransky, "Three More Bulfone-Paus Rejection Notices."

53. *Retraction Watch*, "Tracking Retractions as a Window into the Scientific Process: The Retraction Watch FAQ, Including Comments Policy," accessed April 2015, http://retractionwatch.com/the-retraction-watch-faq.

54. A. Marcus and I. Oransky, "As Last of 12 Bulfone-Paus Retractions Appears, a (Disappointing) Report Card on Journal Transparency," *Retraction Watch*, March 14, 2011, http://retractionwatch.wordpress.com/2011/03/14/as-last-of-12-promised-bulfone-paus-retractions-appears-a-disappointing-report-card-on-journal-transparency/#more-2048.

55. Joerg Zwirner, "SMS Alert at Erlangen: The Mystery of a Cancer Study," September 19, 2011, *Abnormal Science*, http://abnormalscienceblog.wordpress.com/2011/09/19/sms-alert-in-erlangen-the-mystery-of-a-cancer-study/#more-761. [Link defunct]

56. A. Marcus and I. Oransky, "Do Plagiarism, Fraud, and Retractions Make It More Difficult to Trust Research from China?" *Retraction Watch*, October 7, 2010, http://retractionwatch.wordpress.com/2010/10/07/do-plagiarism-fraud-and-retractions-make-it-more-difficult-trust-research-from-china/#more-496.

57. A. Marcus and I. Oransky, "Ahluwalia Did Not Tell UCL He Had Been Dismissed from Cambridge," *Retraction Watch*, February 17, 2011, http://retractionwatch.wordpress.com/2011/02/21/ahluwalia-did-not-tell-ucl-he-had-been-dismissed-from-cambridge/#more-1817.

58. Marcus and Oransky, "Why Was That Paper Retracted?"

59. Joerg Zwirner, "SMS Alert at Erlangen: The Sociological Aspects of Scientific Misconduct," *Abnormal Science*, September 15, 2011, http://abnormalscienceblog.wordpress.com/2011/09/15/sociological-aspects-of-scientific-misconduct/#more-748. [Link defunct]

60. Merton.

61. Martin Raff, *F1000Prime*, accessed July 2014, http://f1000.com/prime.

62. Dan Cohen, "A Conversation with Richard Stallman about Open Access," November 23, 2010, http://www.dancohen.org/2010/11/23/a-conversation-with-richard-stallman-about-open-access.

63. H. Mercier and D. Sperber, "Why Do Humans Reason? Arguments for an Argumentative Theory," *Behavioral and Brain Sciences* 34 (2011): 57–74.

64. H. Mercier and C. Heinze, "Scientists' Argumentative Reasoning," *Topoi*, November 10, 2013, doi: 0.1007/s11245-013-9217-4.

65. H. Mercier, "The Argumentative Theory of Reasoning," accessed April 12, 2013, https://sites.google.com/site/hugomercier/theargumentativetheoryofreasoning.

66. R. F. Baumesiter, E. J. Masicampo, and C. N. DeWall, "Arguing, Reasoning, and the Interpersonal (Cultural) Functions of Human Consciousness," *Behavioral and Brain Sciences* 34 (2011): 74. Abstract (gated).

67. Kevin Chien-Chang Wu, "Deliberative Democracy and Epistemic Humility," *Behavioral and Brain Sciences* 34 (2011): 93–94.

68. Jonathan St. B. T. Evans, "Reasoning Is for Thinking, Not Just for Arguing," *Behavioral and Brain Sciences* 34 (2011): 77–78.

69. Keith Frankish, "Reasoning, Argumentation, and Cognition," *Behavioral and Brain Sciences* 34 (2011): 79–80.

70. T. Connolly and J. Reb, "Regret and Justification as a Link from Argumentation to Consequentialism," *Behavioral and Brain Sciences* 34 (2011): 75.

71. J. S. Uleman, L. M. Kressel, and S. Y. Rim, "Spontaneous Inferences Provide Intuitive Beliefs on Which Reasoning Proper Depends," *Behavioral and Brain Sciences* 34 (2011): 90–91.

72. Darcia Narvaez, "The World Looks Small When You Only Look through a Telescope: The Need for a Broad and Developmental Study of Reasoning," *Behavioral and Brain Sciences* 34 (2011): 83–84.

73. Maralee Harrell, "Understanding, Evaluating, and Producing Arguments: Training is Necessary for Reasoning Skills," *Behavioral and Brain Sciences* 34 (2011): 80–81.

74. Wim De Neys, "The Freak in All of Us: Logical Truth Seeking Without Argumentation," *Behavioral and Brain Sciences* 34 (2011): 75–76.

75. Robert J. Sternberg, "When Reasoning Is Persuasive but Wrong," *Behavioral and Brain Sciences* 34 (2011): 88–89.

76. E. J. N. Stupple and L. J. Ball, "The Chronometrics of Confirmation Bias: Evidence for the Inhibition of Intuitive Judgements," *Behavioral and Brain Sciences* 34 (2011): 89–90.

77. J. E. Opfer and V. Sloutsky, "On the Design and Function of Rational Arguments," *Behavioral and Brain Sciences* 34 (2011): 85–86.

78. H. Mercier and D. Sperber, "Argumentation: Its Adaptiveness and Efficacy," *Behavioral and Brain Sciences* 34 (2011): 93–101.

79. Ibid., 93–94.

80. Ibid., 93.

81. Mercier and Sperber, "Why Do Humans Reason?" 72.

82. Mercier and Sperber, "Argumentation," 95.

83. Harrell, 81.

84. Mercier and Sperber, "Argumentation," 98.

85. Ibid., 100.

86. Ibid., 99.

87. Morendil, "Reasoning Isn't About Logic (It's About Arguing), *Less Wrong*, March 14, 2010, http://lesswrong.com/lw/1wu/reasoning_isnt_about_logic_its_about_arguing

88. "The New Science of Morality," *Edge*, 2010, http://edge.org/events/the-new-science-of-morality.

89. Patricia Cohen, "Reason Seen More as Weapon Than Path to Truth," *New York Times*, June 14, 2011, http://www.nytimes.com/2011/06/15/arts/people-argue-just-to-win-scholars-assert.html?pagewanted=all.

90. Catarina Dutilh Novaes, *New APPS: Art, Politics, Philosophy, Science*, June 15, 2011, http://www.newappsblog.com/2011/06/mercier-and-sperber-on-the-origins-of-reasoning.html.

91. Massimo Pigliucci, *Rationally Speaking*, "Bad Reasoning about Reasoning," June 28, 2011, http://rationallyspeaking.blogspot.com/2011/06/bad-reasoning-about-reasoning.html.

92. Laurie Fendrich, *Chronicle of Higher Education,* "I Argue, There I Am," July 19, 2011, http://chronicle.com/blogs/brainstorm/i-argue-therefore-i-am/37448.

93. "Did Reason Evolve for Arguing?" *Point of Inquiry*, August 15, 2011, http://www.pointofinquiry.org/did_reason_evolve_for_arguing_hugo_mercier.

94. "Dan Sperber on the Enigma of Reason," *Philosophy Bites*, September 25, 2011, http://philosophybites.com/2011/09/dan-sperber-on-the-enigma-of-reason.html.

95. Cohen, comment No. 231.

96. Cohen, comment No. 53.

97. Cohen, comment No. 14.

98. Cohen, comment No. 134.

99. Cohen, comment No. 20.

100. Cohen, comment No. 105.

101. Cohen, comment No. 32.

102. Cohen, comment No. 211.

103. Cohen, comment No. 50.

104. Cohen, comment No. 241.

105. Gary Gutting, "Argument, Truth and the Social Side of Reasoning," *New York Times*, June 29, 2011, http://opinionator.blogs.nytimes.com/2011/06/29/argument-truth-and-the-social-side-of-reasoning.

106. Cohen, comment No. 182.

107. M. C. Hauser, N. Chomsky, W. T. Fitch, "The Faculty of Language: What Is It, Who Has It, and How Did It Evolve?" *Science* 298 (2002): 1569–1579.

108. Cohen, comment No. 23.

109. Cohen, comment No. 28.

110. Hugo Mercier, "Researcher Responds to Arguments over his Theory of Arguing," *New York Times*, June 15, 2011, http://artsbeat.blogs.nytimes.com/2011/06/15/researcher-responds-to-arguments-over-his-theory-of-arguing.

111. D. Sperber, F. Clément, C. Heintz, O. Mascaro, H. Mercier, G. Origgi, and D. Wilson, "Epistemic Vigilance," *Mind & Language* 25, no. 4 (2010): 359–393.

112. Cohen, comment No. 4.

113. Daniel J. Cohen, *Equations from God: Pure Mathematics and Victorian Faith* (Baltimore: Johns Hopkins University Press, 2007).

114. Peter Galison, *Image and Logic: A Material Culture of Microphysics* (Chicago: University of Chicago Press, 1997).

115. Judith V. Grabiner, "Review of Cohen's *Equations from God*," *British Journal for the History of Science* 41 (2008): 298–300.

116. Ivor Grattan-Guinness, "Review of Cohen's *Equations from God*," *American Historical Review*, 113 (2008): 249.

117. Bertrand Russell, *Autobiography* (London: Routledge, 1998), 126–128.

118. Caroline Morehead, *Bertrand Russell: A Life* (New York: Viking, 1992), 73–75.

119. Grabiner, 299.

120. Fernando Q. Gouvêa, "Faith by the Numbers," *First Things: A Monthly Journal of Religion and Public Life* (December 2007): 49–52, http://www.firstthings.com/article/2007/12/002-faith-by-the-numbers.

121. Karen Hunger Parshall, "Review of Cohen's *Equations from God*," *Isis* 99 (2008): 193–194.

122. Ibid., 194.

123. Jeremy Gray, "Review of Cohen's *Equations from God*," *London Mathematical Society Newsletter*, No. 362 (September 2007).

124. Grabiner, 300.

125. K. C. Hannibuss, "Review of Cohen's *Equations from God*," *English Historical Review*, 124 (2009): 728–731.

126. Amazon.com, Blurbs to entry for Cohen's Equations from God, accessed December 29, 2011, http://www.amazon.com/Equations-God-Mathematics-Victorian-Hopkins/dp/0801885531/ref=sr_1_3?ie=UTF8&qid=1325163384&sr=8-3.

127. W. K. H. Panofsky, "Where Engine Grease Meets up with Experimental Results," *Physics Today* (December 1997), p. 65.

128. Martin L. Perl, "Review of Galison's *Image and Logic*," *Science* 279 (1998): 1484.

129. Ed Hinds, "Rhymes with Sparks," *New Scientist* 155 (September 27, 1997): 44.

130. Daniel J. Kevles, "Golden Events," *New Republic* (February 2, 1998): 34–39, 35.

131. Hinds, 44.

132. Joseph C. Pitt, "Review of Galison's *Image and Logic*," *Science, Technology, & Human Values* 24 (1999): 295–300, 296.

133. Florian Hars, "Review of Galison's *Image and Logic*," *History and Technology* 15 (1999): 384–389, 384.

134. Richard Cook, "Colliding Paths," *American Scientist* 86 (1998): 582–583, 583.

135. John Ziman, "An Evolutionary History of High Energy Particle Physics, with Metaphysical Goals," *Minerva* 36 (1998): 289–303, 292.

136. C. W. F. Everitt and Anna Muza, "History, Theory, and the Ziggurat of Physics," *Isis* 91 (2000): 310–313.

137. Andrew Pickering, "Keeping It on an Even Keel," *TLS* (July 24, 1997), p. 23.

138. Zinman, 289.

139. Jeff Hughes, "What Can Particle Physicists Count on?" *Metascience* 8 (1999): 379–388.

140. Hars.

141. Zinman, 292.

142. Kent W. Staley, "Golden Events and Statistics: What's Wrong with Galison's Image–Logic Distinction?" *Perspectives on Science* 7 (1999): 196–230, 224.

143. David Gooding, "What Can Particle Physicists Count on?" *Metascience* 8 (1999): 361–367.

144. William J. McKinney, "What Can Particle Physicists Count on?" *Metascience* 8 (1999): 367–375.

145. Robert P. Crease, "Review of Galison's *Image and Logic*," *Technology and Culture* 40 (1999): 924–925.

146. McKinney, 374.

147. Kyle Gervais, *Bryn Mawr Classical Review*, January 16, 2012, http://www.bmcreview.org/2012/01/20120121.html.

148. Emily Greenwood, *Bryn Mawr Classical Review*, January 16, 2012, http://www.bmcreview.org/2012/01/20120120.html.

149. Daniel J. Cohen and Roy Rosenzweig, *Digital History: A Guide to Gathering, Preserving, and Presenting the Past on the Web*, 2005, http://chnm.gmu.edu/digitalhistory/index.php.

CHAPTER 7

1. Richard Poynder, "A New Declaration of Rights: Open Content Mining," June 8, 2012, http://poynder.blogspot.ca/2012/06/new-declaration-of-rights-open-content.html.

2. Ian Sample, "Harvard University Says It Can't Afford Journal Publishers' Prices," *The Guardian*, April 24, 2012, http://www.theguardian.com/science/2012/apr/24/harvard-university-journal-publishers-prices.

3. Richard Van Noorden, "The True Cost of Science Publishing," *Nature* 495 (2013): 426–429.

4. J. Xia and L. Sun, "Assessment of Self-Archiving in Institutional Repositories: Depositorship and Full-Text Availability," *Serials Review* 33 (2006): 14–21, 19.

5. Jingfeng Xia, "A Comparison of Subject and Institutional Repositories in Self-Archiving Practices," *Journal of Academic Librarianship* 34 (2008): 489–495, 493.

6. C. Creaser, J. Fry, H. Greenwood, C. Oppenheim, S. Probets, V. Spezi, and S. White, "Authors' Awareness and Attitudes Toward Open Access Repositories," *New Review of Academic Librarianship* 16 (2010): 145–161.

7. J. Xia, S. B. Gilchrist, N. X. P. Smith, J. A. Kingery, J. R. Radecki, M. L. Wilhelm, K. C. Harrison, M. L. Ashby, and A. J. Mahn, "A Review of Open Access Self-Archiving Mandate Policies," *Libraries and the Academy* 12 (2012): 85–102, 92.

8. Creaser et al.

9. J. W. Houghton, B. Rasmussen, P. J. Sheehan, C. Oppenheim, A, Morris, C. Creaser, H. Greenwood, M. Summers, and A. Gourlay, *Economic Implications of Alternative Scholarly Publishing Models: Exploring the Costs and Benefits* (London and Bristol: Joint Information Systems Committee, 2009).

10. Research Information Network, *Paying for Open Access Publication Charges*, March 18, 2009, http://www.rin.ac.uk/our-work/research-funding-policy-and-guidance/paying-open-access-publication-charges.

11. Branwen Hide, "The Economics of Open Access Publishing," Conference on Open Access Scholarly Publishing, Research Information Network, September 14, 2009, https://www.youtube.com/watch?v=SLd6bfZiptM.

12. Mary Waltham, "The Future of Scholarly Journal Publishing among Social Science and Humanities Associations: Report on a Study Funded by a Planning Grant from the Andrew W. Mellon Foundation," *Journal of Scholarly Publishing* 41 (2010): 258–324, 304.

13. Ibid., 279.

14. Ibid., 268.

15. Salvatore Mele, "SCOAP3: Sponsoring Consortium for Open Access Publishing in Particle Physics," First Open Access Scholarly Publishing Association Conference, Lund, September 16, 2009, http://scoap3.org/files/25102010_berlin8_mele.pdf.

16. T. C. Bergstrom and C. T. Bergstrom, "Can 'Author Pays' Journals Compete with 'Reader Pays'? *Nature*, 2004, http://www.nature.com/nature/focus/accessdebate/22.html.

17. Donald E. Knuth, "Letter to the Editorial Board of *Journal of Algorithms*," October 25, 2003, http://www-cs-faculty.stanford.edu/~uno/joalet.pdf.

18. B.-C. Björk, A. Roosr, and M. Lauri, "Global Annual Volume of Peer Reviewed Scholarly Articles and the Share Available via Different Open Access Options," Proceedings of the ELPUB Conference on Electronic Publishing, Toronto, Canada, June 2008, http://elpub.scix.net/data/works/att/178_elpub2008.content.pdf.

19. E. Archambault, D. Amyot, P. Deschamps, A. Nicol, L. Rebout, and G. Roberge, "Proportion of Open Access Peer-Reviewed Papers at the European and World Levels—2004–2011" (Brussels: Science Metrix Inc., European DG Research and Innovation, August 2013), http://www.science-metrix.com/pdf/SM_EC_OA_Availability_2004-2011.pdf.

20. Australian Open Access Support Group, "Developments in OA Monograph Publishing," September 2013, http://aoasg.org.au/oa-monographs-developments.

21. Ernest L. Boyer, *Scholarship Reconsidered: Priorities of the Professoriate* (Princeton: Carnegie Foundation for the Advancement of Teaching, 1990).

22. Walter P. Metzger, "The 1940 Statement of Principles of Academic Freedom and Tenure," in William W. Van Alstyne, ed., *Freedom and Tenure in the Academy* (Durham: Duke University Press, 1993), 71.

23. Modern Language Association, "Guidelines for Evaluating Work in the Digital Humanities and Digital Media," 2012, http://www.mla.org/guidelines_evaluation_digital?ot=letterhead.

24. The Chesapeake Digital Preservation Group, "'Link Rot' and Legal Resources on the Web: A 2013 Analysis by the Chesapeake Digital Preservation Group," 2013, http://cdm16064.

contentdm.oclc.org/ui/custom/default/collection/default/resources/custompages/reportsand-publications/2013LinkRotReport.pdf.

25. Jennifer Howard, "Born Digital, Projects Need Attention to Survive," *Chronicle of Higher Education* 60, no. 17 (2014): A30–A32.

26. University of Virginia Library, Digital Curation, Services, "Sustaining Digital Scholarship," accessed July 2014, http://www.digitalcurationservices.org/sustaining-digital-scholarship.

27. University of Virginia Library, Digital Curation, Services, "Valley of the Shadow," accessed July 2014, http://www.digitalcurationservices.org/sustaining-digital-scholarship/valley-of-the-shadow.

28. Julia Martin and David Coleman, "Change the Metaphor: The Archive as an Ecosystem," *Journal of Electronic Publishing* 7, no. 3 (2012), http://quod.lib.umich.edu/j/jep/3336451.0007.301?view=text;rgn=main.

29. Digital Preservation Management, "Timeline: Digital Technology and Preservation," accessed July 2014, http://www.dpworkshop.org/dpm-eng/timeline/popuptest.html.

30. M. W. Foster and R. R. Sharp, "Share and Share Alike: Deciding How to Distribute the Scientific and Social Benefits of Genomic Data," *Nature Reviews Genetics* 8 (2007): 633–639.

31. A. K. Rai, J. H. Reichman, P. F. Uhlir, and C. Crossman, "Pathways Across the Valley of Death: Novel Intellectual Property Strategies for Accelerated Drug Discovery," *Yale Journal of Health Policy, Law, and Ethics* 8 (2008): 55–89, 63–64.

32. D. C. Mowery, R. R. Nelson, B. N. Sampat, and A. A. Zeidonis, *Ivory Tower and Industrial Innovation: University-Industry Technology Transfer Before and After the Bayh-Dole Act in the United States* (Stanford: Stanford University Press, 2004), 185–186.

33. Alison McLennan, "Building with Biobricks: Constructing a Commons for Synthetic Biology," in Matthew Rimmer and Alison McLennon, eds., *Intellectual Property and Emerging Technologies: The New Biology* (Cheltenham: Edward Elgar, 2012), 190.

34. Amina Agovic, "Stem Cell Patents: Looking for Serenity," in Matthew Rimmer and Alison McLennon, eds., *Intellectual Property and Emerging Technologies: The New Biology* (Cheltenham: Edward Elgar, 2012), 247.

35. *Retraction Watch*, "JPET Peeves: Paper Withdrawn after Drug Company Won't Disclose Chemical Structure," June 20, 2012, http://retractionwatch.com/2012/06/20/jpet-peeves-paper-withdrawn-after-drug-company-wont-disclose-chemical-structure.

36. Victoria Stodden, "Enabling Reproducible Research: Licensing Scientific Innovation," *International Journal of Communications Law and Policy* 13 (2009): 1–25.

37. A. McLennan and M. Rimmer, "Cosmo, Cosmolino: Patent Law and Nanotechnology," in Matthew Rimmer and Alison McLennon, eds., *Intellectual Property and Emerging Technologies: The New Biology* (Cheltenham: Edward Elgar, 2012), 255–292.

38. Richard R. Nelson, "The Market Economy, and the Scientific Commons," *Research Policy* 33 (2004): 455–471.

39. McLennan and Rimmer.

40. Agovic, 228–254.

41. A. Bostanci, J. Calvert, and P. B. Joly, "Regulating Gene Regulation: Patenting Small RNAs," in Matthew Rimmer and Alison McLennon, eds., *Intellectual Property and Emerging Technologies: The New Biology* (Cheltenham: Edward Elgar, 2012), 205–227.

42. J. H. Reichman and R. L. Okediji, "Empowering Digitally Integrated Research Methods on a Global Scale," *Minnesota Law Review* 96 (2012): 1362–1480, 1459.

43. Agovic, 244–247.

44. M. A. Heller and R. S. Eisenberg, "Can Patents Deter Innovation? The Anticommons in Biomedical Research," *Science* 280 (1998): 699–701.

45. Eva Hemmungs Wirtén, "Of Plants, Pills, and Patents: Circulating Knowledge," in Matthew Rimmer and Alison McLennon, eds., *Intellectual Property and Emerging Technologies: The New Biology* (Cheltenham: Edward Elgar, 2012), 39–59.

46. Miriam Bitton, "Protection for Informational Works after *Feist Publications, Inc. v. Rural Telephone Service Co.*," *Fordham Intellectual Property, Media, and Entertainment Journal* 21 (2010–11): 611–669.

47. J. H. Reichman and P. F. Uhlir, "A Contractually Reconstructed Research Commons for Scientific Data in a Highly Protectionist Intellectual Property Environment," *Law and Contemporary Problems* 66 (2003): 315–462, 354, 386–387, 398.

48. D. C. Mowery, R. R. Nelson. B. M. Sampat, and A. A. Ziedonis, "The Growth of Patenting and Licensing by U.S. Universities: An Assessment of the Effects of the Bayh-Dole Act of 1980," *Research Policy* 30, no. 1 (2001): 99–119, 102.

49. Rai et al.

50. Dov Greenbaum, "Are We Legislating Away our Scientific Future?" *Duke Law and Technology Review* 2, No. 1, 2003, http://scholarship.law.duke.edu/dltr/vol2/iss1/20.

51. Eric Von Hippel, *Democratizing Innovation* (Cambridge, MA: MIT Press, 2005), 96.

52. J. Yann, E. S. Dove, B. M. Knopper, M. Bobrow, and D. Chalmers, "Data Sharing in the Post-Genomic World: The Experience of the International Cancer Genome Consortium (ICGC) Data Access Compliance Office (DACO)," *PLOS Computational Biology* 8, no. 7 (2012): e1002549.

53. Rai et al.

54. Donna M. Gitter, "The 1000 Genomes Project," in Matthew Rimmer and Alison McLennon, eds., *Intellectual Property and Emerging Technologies: The New Biology* (Cheltenham: Edward Elgar, 2012), 158–175.

55. M. W. Weiner, D. P. Veitch, P. S. Aisen, L. A. Beckett, N. J. Cairns, R. C. Green, D. Harvey, C. R. Jack, W. Jagust, E. Liu, J. C. Morris, R. C. Petersen, A. J. Saykin, M. E. Schmidt, L. Shaw, J. A. Siuciak, H. Soares, A. W. Toga, J. Q. Trojanowski, and Alzheimer's Disease Neuroimaging Initiative, "The Alzheimer's Disease Neuroimaging Initiative: A Review of Papers Published Since its Inception," *Alzheimers Dementia* 8, no. 10 (2012): S1–68.

56. C. S. Wagner and L. Leydesdorff, "Mapping the Network of Global Science: Comparing International Co-authorships from 1990 to 2000," *International Journal of Technology and Globalisation* 1 (2005): 185–208.

57. K. H. Jacobsen, "Patterns of Co-Authorship in International Epidemiology," *Journal of Epidemiology and Community Health* 63 (2009): 665–669.

58. Victoria Stodden, "Enabling Reproducible Research: Open Licensing for Scientific Innovation," *International Journal of Communications Law and Policy* 13 (2009): 1–25.

59. Katherine M. Nolan-Stevaux, "Open Source Biology: A Means to Address the Access and Research Gaps?" *Santa Clara Computer and High Technology Law Journal* 23 (2006–7): 271–316.

60. P. Arzberger, P. Schroeder, A. Beaulieu, G. Bowker, K. Casey, L. Laaksonen, D. Moorman, P. Uhlir, and P. Wouters, "An International Framework to Promote Access to Data," *Science* 303 (2004): 1777–1778.

61. Reichman and Uhlir.

62. Nelson.

63. Marc A. Rodwin, "Patient Data: Property, Privacy & the Public Interest," *American Journal of Law and Medicine* 36 (2010): 586–618.

64. J. Yann et al.

65. Rodwin, 616.

66. Reichman and Okediji, 1478.

67. Jonathan Schwieger, "DOE Energy Storage Hub: A New Model for Science, Engineering and Business," December 13, 2013, http://www.nextenergy.org/wp-content/uploads/2013/12/UM-NextEnergy-_20131213_CET.pdf.

68. Ruth Bader Ginsberg, "*Eric Eldred, et al., Petitioners v. John D. Ashcroft, Attorney General*: On a Writ of Ceteriorari to the United States Court of Appeals for the District of Columbia Circuit," 01-618, 537 U. S, 186 (January 15, 2003), 32.

69. Ibid., 17.

70. L. R. Patterson and S. W. Lindberg, *Nature of Copyright: A Law of Users' Rights* (Athens: University of Georgia Press, 1991).

71. L. R. Patterson and S. F. Birch, Jr., "A Unified Theory of Copyright," *Houston Law Review* 46 (2009–10): 223–395.

72. A. G. Gross and J. E. Harmon, *Science from Sight to Insight: How Scientists Illustrate Meaning* (Chicago: University of Chicago Press, 2013).

73. Stephen Breyer, "*Eric Eldred, et al., Petitioners v. John D. Ashcroft, Attorney General*: On a Writ of Ceteriorari to the United States Court of Appeals for the District of Columbia Circuit," 01-618, 537 U. S, 186 (January 15, 2003), 9.

74. Kathryn M. Rudy, "Open Access: Imaging Policies for Medieval Manuscripts in Three University Libraries Compared," *Visual Resources: An International Journal of Documentation* 27 (2011): 345–359.

75. S. Katyal, P. Aikent, L. Quilter, D. O. Carson, J. G. Palfrey, Jr., and H. C. Hansen, "Panel III: Fair Use: Its Application, Limitations and Future." *Fordham Journal of Intellectual Property, Media and Entertainment Law Journal* 17 (2007): 1017–1082, 1055–1056.

76. Ibid., 1062.

77. Michael W. Carroll, "Fixing Fair Use," *North Carolina Law Review* 85 (2007): 1087–1154, 1098–1099 and fn.

78. *Copyright Law of the United States of America and Related Laws Contained in Title 17 of the United States Code*, in Section 107, "Limitations on Exclusive Right: Fair Use," accessed July 2014, http://www.copyright.gov/title17/92chap1.html#107.

79. David Nimmer, "'Fairest of Them All' and Other Fairy Tales of Fair Use," *Law and Contemporary Problems* 66 (2003): 264–287.

80. Pamela Samuelson, "Unbundling Fair Uses," *Fordham Law Review* 77 (2008–9): 2537–2621, 2619.

81. Pierre N. Leval, "Toward a Fair Use Standard," *Harvard Law Review* 103 (1990): 1105.

82. Chris McElwain, "Fact in the World: The Referential Model of Fair Use," *Journal of the Copyright Society* 58 (2011): 855–891.

83. Michael J. Madison, "A Pattern-Oriented Approach to Fair Use," *William and Mary Law Review* 45 (2004): 1525–1690.

84. P. Aufderheide and P Jaszi, *Reclaiming Fair Use: How to Put Balance Back in Copyright* (Chicago: University of Chicago Press, 2011).

85. International Communication Association, *Code of Best Practices in Fair Use for Scholarly Research in Communication*, June 2010, http://www.icahdq.org/pubs/reports/fairuse.pdf.

86. Samuelson, 2619.

87. Tom McClean, "Review of *Freedom of Information and the Developing World: The Citizen, the State, and Models of Openness* by Colin Darch and Peter G. Underwood," *Governance: An International Journal of Policy, Administration, and Institutions* 24 (2011): 745–747.

88. Jeanine E. Relly, "Freedom of Information Laws and Global Diffusion: Testing Rogers's Model," *Journal of Mass Communication Quarterly* 89 (2012): 431–457.

89. E. Shepherd, A. Stevenson, and A. Flinn, "Freedom of Information and Records Management in Local Government: Help or Hindrance?" *Information Polity* 167 (2011): 111–121.

90. S. Springer, H. Chi, J. Crampton, F. McConnell, J. Cupples, K. Glynn, B. Warf, and W. Attewell, "Leaky Geopolitics: The Ruptures and Transgressions of WikiLeaks," *Geopolitics* 17 (2012): 681–711.

91. Darby A. Morrisroe, "Freedom of Information and the American Presidency: A Researcher's Perspective," in A. Flinn and H. Jones, eds., *Freedom of Information: Open Access, Empty Archives?* (London: Routledge, 2009), 102–112.

92. Miklos Lojko, "Political and Digital Divides: The Dual Challenge for Central European Archives," in A. Flinn and H. Jones, eds., *Freedom of Information: Open Access, Empty Archives?* (London: Routledge, 2009), 182–193.

93. K. Östberg and F. Eriksson, "The Problematic Freedom of Information Principle: The Swedish Experience," in A. Flinn and H. Jones, eds., *Freedom of Information: Open Access, Empty Archives?* (London: Routledge, 2009), 119.

94. Gill Bennett, "Opening Government? The Freedom of Information Act and the Foreign and Commonwealth Office," in A. Flinn and H. Jones, eds., *Freedom of Information: Open Access, Empty Archives?* (London: Routledge, 2009), 29.

95. Kevin Dunion, "Viewpoint: In Defense of Freedom of Information," *Information Polity* 16 (2011): 93–96, 95.

96. Geoffrey R. Stone, "WikiLeaks and the First Amendment," *Federal Communications Law Journal* 64 (2012): 477–491.

97. WikiLeaks, "Collateral Murder," April 3, 2010, https://www.youtube.com/watch?v=5rXPrfnU3Go.

98. C. Beckett and J. Ball, *WikiLeaks: News in the Networked Era* (Cambridge: Polity Press, 2012), 65.

99. Stone.

100. Patricia J Bellia, "WikiLeaks and the Institutional Framework for National Security Disclosures," *Yale Law Journal* 121 (2012): 1448–1526.

101. Amartya Sen, "Rational Fools: A Critique of the Behavioral Foundations of Economic Theory," *Philosophy & Public Affairs* 6 (1977): 317–344, 335–336.

102. Mancur Olson, *The Logic of Collective Action: Public Goods and the Theory of Groups* (Cambridge, MA: Harvard University Press, 1965).

103. Douglass C. North, *Structure and Change in Economic History* (New York: Norton, 1981), 58.

104. Elinor Ostrom, *Governing the Commons: The Evolution of Institutions for Collective Action* (Cambridge: Cambridge University Press, 1990).

105. C. Hess and E. Ostrom, eds., *Understanding Knowledge as a Commons: From Theory to Practice* (Cambridge, MA: MIT Press, 2007).

106. Yochai Benkler, *The Penguin and the Leviathan: How Cooperation Triumphs over Self-Interest* (New York: Crown Business, 2011).

107. Hess and Ostrom, 51.

108. Ostrom, 211.

109. Hess and Ostrom, 136–137.

110. A. R. Poteete, M. A. Janssen, and E. Ostrom, eds., *Working Together: Collective Action, the Commons, and Multiple Methods in Practice* (Princeton: Princeton University Press, 2010), 239.

111. Hess and Ostrom, 7.

112. Yochai Benkler, *The Wealth of Networks: How Social Production Transforms Markets and Freedom* (New Haven: Yale University Press, 2006), 456.

Index

"Abnormal Science," 157–158, 165–167, 169, 170, 186

Abstract of abstract, 28, 29f, 30f

Academic cultures, 4

Academic work, 3–4

Accessibility, scientific article, 24–26, 25f, 26f

ACM Transactions on Algorithms, 192–193

"A Cradle Song" (Blake), 98

Adachi, K., 105

Adams, Dean C., 48

AJAX tabs, 21

Altruism, 207

"A March in the Ranks Hard-Prest" (Whitman), 93–94

Ancient Lives Project, 114

Anderson, Kent, 21

"And Yet Not You Alone" (Whitman), 94–95, 95f, 96f

An Inquiry into Modes of Existence (Latour), 86

Anonymous, 205

Apache gunship incident, 204–205

Archival websites, 88–121. *See also specific types*
    accessibility, 89–90
    Ancient Lives Project, 114
    arXiv, 7, 50, 107–110, 108f, 190, 191, 192
    codification, existing knowledge, 115–120, 117f, 119f

content, disciplinary needs, 120

Corpus of Historical American English, 91

costs, 90

CREDO, 105

data reliability, 120–121

data storage, scientific research, 104–107

digital archive, 90

digital repository, 90

Encyclopedia of Life, 13, 90, 116–118, 117f

Figshare–PLOS alliance, 110

finding system, 121

Foldit, 110

Folger Digital Texts, 91

Galaxy Zoo, 7, 13–14, 90, 110–114, 111f, 113f–114f, 120 (*See also* Galaxy Zoo)

institutional base, 121

knowledge creation, volunteers, 110–115, 111f, 113f–114f

as new genre, 90

Online Mendelian Inheritance in Man, 104

Open Tree of Life, 118, 119f

Oxford Scholarly Editions Online, 91

The Oxyrhynchus Papyri, 115

Perseus Digital Library, 91–92

vs. physical archives, advantages, 89–90

Planet Hunters, 110

Princeton Dante Project, 92

Archival websites (*Cont.*)
 Protein Data Bank, 104–107, 106f
 recognition and reward, institutional, 121
 resources, scholarship, 91–104
 revisions, continuous, 89, 90
 Rome Reborn, 115
 Social Science Research Network, 109, 190, 191
 Soweto posters, 88
 Stanford Encyclopedia of Philosophy, 115
 storage, scientific/scholarly paper,
  107–110, 108f
 thematic links and organization, 90–91
 Tolstoy:ru, 115
 Victorian Web, 91, 120
 Walt Whitman Archive, 89, 90, 92–95, 103,
  104 (*See also* Walt Whitman Archive)
 William Blake Archive, 89, 92, 95–104
  (*See also* William Blake Archive)
Archives
 physical, 88–89
 self-archiving, 190–191
Argumentative competence, peer review
 humanities, 146, 147–148
 sciences, 129, 130
Argument, scientific, 18
Argument theory, 126–129
Art, 60–64, 62f
Article, journal
 efficient design, 7
 postpublication peer review, 172–178
 scientific (*See* Scientific article)
"The Article of the Future" (Elsevier
  Publishing), 20–21, 22f
Arts, 1–2
Artus Quellinus the Elder, 100–101, 102f
arXiv, 7, 50, 107–110, 108f, 190, 191, 192
Atmospheric Chemistry and Physics, 136–138
Aufderheide, P., 203
Authorship, scientific article, 25f, 26–27, 26f
Author summary, 18, 27–28
Ayers, Edward L., 4, 64–69, 66f, 68f–70f, 196

Barenboim, Daniel, 77
"Baroque Expressiveness and Stylishness
  in Three Recordings of the D minor
  Sarabanda for Solo Violin by J. S. Bach"
  (Fabian and Schubert), 78–79
Bayh-Dole, 198
Beall, Jeffrey, 23–24
Behavioral and Brain Sciences, 172–178, 186–187
Benkler, Yochai, 10, 206, 208
Bennett, Gill, 204

Bilson, Malcolm, 78
Björk, Bo-Christer, 193
Blake, William. *See* William Blake Archive
Blunt, Anthony, 101
Book reviews, scholarly, 178–186, 185f, 187
 aggregate websites, 183
 Bryn Mawr Classical Review, 184–186
 *Equations from God: Pure Mathematics and
  Victorian Faith,* 178–181, 187
 gated access, 184, 187
 H-France Review, 184
 *Image and Logic: A Material Culture of
  Microphysics,* 178, 181–183, 185f, 187
 Metascience's "Review Symposium," 184
 Open Humanities Press, 184
 Rotten Tomatoes, 184
Books
 humanities (*See* Essays and books,
  humanities; *specific books*)
 peer review, postpublication, 178–186, 185f, 187
 print *vs.* online, 193
Bookstein, Fred, 39, 46, 49
Bornmann, Lutz, 124, 137–138
Boyer, Ernest, 193–194
Browsing (browsers), 10
 journal, 12
 OneZoom, 118
 scientific articles, 18, 31
 Victorian Web, 121
Bryn Mawr Classical Review, 184–186
Bulfone-Paus, Silvia, 158–163, 162f, 166

Cambridge University Press v. Becker et al., 203
Caplin, William E., 78
Caubert, Sylvain, 63
Ceci, S. L., 124–125
Cell, pane format article, 21, 22f
Censer, Jack, 60–64, 62f
Cerf, Vinton, 11
ChemSpider, 21, 120–121
Chubin, D. E., 128
Citations, 28–31
Civil War, visual reinterpretation, 64–69, 66f,
  68f–70f
Clarity of expression, 129, 131, 146, 148–150
Clicking
 Elsevier's "The Article of the Future," 20–21
 Galaxy Zoo, 111
 Internet scientific article, 36
 LA, 71
 *Los Angeles and the Problem of Urban Historical
  Knowledge* (Ethington), 70–72, 71f, 73f

Pohlandt-McCormick's "*I Saw a Nightmare*," 57
Climategate, 129–131
Climate of the Past, 138–144, 139f
  vs. ideal speech situation, 151
Cohen, Daniel J., 171–172, 178–181, 184, 187
Cole, Stephen, 125
Collaboration
  humanities, 7–8
  sciences, 6, 12, 26–27
  university communities, 199–200
  university–industry, 199
Comments, reader, 33–34
Commons, 206
Communication channels, 169
Communities, research, 199
Complete Writings of William Blake (Keynes), 97
Complexity, scientific article, 27–28, 29f, 30f
Confirmation bias, 127, 173
Contents, 31–33, 32f
Contents page, journal, 31, 32f
Copyright, 198–203
  Bayh-Dole, 198
  Cambridge University Press v. Becker et al., 203
  Eldred v. Ashcroft, 200–201
  vs. fair use, 201–203
  Feist v. Rural, 198
  New Era Publishing International v. Carol Publishing, 202
Copyright Term Extension Act (CTEA), 200
Coquerelle, M., 47–48, 47f, 49f
Corpus of Historical American English, 91
CREDO, 105
Cromwell, Oliver, 42–46, 44f, 45f, 46t
CrossRef, 195
Cuvier, Georges, 39

Darnton, Robert, 55–56, 87
"Death in Motion" (Favro and Johanson), 75–77, 76f
Descartes, René, 4
The Differences Slavery Made: A Close Analysis of Two American Communities (Thomas and Ayers), 64–69, 66f, 68f–70f
Digital archive, 90. *See also* Archival websites
Digital History (Cohen and Rosenzweig), 184
Digital humanities, 91
"Digital Humanities Blog," 171–172
Digitally networked sites, 200
Digital Object Identifiers (DOIs), 195
Digital preservation, 195–196
Digital repository, 90. *See also* Archival websites

Digitization, 195
Dissemination, scientific research, 5
Division of labor, 6
The Division of the Kingdoms, 103–104

Eaves, Morris, 95–97
Economics Bulletin, 193
Eisenstein, Elizabeth, 10–11
Eldred v. Ashcroft, 200–201
Elsevier's "The Article of the Future," 20–21, 22f
Email addresses, in publications, 108
EMBO Journal, 135, 154
Encyclopedia of Life (EOL), 13, 90, 116–118, 117f
Engerman, Stanley, 64
Epistemic vigilance, 127, 173
Equations from God: Pure Mathematics and Victorian Faith (Cohen), 178–181, 187
Error. *See also* Watchdog blogs
  "Abnormal Science," 157–158, 165–167, 169, 170, 186
  "Retraction Watch," 156–157, 165–166, 169, 186
Essays and books, humanities, 4, 7–10, 52–87
  art, 60–64, 61f, 62f
  Civil War reinterpretation, visualization, 64–69, 66f, 68f–70f
  film scholars, 79–85, 81f–85f
  future, 86–87
  Internet innovation and, 52–55
  Kairos, 53–54
  musicians, 77–79
  photographs, 55–60, 58f, 59f, 61f
  Roman Forum, 75–77, 76f
  urban history, multimedia Los Angeles, 69–75, 71f–74f
  Vectors: Journal of Culture and Technology in a Dynamic Vernacular, 52–55
Essick, Robert N., 95–97
Ethington, Philip, 69–75, 71f–74f
Europe (Blake), 100–101, 102f–103f
European Geosciences Union (EGU), 135, 153, 192
European Journal of Comparative Economics, 192
Evaluation, post-publication, 155–187
  peer review, articles, 172–178
  peer review, books, 178–186, 185f
  peer review, humanities, 169–172
  watchdog blogs, sciences, 155–169 (*See also* Watchdog blogs)
Expression, clarity of, 129, 131, 146, 148–150

Fabian, Dorottya, 78–79
Faculty of 1000, 170
Fair use, 201–203
Favro, Diane, 75–77, 76f
Figshare, 110
File sharing, 208
Film scholars, 79–85, 81f–85f
Finding systems
    master, 31–33, 32f
    Protein Data Bank, 120, 121
    reliable and easy, 121
    Victorian Web, 121
Fitzpatrick, Kathleen, 151–153
Flick, Robbert, 71, 72f
Fogel, Robert, 64
Foldit, 110
Folger Digital Texts, 91
Folsom, Ed, 92
Fractal tree diagram, 118, 119f
Fraud. *See also* Watchdog blogs
    "Abnormal Science," 157–158, 165–167, 169,
        170, 186
    prevalence, 163–164
    retractions, 158–163, 162f
    "Retraction Watch," 156–157, 165–166, 169, 186
Freedom of Information acts, 203–205
Free sourcing, 151–153
French Revolution, 60–64, 62f
Friedberg, Anne, 54, 55
Frost, Martin, 159–160

Galaxy Zoo, 7, 13–14, 90, 110–115, 120
    "Classify Galaxies," 111
    collaborative problem solving, 111–113, 111f
        113–114f
    data reliability, 121
    "Hanny's Voorwerp," 112–114, 112f–114f
Galiher, Clifford, 82–85, 84f, 85f
Galison, Peter, 181–183, 185f, 187
Garfield, Eugene, 52
Gated access, 189–193
    book reviews, 184, 187
Geertz, Clifford, 8
Geometric morphometrics, 12, 46–50, 47f–50f
*Ghost Metropolis: A Global History of Los Angeles
    Since 13,000* (Ethington), 75
Ginsparg, Paul, 7, 50, 107–109
Goldacre, Ben, 157
Governing the Commons (Ostrom), 206
Grant proposals, review process, 125–126
Gross, A. G., 201
Grumiaux, Arthur, 78–79
Gutenberg-e series, 55–56

Habermas, Jürgen, 127–128
Habits, social, 3
Hackett, E. J., 128
Haldane, J. B. S., 41–42
Hanley, Wayne, 64
"Hanny's Voorwerp," 112–114, 111f, 113–114f
Harmon, J. E., 201
Harnad, Stevan, 17
Harrington, D. J., 105
Hepokoski, James, 78
H-France Review, 184
Hickman, Barbara Day, 63
Hogan, C. Michael, 118
Honigmann, E. A. J., 104
Humanists
    culture, 7–10
    ideal type, 7–10
    vs. scientists, 1–4
Humanities, 1–2, 4. *See also specific topics*
    collaboration, 7–8
    digital, 91
    essays and books (*See* Essays and books,
        humanities)
    Internet projects, 11
    transformation, 10–12
Hunt, Lynn, 60–64, 62–63, 62f
Huston, John, 82–85, 84f, 85f
Huxley, Julian, 39, 40–42, 41f
Hyperlinks
    Cell, 21, 22f
    Elsevier's article of future, 20–21
    Ethington's *Ghost Metropolis,* 75
    Mamber's *Who Shot Liberty Valance?,* 81,
        81f, 82f
    open access peer-reviewed publication, 190
    Pohlandt-McCormick's "*I Saw a
        Nightmare*," 56
    scientific articles, 6, 28, 30
    Thomas and Ayers' *The Differences Slavery
        Made,* 66–67, 66f, 69
    Victorian Web, 91
Hypertext, 7, 28, 54
    The Differences Slavery Made, 64
    humanities essays, future, 86
    humanities websites, 90, 91
    Pohlandt-McCormick's e-book, 58, 58f
    "*Singin' in the Rain:* A Hypertextual
        Reading", 64
    Vectors, 54

Ideal speech situation (ISS)
    application, 129–135
    Behavioral and Brain Sciences, 172–178, 186–187

vs. Climate of the Past open peer review, 151
vs. Shakespeare Quarterly open peer
    review, 151
theory, 127–128
Ideal types, 2–4
    humanist, 7–10
    scientist, 5–7
Image and Logic: A Material Culture of Microphysics
    (Galison), 178, 181–183, 185f, 187
Imaging the French Revolution (Censer and
    Hunt), 60–64, 62f
Immaculate Conception (Tiepolo), 99–100,
    100f–101f
Interactivity, 122. *See also specific types*
International Journal of Communication,
    191–192
The Interpretation of Cultures (Geertz), 8
Intertextuality, 28–31, 32f
Intratextuality, 31–33, 32f
Investigative journalism, 166
*"I Saw a Nightmare" ... Doing Violence to
    Memory: The Soweto Uprising, June 16,
    1976* (Pohlandt-McCormick), 56–60, 58f,
    59f, 61f

Jaszi, P., 203
Johanson, Christopher, 75–77, 76f
Joint Information Systems Committee, 191
Journal
    article (*See* Article, journal)
    contents page, 31, 32f
    print *vs.* online, 192–193
Journal des Sçavans, 5
Journal of the Learned, 5
Journal of the Society of Architectural Historians,
    75–77, 76f, 87
Journal of Visualized Experiments, 19–20
Journal, scientific. *See also* Scientific article
    first, 5
    most cited, 17–18
    multimedia centers, 33
    visual-verbal text interaction, 18

Kahn, Robert, 11
Kairos, 53–54
Kendall, David, 46, 49
Keynes, Geoffrey, 97
King Lear (Shakespeare), 104
Knoepfler, Paul, 164
Knowledge dissemation, 5
Kolb, David, 53–54
Kolker, Robert, 79–80
ktwop, 168

Labor, division of, 6
Lamont, Michèle, 125, 128–129
Landes, Joan, 63–64
Landow, George, 91
Latour, Bruno, 86
Leaves of Grass (Whitman), 92
Libraries. *See also PLOS (Public Library of
    Science)*
    Perseus Digital Library, 91–92
    virtual, 31
Link rot, 195
"London" (Blake), 98
*Los Angeles and the Problem of Urban
    Historical Knowledge* (Ethington), 69–75,
    71f–74f
Luca, Sergiù, 78–79
Lysis (Plato), 170

MacNeale, Kate, 118
Majors, Tristy Vick, 116
Mamber, Stephen
    "Simultaneity and Overlap in Stanley
        Kubrick's *The Killing,*" 82, 83f, 84f
    Who Shot Liberty Valance?, 80–81, 81f, 82f
Marcus, Adam, 156–157, 166–167
Master finding system, 31–33, 32f
Mathematical visualization, 42–46, 44f,
    45f, 46t
MediaCommons Press, 144, 152
Menuhin, Yehudi, 78–79
Mercier, Hugo, 126–127, 172–178, 187
Merton, Robert, norms of, 161, 169–170
Metascience's "Review Symposium," 184
Metzger, Walter, 194
Miles, Adrian, 80
Mitchell, W. T. J., 98, 100–101, 100f–103f
Modern Language Association, 194
Morant, G. M., 42–46, 44f, 45f, 46t
Morphometrics, geometric, 12, 46–50,
    47f–50f
Multimedia
    digital repositories, 109
    Figshare, 110
    Ghost Metropolis, 75
    Kairos, 53
    Rome Reborn, 115
    scientific article, 12, 20, 21, 33
    "Three Fates of the Maltese Falcon:
        Hammett's Novel at Warner Bros.," 82–83,
        84f, 85f
    Tout-Fait, 53
    Vectors, 54
    Victorian Web, 91

Multimedia Los Angeles, urban history, 69–75, 71f–74f
Musicians, 77–79
Music Theory Online, 77–79, 87, 192

Natural sciences, 4
Nature, 135, 153
Nemesis affair, 122
Networked sites, 200. *See also specific websites*
New Era Publishing International v. Carol Publishing, 202
Nielsen, Michael, 20, 33–34, 114
North, Douglass C., 206

Obokata, Haruko, 164–176
Olson, Mancur, 206
OneZoom, fractal tree diagram, 118, 119f
On Growth and Form (Thompson), 39–40, 39f
Online journals, 192–193. *See also specific journals*
    humanities, 53
    scientific (*See* Scientific article, Internet)
Online Mendelian Inheritance in Man (OMNI), 104
Open access peer-reviewed publication, 171–172, 190
Open-access publishing, 191–192
"Open Access Publishing and Scholarly Values," 171–172
Open Humanities Press, 52, 184, 193
Open Journal Systems (OJS), 124
Open peer review, 122–154
    argument theory, 126–129
    case for and against, 123–126
    epistemic vigilance, theory of, 127
    free sourcing, 151–153
    humanities *(Shakespeare Quarterly),* 144–151 (*See also Shakespeare Quarterly,* open peer review)
    ideal speech situation, 127–135 (*See also* Ideal speech situation (ISS))
    interactivity, 122
    knowledge, 123
    Nemesis affair, 122
    Open Journal Systems, 124
    peer-to-peer review, 151–153
Open peer review, sciences, 135–144, 139f
    Atmospheric Chemistry and Physics, 136–138
    Climate of the Past, 138–144, 139f
    European Geosciences Union journals, 135
    Nature, 135, 153
Open Tree of Life, 118, 119f

Opportunities, 188–189
Oransky, Ivan, 156–157, 166–167
Organizations, first scientific, 5
Originality, 129, 130
Ostrom, Elinor, 206
Owen, John Stewart MacKenzie, 17
Oxford Scholarly Editions Online, 91
The Oxyrhynchus Papyri, 115

Patents, 197–203
Path forward, 205–208
Pearson, Karl, 42–46, 44f, 45f, 46t
Peer review, 5, 124
    argumentative competence, 129, 130
    argument theory, Mercier and Sperber's, 126–127
    central tendencies, 128–129
    clarity of expression, 129, 131, 146, 148–150
    confirmation bias, 127
    costs, 126
    criteria, unified set, 129
    definition, 123
    efficacy, 124–125
    epistemic viligance, 127
    ideal speech situation, 127–135 (*See also* Ideal speech situation (ISS))
    importance, 122
    judgments and citation success, 124
    open (*See* Open peer review)
    originality, 129, 130
    origins and practice, 123
    preference ordering, 127
    procedure, violation, 131–132
    vs. rational consensus, 127–128
    revision request, 132–133
    significance to field, 129, 130–131
Peer review, postpublication
    articles, 172–178
    books, 178–186, 185f, 187
Peer-to-peer review, 151–152
The Penguin and the Leviathan (Benkler), 206
Perelman, Grigoriy, 109
Periodicals, first scientific, 5
Perseus Digital Library, 91–92
Peters, D. P., 124–125
Philosophical Transactions, 5
Photographs, 55–60, 58f, 59f, 61f
Pillai, Krishna, 168
Plagiarism. *See also* Watchdog blogs
    "Abnormal Science," 157–158, 165–167, 169, 170, 186
    retractions, 158

"Retraction Watch," 156–157, 165–166, 169, 186
significance, 158–159
Planet Hunters, 110
Planned Obsolescence (Fitzpatrick), 151–153
Plato, 170
PLOS (Public Library of Science), 23
Figshare alliance, 110
financing, 26
mission, 25–26
reader statistics, 34
PLOS Biology, sample article, 24, 25f
PLOS One, peer review, 124
Pohlandt-McCormick, Helena, 56–60, 58f, 59f, 61f, 88
Ponce de León, Maria, 48–49, 50f
Pöschl, Ulrich, 136, 153
Postmodern Culture, 79–85, 87
"Simultaneity and Overlap in Stanley Kubrick's *The Killing,*" 82, 83f, 84f
"*Singing in the Rain:* A Hypertextual Reading," 80
"The Moving Image Reclaimed," 79–80
"Three Fates of the Maltese Falcon: Hammett's Novel at Warner Bros.," 82–85, 84f, 85f
Who Shot Liberty Valance?, 80–81, 81f, 82f
Post-peer review, humanities, 169–172
Post-publication evaluation, 155–187
peer review, articles, 172–178
peer review, books, 178–186, 185f, 187
peer review, humanities, 169–172
watchdog blogs, sciences, 155–169 (*See also* Watchdog blogs)
Preference ordering, 127
Preservation, digital, 195–196
Price, Kenneth M., 92
Prieur, Jean-Louis, 61–63, 62f
Princeton Dante Project, 92
The Printing Press as an Agent of Change: Communications and Cultural Transformations in Early Modern Europe (Eisenstein), 10–11
Pritsker, Moshe, 19
Problems of Relative Growth (Huxley), 40–42, 41f
Profit incentive, on universities, 197
The Promise of the New South (Ayers), 64–65
Promotion policies, 194–195
Protein Data Bank, 14, 90, 104–107, 106f
article links, 31
data reliability, 121
finding system, 121

The Protestant Ethic and the Spirit of Capitalism, 3
Public access, free, 24–25
Public Knowledge Project, Open Journal Systems, 124
Public Library of Science (PLOS). *See* PLOS *(Public Library of Science)*
PubMed, 190, 191
"PubPeer," 164, 186

Raff, Martin, 170
Rational actor theory, 206
Rational consensus, *vs.* peer review, 127–128
Rationality, 128
Raup, David, 122, 152
Reader comments, 33
Reader statistics, 34
Reasoning, 172
Reclaiming Fair Use (Aufderheide and Jaszi), 203
Reich, Eugenie Samuel, 160
Rennie, John, 157
Research dissemination, 5
Research front, 5
Research Information Network, 191
Research Papers in Economics (RePEc), 190, 191
Research university, 206. *See also* Universities
Retractions
plagiarism and fraud, 158–163, 162f
prevalence, 163–164
"Retraction Watch," 156–157, 165–166, 186
Bulfone-Paus, Silvia, 158–163, 162f, 166, 186
narrative with irony, 169
as public forum, 167
reader commentary, 168–169
sarcasm and ridicule, 166–167
successes, 169
Review. *See also* Open peer review; Peer review
grant proposals, 125–126
"Review Symposium," 184
Roberts, Warren, 62–63
Rolf, F. James, 46
Roman Forum, reimagining, 75–77, 76f
Rome Reborn, 115
Rosenzweig, Roy, 184
Rosindell, James, 118, 119f
Rotten Tomatoes, 184
Royer, W. E., Jr., 105
Rudé, George, 62

Scafidi, Susan, 201–202
Schilpp, Paul, 4
Schmalfeldt, Janet, 78

Scholarship, 193–194
Scholarship Reconsidered (Boyer), 193–194
Schubert, Emery, 78–79
Science from Sight to Insight: How Scientists Illustrate Meaning (Gross and Harmon), 201
Science, on journal data, 104
Sciences, 1–2. *See also specific topics*
  collaboration, 6, 12, 26–27
  Internet projects, 11
  shared norms, 161–163
  transformation, 10–12
Scientific article
  argument, 18
  argumentative structures, 18–19
  collaboration, 12
  reinvented, 188
Scientific article, Internet, 17–51
  abstract of abstract, 28, 29f, 30f
  accessibility, 24–26, 25f, 26f
  argumentative structure, *vs.* print articles, 18
  authorship, 25f, 26–27, 26f
  author summary, 18, 27–28
  citations, 28–31
  complexity, 27–28, 29f, 30f
  contents page, journal, 31, 32f
  Elsevier's "The Article of the Future," 20–21, 22f
  geometric morphometrics, 46–50, 47f–50f
  hyperlinked text, 6
  inter- and intratextuality, 28–33, 32f
  Journal of Visualized Experiments, 19–20
  journals analyzed, 23–24
  mathematical visualization, 42–46, 44f, 45f, 46t
  methods section, 19
  most cited journals, 17–18
  Owen on, 17
  public access, free, 24–25
  reader comments and reader statistics, 33–34
  revolution *vs.* evolution, 17–23, 22f
  shape, science of, 38–50 (*See also* Shape, science of)
  startups, ecosystem, 20
  Supplemental Information, 19
  virtual libraries, 31
  visualization, 34–38, 35f, 37f
Scientific culture, 5–7
Scientific organizations, first, 5
Scientific periodicals, first, 5
Scientific Research Publishing, 23–24

Scientists
  collaboration, 7
  vs. humanists, 1–4
  on humanities, 2–3
  ideal type, 5–7
Scrolling
  Nature, 36
  Walt Whitman Archive, 95
Scruton, Roger, 77
Search engines, 10, 89, 90
Searching
  algorithms, 13
  encyclopedia and database websites, 120
  Google, 10
  Google Scholar, 190
  humanities, 13, 53
  Protein Data Base, 120, 121
  search engines, 10, 89, 90
Self-archiving, 190–191
Sen, Amartya, 127, 206
Sepkoski, Jack, 122
Shakespeare, *King Lear,* 104
Shakespeare Quarterly, open peer review, 144–151, 145f, 147
  argumentative competence, 146, 147–148
  clarity, 146, 148–150
  criteria, 144
  vs. ideal speech situation, 151
  methodological questions, 150
  open commentary, 144–146, 145f
  significance to field, 146–147
  special issues, 144
Shape, science of, 38–50
  birth, 39–42, 39f, 41f
  geometric morphometrics, 46–50, 47f, 49f, 50f
  Haldane, J. B. S., 41–42
  Huxley, Julian, 39, 40–42, 41f
  Internet, 46–50, 47f, 49f, 50f
  mathematical visualization, 42–46, 44f, 45f, 46t
  pre-history, 38–39
  Thompson, D'Arcy, 39–40, 39f
Sickle cell disease, inheritance, 105
Significance to field, 129, 130–131
Silverman, Craig, 157
"Simultaneity and Overlap in Stanley Kubrick's *The Killing* (Mamber), 82, 83f, 84f
"*Singin' in the Rain:* A Hypertextual Reading" (Miles), 80
Smith, Reginald, 158
Snow, C. P., 1–3
Social media, Internet scientific article, 12, 20, 21, 34

Social Science Research Network (SSRN), 109, 190, 191
Social sciences, 4
"Song of Myself" (Whitman), 92–93, 93f
Songs of Innocence and of Experience (Blake), 97–103
  "A Cradle Song," 98
  Immaculate Conception, 99–100, 100f–101f
  "London," 98
  Mitchell, 98, 100
  Shewing the Two Contrary States of the Human Soul, 98–99
  "The Clod and the Pebble," 99
  "The Human Abstract," 100
  "The Lamb," 98
  "The Little Black Boy," 100
  "The Poison Tree," 98
  Tiepolo's *Immaculate Conception,* 99–100, 100f
Soweto uprising, 56–60, 58f, 59f, 88
Sperber, Dan, 126–127, 172–178, 187
Sponsoring Consortium for Open Access Publishing in Particle Physics (SCOAP), 192
Stallman, Richard, 171
Stanford Encyclopedia of Philosophy, 115
Statistics, reader, 34
Summary, author, 18, 27–28
Supplemental Information, 19
Symposium, 184

Tempest, 77–78
Tenure rules, 193–195
"The Clod and the Pebble" (Blake), 99
"The Human Abstract" (Blake), 100
"The Lamb" (Blake), 98
"The Little Black Boy" (Blake), 100
"The Moving Image Reclaimed" (Kolker), 79–80
Theory of epistemic viligance, 127, 173
"The Poison Tree" (Blake), 98
Thomas, William G., III, 4, 64–69, 66f, 68f–70f
Thompson, D'Arcy, 39–40, 39f, 46, 49, 77
3D interactive visuals
  "Death in Motion," 76–77, 76f
  Rome Reborn, 115
  Who Shot Liberty Valance?, 80–81, 81f, 82f
"Three Fates of the Maltese Falcon: Hammett's Novel at Warner Bros." (Galiher), 82–85, 84f, 85f
Thumbnail
  Elsevier's "The Article of the Future," 20
  Internet scientific article, 36

Tiepolo, Giovanni Battista, *Immaculate Conception,* 99–100, 100f–101f
Time on the Cross: The Economics of American Negro Slavery (Fogel and Engerman), 64
Tolstoy:ru, 114
Transparency, 122–123
Traweek, Sharon, 3
Tree of Life, 13, 90
Two Cultures and a Second Look (Snow), 1–3

Understanding Knowledge as a Commons (Ostrom), 206
Universities
  license revenues, 198
  profit incentive, 197
  research, 206
University–industry partnerships, 199
Urban history, multimedia Los Angeles, 69–75, 71f–74f

Valley of the Shadow, 196
Van Arkel, Hanny, 112–114, 111f, 113f–114f
Vectors: Journal of Culture and Technology in a Dynamic Vernacular, 52–55
Victorian Web, 91, 120, 121
Virtual libraries, 31
"The Virtual Window Interactive," 54, 55
Viscomi, Joseph, 95–98
Visualization, 38–47. *See also* Shape, science of
  color, 36
  geometric morphometrics, 46–50, 47f–50f
  mathematical, 42–46, 44f, 45f, 46t
  multicomponent figures, 36–38, 37f
  quantity and density, 34–35, 35f
  scientific articles, 34–38, 35f, 37f

Waltham, Mary, 191–192
Walt Whitman Archive, 89, 90, 92–95, 104
  "A March in the Ranks Hard-Prest," 93–94
  "And Yet Not You Alone," 94–95, 95f, 96f
  Leaves of Grass, 92
  "Song of Myself," 92–93, 93f
Watchdog blogs
  "Abnormal Science," 157–158, 165–167, 169, 170, 186
  Bulfone-Paus, Silvia, 158–163, 162f, 166
  mechanisms, 165–169
  Obokata article, 164–176
  "PubPeer," 164, 186
  "Retraction Watch," 156–157, 165–166, 169, 186
  revelations, 158–165, 162f
  sciences, 155–158

Wayback Machine, 195
WebCite, 195
Webe, Maz, 3
Websites. *See also specific sites*
   archival, 88–121 (*See also* Archival websites)
Whistleblowers, 204
Whitman, Walt. *See* Walt Whitman Archive
Who Shot Liberty Valance? (Mamber), 80–81,
   81f, 82f
Wiebauer, Karin, 159–161
WikiLeaks, 204–205
"The Wilkinson Head of Oliver Cromwell
   and its Relationship to Busts, Masks, and
   Painted Portraits" (Pearson and Morant),
   42–46, 44f, 45f, 46t
William Blake Archive, 89, 92, 95–104
   "A Cradle Song," 98
   Blunt, Anthony 101

Europe, 100–101, 102f–103f
   founders, 95–97
   goal, 97
   Immaculate Conception, 99–100, 100f–101f
   "London," 98
   Songs of Innocence and of Experience, 97–103
   "The Lamb," 98
   "The Poison Tree," 98
   Viscomi, Joseph 97–98
   visual–verbal interaction, 98, 102–103
Wilson, E. O., 116
World Wide Web, 10

Zollikofer, Christoph, 48–49, 50f
Zooming, 188
   Elsevier's "The Article of the Future," 21
   OneZoom, 118–120, 119f
Zwirner, Joerg, 157–158, 165–168